News Corp

A comprehensive scholarly look at the dominance, power, and influence of News Corp as one of the most potent communication giants of current times.

Drawing on a wealth of empirical evidence, this book offers an authoritative, wide-ranging, and accessible analysis of the development, operations, and political influence of the most widely commented on media company of modern times, directed by the world's most famous media mogul, Rupert Murdoch. It details News Corp's ownership and control, traces its global expansion in print, television, and film, examines the crises that have prompted sell-offs, withdrawals, and retrenchment, and explores losses and gains in its responses to the rise of digital media. The book explores Rupert Murdoch's close relations with successive prime ministers and presidents, examines the mobilisation of his news outlets to make and break political reputations, and details the consistent promotion of right-wing populist ideology on a range of key issues across the company's tabloid outlets.

This is an invaluable resource to students and scholars of global media industries, the political economy of media, media policy, and media and politics.

Graham Murdock is Emeritus Professor of Culture and Economy at Loughborough University, UK. He is internationally known for his work in the sociology and political economy of communication. He has held visiting professorships at the universities of Auckland, Bergen, Brussels, California, Curtin, and Fudan in Shanghai. His writings are available in 21 languages. His books include, as co-editor, *Money Talks: Media, Markets, Crisis* (2015), *Carbon Capitalism and Communication: Confronting Climate Crisis* (2017), and *Contested Connections: Pandemic and Digital Media* (2022), and, as co-author, *Researching Communications* (2021).

Benedetta Brevini is Visiting Professor at the Institute for Public Knowledge, New York University, USA, and Associate Professor of Political Economy of Communication at the University of Sydney, Australia. Before joining the academy, she worked as a journalist in Milan, New York, and London for CNBC, RAI, and *The Guardian*. She is the author of several books including *Public Service Broadcasting Online* (2013), *Amazon: Understanding a Global Communication Giant* (2020), and *Is AI Good for the Planet?* (2022), and the editor of *Beyond Wikileaks* (2013), *Carbon Capitalism and Communication: Confronting Climate Crisis* (2017), and *Climate Change and the Media* (2018).

Michael Ward teaches Australian media as part of Boston University's global program in Sydney and is a sessional academic in media and communication at the University of Sydney, Australia. He was a senior executive with the Australian Broadcasting Corporation.

Global Media Giants

Series Editors: Benjamin J. Birkinbine, Rodrigo Gomez and Janet Wasko

Since the second half of the 20th century, the significance of media corporate power has been increasing in different and complex ways around the world; the power of these companies in political, symbolic and economic terms has been a global issue and concern. In the 21st century, understanding media corporations is essential to understanding the political, economic and socio-cultural dimensions of our contemporary societies.

The **Global Media Giants** series continues the work that began in the series editors' book *Global Media Giants*, providing detailed examinations of the largest and most powerful media corporations in the world.

Alibaba
Infrastructuring Global China
Hong Shen

Bertelsmann
A Transnational Media Service Giant
Mandy Tröger and Jörg Becker

Baidu
Geopolitical Dynamics of the Internet in China
ShinJoung Yeo

Nintendo
Playing with Power
Randy Nichols

News Corp
Empire of Influence
Graham Murdock, Benedetta Brevini, and Michael Ward

For more information about this series, please visit:
https://www.routledge.com/Global-Media-Giants/book-series/GMG

News Corp

Empire of Influence

Graham Murdock, Benedetta Brevini, and Michael Ward

NEW YORK AND LONDON

First published 2025
by Routledge
605 Third Avenue, New York, NY 10158

and by Routledge
4 Park Square, Milton Park, Abingdon, Oxon, OX14 4RN

Routledge is an imprint of the Taylor & Francis Group, an informa business

Library of Congress Cataloging-in-Publication Data
Names: Murdock, Graham, 1946- author. | Brevini, Benedetta, 1982- author. | Ward, Michael, 1958- author.
Title: News Corp : empire of influence/Graham Murdock, Benedetta Brevini and Michael Ward.
Description: New York: Routledge, 2025. | Series: Global media giants | Includes bibliographical references and index.
Identifiers: LCCN 2024014112 (print) | LCCN 2024014113 (ebook) | ISBN 9781032180328 (hardback) | ISBN 9781032185491 (paperback) | ISBN 9781003255086 (ebook)
Subjects: LCSH: News Corporation. | Murdoch, Rupert, 1931- | Mass media--Influence.
Classification: LCC PN4734.5.N48 M87 2025 (print) | LCC PN4734.5.N48 (ebook) | DDC 070.1/720904--dc23/eng/20240617
LC record available at https://lccn.loc.gov/2024014112
LC ebook record available at https://lccn.loc.gov/2024014113

ISBN: 978-1-032-18032-8 (hbk)
ISBN: 978-1-032-18549-1 (pbk)
ISBN: 978-1-003-25508-6 (ebk)

DOI: 10.4324/9781003255086

Typeset in Times New Roman
by KnowledgeWorks Global Ltd.

Contents

Figures and Tables

Figures

Tables

1 An Empire in Decline?

Visitors entering the deconsecrated space of St Saviour's Church of Exiles in Melbourne on Saturday 6 November 2021 were confronted with life-sized sculptures of Rupert Murdoch and his son Lachlan arranged as a classic corporate portrait. Murdoch senior is seated, his hands crossed and resting on his thigh. Lachlan, the heir apparent, is standing behind him. Two other adult children, James and Elisabeth, both once tipped as future successors, are missing. Elisabeth left the company to launch a new independent production company. James resigned in August 2020, citing disagreements over editorial content after having previously objected to the company's coverage of the climate emergency. Constructed as giant candles in wax, the figures were slowly melting.

In September 2023, the tableau was reversed. Lachlan became sole chair of the company's two principal divisions. Rupert Murdoch moved to emeritus positions but remained fully engaged with shaping policy. As he assured staff in his resignation letter, "I can guarantee you that I will be involved every day in the contest of ideas … and reaching out to you with thoughts, ideas and advice." [1]

It was clear that major decisions will continue to require his consent.

1.1 News Corp and Rupert Murdoch: Between Biography and History

News Corp is unique among the longer-established global media giants as "the only media conglomerate created, built and dominated by the vision and tenacity of one individual" from its foundation to the present. [2]

Rupert Murdoch has come to represent the archetypal media mogul ruthlessly pursuing profit and political influence. He is immediately recognisable as the ageing media potentate, Logan Roy, in one of the most popular and critically acclaimed television drama series of recent years, HBO's *Succession.* Broadcast from 2018 to 2023 and based on Shakespeare's *King Lear*, it follows the patriarch's fraught relations with his children competing for his favour. Art has come close to imitating life with persistent rumours that James suggested plot lines and Rupert Murdoch's divorce agreement with his last

DOI: 10.4324/9781003255086-1

wife, Jerry Hall, allegedly containing a clause forbidding her to contact the production team.

The unmissable echo of 'Roi', the French word for 'king', in Logan Roy's surname plays on the image of the Sun King popularised by Andrew Neil, who edited Murdoch's British Sunday broadsheet *The Sunday Times*. Louis XIV, the original Sun King, ruled France for over 72 years. Rupert Murdoch, now in his 90s, inherited his father's Australian newspapers at the age of 22 and, like Louis, has directed his domain with an unshakeable sense of entitlement reminiscent of the divine right claimed by hereditary rulers. In Neil's account:

> When you work for Rupert Murdoch … you are a courtier at the court of the Sun King … all authority comes from him. He is the only one to whom allegiance must be owed, and he expects his word to be final. [3]

Rupert Murdoch's gambles, mistakes, ideological affiliations, and political networks have played a decisive role in News Corp's development, but his options for action have been determined by fundamental shifts in the company's operating environment propelled by two forces: marketisation and digitalisation.

From the mid-1980s, government policies informed by neoliberal economics gained increasing momentum in News Corp's major English-speaking markets. Restricted sectors were opened up and public interest regulations relaxed. Aided and abetted by active support from key political actors, Rupert Murdoch took full advantage, consolidating his newspaper holdings and diversifying into book publishing, broadcasting, and film to build an archetypal media conglomerate.

Versions of marketisation were also adopted in emerging economies led by China and India, but News Corp's efforts to establish a global satellite broadcasting system proved more problematic. Loosening state economic management opened new opportunities for foreign investors, but market entry remained conditional on compliance with national policies and priorities, placing limits on News Corp's globalising ambitions.

The key moments in News Corp's development as a transnational conglomerate, with interests in the range of traditional print and audiovisual industries, and the successive miscalculations and crises that have forced retrenchments are detailed in Chapter 2.

Over this same period, the company's operating environment was altered in fundamental ways by a second structural shift: digitalisation. The rapid rise of digital networks and desktop computerisation transformed every aspect of media production, access, and use, undermining established labour practices, subverting established business models, and generating new sources of profit.

Rupert Murdoch has employed successive innovations to cut labour costs in his press divisions. In an early confrontation, provoking a year-long strike by London compositors, traditional typesetting was replaced by direct computer inputting. More recently, artificial intelligence (AI) systems have been deployed to write stories for his local news outlets in Australia, filling gaps created by shedding journalists.

Elsewhere, News Corp's engagements with digitalisation have been marked by threats to revenues and successive failures to capitalise on opportunities. Here again, neoliberal economics played a decisive role. Between 1992 and 1994, the internet ceased to be a publicly administered resource and was opened to commercialisation. In the absence of effective curbs on acquisitions, control over the most popular uses, search and social media, rapidly coalesced in the hands of newly launched US-based digital platforms led by Google and Facebook. Their novel business model offered free access in return for exclusive rights to collect and market users' personal data to advertisers wanting to target appeals more effectively. News Corp, anchored in print and broadcasting, rapidly dubbed 'legacy' media, faced a formidable new source of competition for audience attention and advertiser expenditure.

Its responses have met with mixed fortunes. Attempts to establish an independent presence on the public internet failed. Press revenues have been partially retrieved by introducing subscriptions where feasible and by forcing digital platforms to pay for carrying News Corp content, although the platforms continue to enjoy the balance of advantage. AI has opened a new point of contention with struggles over payment for using News Corp content to train systems and the prospect of news provision operating outside the established news organisations.

The single undisputed success in News Corp's response to digital disruption has come from its successive investments in digital data services, now a major profit centre. The overall impact of digitalisation on the company's operations is reviewed in Chapter 3.

1.2 Decline and Fall?

Observers might be tempted to interpret the Melbourne wax installation as a metaphor, confirming the slow disintegration of an Australian family-controlled newspaper business that rose to become a global media empire, but with the sale of the transnational satellite television interests and the US film production holdings is now a dwindling force. It is a view popularised by Michael Wolff, a journalist with personal access to Rupert Murdoch and his operations. His first book, published in 2008, was bullishly entitled *The Man Who Owns the News*. His latest, *The Fall: The End of the Murdoch Empire*, issued in 2023, is a valediction. [4]

Annual company reports for the 2023 fiscal year, using the EBITA measure of profitability (calculating earnings before interest, taxation, and amortisation) appear to support this judgement. Fox Corporation, with Fox News as its main revenue source, saw a 15 per cent drop in overall earnings from 2022 [5] and News Corporation a 75 per cent fall from the previous year. For the first time, over 50 per cent of News Corporation's earnings came from the portfolio of online information provision in finance, real estate, energy, and chemicals [6].

As a company press release noted, the rise of digital services has marked "a profound transformation during the last decade", from a primary revenue base in newspapers, book publishing, and broadcasting to a profit centre in data. [7] This shift is detailed in Chapter 4.

The press and broadcasting divisions may no longer be the primary economic core of News Corp's operations, but they remain central to its continuing political role as a megaphone for right-wing populism. Data services circulate in restricted business circles. Newspapers and broadcast and cable channels relay information and comment on public issues to a general audience, helping to shape political agendas and attitudes.

Rupert Murdoch's news outlets continue to occupy a central position in the information ecology of three leading democracies. Detailed figures and sources are presented in Chapter 4. They list News Corp's two US titles, the *Wall Street Journal* and the *New York Post*, among the country's top five newspapers by print circulation. They show Murdoch's British newspapers accounting for almost a third (32.3%) of the total tabloid market and almost a half (49.38%) of the broadsheet market, and his Australian papers commanding 57.6 per cent of the country's total press market. They confirm that his major Australian television operation, Foxtel, is watched by 15 per cent of the primetime audience, supplemented by viewers for his Sky News Service closely modelled on Fox News, which remains the top- rated US cable news channel. Audiences for Murdoch's major tabloid outlets are further boosted by online traffic, with Fox News (ranked 8th), the *New York Post* (ranked 12th), and the *Sun* (ranked 13th) among the world's most popular global news sites.

The reach of News Corp's news outlets remains unmatched among the leading communications conglomerates, raising major questions about the company's role in the politics of Australia, Britain, and the United States. Chapters 5 and 6 investigate the organisation of ownership and control in Rupert Murdoch's companies and explore his political ties, influence, and ideology.

In opposition to commentators who present his relations with politicians as transactional, wielded purely in pursuit of his business interests, we draw on a wealth of detailed empirical research showing that his news outlets have consistently promoted populist ideology across a range of key issues, from immigration to climate change.

The Wealth of Nations, Adam Smith's enduringly influential manifesto for minimal state intervention in capitalist markets, appeared in 1776 within months of Britain's American colonies declaring independence from the Crown and establishing a republic based on the popular vote. Newspapers, and later broadcasting, were assigned a pivotal role in democratic politics as indispensable sources of the comprehensive information, analysis, and argument citizens needed to make considered choices. How far this ideal has been subverted by media owners pursuing their own economic and political interests and ideologies has been a continuing focus of debate. The history of News Corp adds an instructive and possibly unique chapter.

Over the years, the Murdoch family interests have operated under a series of names. The original company, based in Australia, was incorporated as News Limited. In 1968, the British operations, the first major foray overseas, were grouped together as News International. Following newspaper acquisitions in the US, News Corporation was established in 1979 as a general holding company for the family's increasingly global interests. Incorporated initially in Australia, it was reincorporated in the US where Murdoch had established a significant presence in film and television after buying the 20th Century Fox studios, acquiring television stations in major cities as the basis for a fourth national network, and launching the Fox cable channels.

In 2013, following the scandal surrounding the illegal hacking of newsworthy individuals' mobile phones at the British tabloid paper *The News of the World*, the company was split into two. The newly created 21st Century Fox oversaw the audiovisual interests. 'New' News Corp directed the print interests. In 2019, following the sale of the Sky satellite television network to Comcast and the film production interests to Disney, the two divisions were renamed again. The remaining US-based audiovisual holdings are now overseen by the Fox Corporation, while the print and online divisions and the Australian subscription television services are managed by a reconfigured News Corporation. The logo is based on Rupert Murdoch's handwriting, a visible reminder that every major decision shaping the company's direction has born his signature.

References

[1] Rupert Murdoch (2023) 'Rupert Murdoch's resignation letter, in full', 22 September. Available at www.afr.com/companies/media-and-marketing/rupert-murdoch-s-resignation-letter-in-full-20230922-p5e6qt

[2] Daya Kishan Thussu (2007) 'The "Murdochization" of news? The case of Star TV India', *Media, Culture and Society*, Vol. 29, No. 4, p. 595.

[3] Andrew Neil (1996) 'Murdoch and Me', *Vanity Fair*, December. Available at https://archive.vanityfair.com/article/1996/12/murdoch-and-me

[4] Michael Wolff (2008) *The Man Who Owns the News: Inside the Secret World of Rupert Murdoch*. New York. Broadway Books; (2023) *The Fall: The End of the Murdoch Empire*. London. The Bridge Street Press.

[5] Fox Annual Report (2023) Company's Segment EBITA for fiscal 2023, 2022, 2021, p. 102.

[6] News Corp Annual Report (2023) Company Revenue and Segment EBITA 2023, 2022, p. 117.

[7] News Corp (2023) 'News Corp Reports Fourth Quarter and Full Year Results for Fiscal 2023'. Press Release, 10 August. Available at https://investors.newscorp.com/news-releases/news-release-details/news-corporation-reports-fourth-quarter-and-full-year-results-1

2 The Making of a Global Media Conglomerate

This chapter traces the company's transformation from a 'local' newspaper company based in Australia to a global media conglomerate headquartered in the United States with significant interests in newspapers, magazines, book publishing, television, and film. It is organised around four core strategies driving expansion: *Concentration* traces the accumulation of print interests in Australia, the UK, and the USA; *Diversification* follows moves into broadcasting in Britain and Australia; *Americanisation* charts the careers of the US television, cable, and film interests; and *Globalisation*, which explores the satellite ventures in Europe, Asia and Latin America.

At various points in the company's development, the pursuit of expansion and profit maximisation has generated financial and reputational crises with major consequences for corporate organisation and operations. The final section of the present chapter details three key moments: the 1991 debt crisis, the 2011 *News of the World* phone-hacking crisis, and the 2021 crisis around Fox News's promotion of Donald Trump's 'stolen election' lies.

2.1 Disputed Inheritance: From Gallipoli to Gun Alley

Rupert Murdoch's enduring personal control over corporate decisions has shaped News Corporation's expansion around his ambitions, personality, and ideological convictions. Consequently, to fully understand the motivations and managerial style informing the succession of acquisitions, disposals, and miscalculations, we first need to revisit the company's origins in the Australian newspaper business created by his father, Keith, and the enduring influence of his conflicted legacy.

The origins of the story News Corp tells about itself lie with the First World War military disaster at Gallipoli and the letter, which has taken on a mythical quality, circulated by Rupert Murdoch's father, Keith, criticising the British command's ineptitude.

In 1915, Keith Murdoch was appointed manager of United Cable Service (UCS), which was jointly owned by the Sydney *Sun* and the Melbourne *Herald*.

DOI: 10.4324/9781003255086-2

Based in London, it was the main source for Australian news of the war. At the request of the Australian prime minister, Andrew Fisher, a friend of Keith's well-connected father, a Presbyterian minister in Melbourne, he was asked to delay his journey to England in Egypt to report on complaints about delays in mail reaching Australian troops. He had no need to go to Gallipoli but, knowing that it was the epicentre of the Allied campaign in the Dardanelles, he wrote to the Commander-in-Chief Sir Ian Hamilton and "begged to be allowed to visit". [1] His brief four-day stay confirmed his impression that the campaign was a disaster but, as Ellis Ashmead-Bartlett covering the conflict for the London *Daily Telegraph* later recalled, since he "has only been here a short time … he does not feel that his word will carry sufficient weight." [2] Ashmead-Bartlett's own exposé of conditions was blocked by the military censors. Murdoch agreed to take it to England, but was intercepted on the way and the manuscript confiscated. On arrival in London, he compiled his own letter, addressed to Fisher, and distributed it within elite circles in London.

Troops from the Australian and New Zealand Army Corps, the ANZACs, were heavily involved in the battles around Gallipoli, but the campaign was ill-conceived and unwinnable from the outset. The casualties and needless losses were attributed to the incompetence of the British high command, driving a wedge between Australia and the 'motherland' and reaffirming a distinctive national character rooted in the bravery and mateship of the troops under fire. Each year, the initial landings are memorialised in Australia and New Zealand on Anzac Day, a national holiday. Rupert Murdoch played an active role in mythologising events when Associated R&R Films, the production company he had formed with the music entrepreneur Robert Stigwood, agreed to finance Peter Weir's 1981 feature film *Gallipoli.* With a budget of $2.8 million, it was the costliest production made in Australia to that time. It went on to win multiple awards and became an iconic contribution to national cinema. A six-part television miniseries, *Gallipoli,* released in 2015 to mark the campaign's hundredth anniversary, assigned Keith Murdoch a central role.

News Corp has repeatedly evoked the Gallipoli Letter to present the company as the proud inheritor of a tradition of resolutely independent journalism holding power to account. Rupert Murdoch made a point of mentioning it during his campaign to acquire Dow Jones and *The Wall Street Journal* in May 2007. In a letter to the majority owners, the Bancroft family, he assured them that their legacy was safe in his hands:

> Your record of journalistic independence and integrity is second to none. … Our interest … comes from an appreciation of this tradition, one that runs in my family as well. My father, Sir Keith Murdoch, was himself a celebrated journalist, best known for uncovering the British debacle at Gallipoli in 1915. As a father myself, nothing makes me prouder than to see that my own children have inherited the passion that my father nurtured in me. [3]

His insistence that the company was fully committed to integrity was needed. Six months before, in January 2007, Clive Goodman, the royal editor of Murdoch's best-selling British Sunday tabloid, the *News of the World*, had been convicted and jailed for paying a private investigator, Glenn Mulcaire, to illegally access the voicemail messages of members of the royal household. The Bancroft family accepted Murdoch's assurance that Goodman was a lone "rogue" reporter and the acquisition of *The Wall Street Journal* (*WSJ*) was finalised in August 2007.

In July 2009, an investigation by *The Guardian* in London established that hacking into the smartphones of newsworthy individuals was widespread at the *News of the World*, which ran contrary to the company's claims. In July 2011, subsequent inquiries revealed that the targets had included a murdered teenager, Milly Dowler. When asked if he now regretted selling to Murdoch, Christopher Bancroft, who had controlled the key block of family shares in Dow Jones (former owner of *WSJ*), admitted that "If I had known what I know now I probably would have pushed harder against [and] held out". [4]

That same month, Rupert Murdoch was called to testify before a British Parliamentary Committee investigating the extent of phone hacking in his British newspapers. He was asked directly if "there is pressure on editors to get scoops that leads them to push boundaries". After insisting that there is "no excuse for breaking the law at any time", he once again evoked Gallipoli to present the company as fully committed to upholding the public good and speaking truth to power.

> I was brought up by a father who was not rich, but who was a great journalist, and he, just before he died, bought a small paper, specifically in his will saying that he was giving me the chance to do good … He was hated in this country for exposing the scandal at Gallipoli, which I remain very, very proud of … it being a family business. I would love to see my sons and daughters follow if they are interested. [5]

A closer look at the Gallipoli Letter and Keith Murdoch's subsequent journalistic career, however, points to a different legacy organised solidly around the pursuit of profit and political influence, employing strategies of tabloidisation that News Corp has continued to build on under Rupert Murdoch.

In August 1917, Keith Murdoch was summoned to testify before an official Commission of Inquiry into the Dardanelles campaign held behind closed doors. He conceded that his overarching aim of forcing a withdrawal had been supported by unsubstantiated allegations, claiming, "I only formed impressions. That was all I ever claimed to have. While I was there, I formed one exceedingly strong impression on which I acted to my utmost power." [6] When asked for the source of a central claim in the Letter – that officers had been ordered to shoot "without mercy any soldier who lagged behind in advance" – he claimed to have forgotten "where I got it". [7]

Questioned further, he admitted not only that many of the most damaging claims in the Letter were either wrong or based on hearsay but "that he had deliberately lied to ensure his objective 'to startle the government' into abandoning the Dardanelles campaign". [8]

Far from being an exemplary example of investigative journalism based on first-hand observation and interviews, the Gallipoli Letter is more accurately described, in the words of one historian of journalism, as "an amazing mixture of error, fact, exaggeration, prejudice and the most sentimental patriotism". [9]

Nor, contrary to claims later made by the Murdoch family, was the Letter responsible for alerting the British government to the unfolding disaster. Murdoch had sent a copy to Prime Minister Asquith, who circulated it as a cabinet paper, but the government had already received a detailed report from a senior officer on the ground, Major Guy Dawnay, weeks before. Dawnay's dispatch remained confidential, leaving Keith Murdoch to take the credit for the cancellation of the campaign.

The Gallipoli Letter was particularly admired by Lord Northcliffe, Britain's leading press proprietor at the time, who became an unofficial mentor and a major influence on Murdoch's views on journalism, politics, and the exercise of power. Keith returned to Australia as Editor-in-Chief of the Melbourne *Herald*, bringing with him the ready-made template for tabloid journalism developed in Northcliffe's *Daily Mail.* Based on a combination of entertainment, sensation, and populist campaigning, it earned him the nickname "Lord Southcliffe".

He ran campaigns on hospitals and tramways and planned a beauty contest and a crime fiction serial, but circulation remained modest. Northcliffe had urged him to "watch the sales during a big murder mystery especially if there is a woman in it". [10] His chance came at the end of 1921 when the body of a 12-year-old schoolgirl who had been raped and strangled was found in a passageway known as "Gun Alley". Circulation soared as the *Herald* gave the hunt for the killer, and the subsequent trial and execution, saturation coverage. The approach was widely recognised as a new style of journalism. The *West Australian* dismissed the initial front-page story as "an outrage of decent journalism". The defence lawyer for the man accused of the murder denounced the trial coverage as "lynch law", arguing that the jury had been "stampeded by newspaper … into preconceived ideas of guilt." [11]

In addition to offering Keith Murdoch advice on boosting circulation, his time spent with Northcliffe underlined two central political lessons: the need to cultivate political links to ensure a favourable corporate environment and the power of publicity to make and break politicians' careers. Northcliffe was widely credited with playing a central role in bringing down the Asquith government in Britain and installing Lloyd George as prime minister in 1916.

They were lessons well learned. In 1936, Keith Murdoch, disappointed in the performance of Joseph Lyons, whose successful 1931 Australian Prime

Ministerial campaign he had supported, remarked, "I put him there and I'll put him out." [12]

Decisions on whether or not to endorse particular political candidates are tactical, guided by the balance of advantage at the time. Over the longer term, however, as we will show in later chapters, coverage is anchored in ideological frames organised around a stable cluster of general views and values.

News Corp began life in 1923 as News Limited, the holding company for two newspapers, the Broken Hill *Barrier Miner* and the Port Pirie *Recorder* located at the two ends of the production chain linking the huge metal mining complex at Broken Hill with the world's largest smelting works. Ostensibly controlled by the former editor of the Melbourne *Herald*, James Davidson, the financial backing, concealed at the time, came from leading corporate interests with the express aim of advancing pro-business views to counter the trade union-owned newspaper at Broken Hill, the *Barrier Truth*. As one official from the mining group noted, "There is great room for propaganda in Broken Hill and Port Pirie … Let us try and educate our men, and the public too." [13] The term "propaganda" here points to a worldview based on maximum freedom of action for corporate interests and minimal state intervention.

News Limited's connection to Keith Murdoch was established when he purchased shares in *The News*, the daily paper Davidson had launched in Adelaide. He moved to acquire *The News* after becoming chair of the company publishing Adelaide's morning *Advertiser* in 1931, in an effort to consolidate control over the city's press market. The acquisition was part of a wider programme of expansion into other states pursued on behalf of the Herald group. In 1933, he had purchased a stake in the *Courier-Mail*, followed by an interest in Perth's only afternoon daily, *The Daily News*.

This concerted push towards greater concentration within the newspaper market was accompanied by moves into other areas of activity. Attracted by the profits offered by the growth of broadcasting and cinema, he invested in radio stations and branched out into newsreels, establishing diversification as a core corporate strategy.

By the time he died in 1952, Keith Murdoch had built an unrivalled newspaper chain with newspapers in every state in Australia except New South Wales.

His will expressed the desire that his son "should have the great opportunity of spending a useful altruistic and full life in newspaper and broadcasting activities and of ultimately occupying a position of high responsibility in that field". [14]

The "opportunity" was rather more modest than Rupert had hoped, however. His father only owned four of the newspapers he had managed: the Brisbane *Courier-Mail*, the two Adelaide titles, *The News* and the *Sunday Mail*, and the *Barrier Miner* at Broken Hill, plus a stake in Southdown Press, publishers of the women's magazine *New Idea*. After his father's funeral, Rupert returned to Oxford University to complete his degree. While he was away, the family were persuaded to sell the Brisbane shares, leaving only *The News* as the principal press holding.

The absence of substantial material assets was partially offset by the social capital provided by his father's network of contacts in London. They included Lord Beaverbrook, the Canadian-born proprietor of the London *Daily Express*, at the time the best-selling daily newspaper in the world. Before returning to manage News Ltd, Murdoch spent months at the *Express*, learning the newspaper business and mastering sub-editing and what Beaverbrook referred to as the "dark arts of journalism". His time with Beaverbrook also underlined the lesson learned from his father's legacy that ownership delivered control. For the next decade, he dedicated himself to assembling a national chain of Australian newspapers to match the holdings his father had once managed.

2.2 Concentration: The Making of a Modern Print Baron

2.2.1 Australia: Rebuilding a Nationwide Press Chain

Unlike Britain, where nationally distributed newspapers co-exist with local and regional titles, the Australian press market that Murdoch entered was regionalised. Competition centred around rival titles serving the major cities, generating news diversification. From the famous account of Henry Mayer in *The Press in Australia*, we learn that the highpoint of diversity of voices in the sector was in fact reached in the mid-1920s: at the time, there were 26 capital city daily newspapers and 21 were independently owned. [15] In 1954, Murdoch acquired the *Sunday Times* in Perth and began crafting the sensationalist tabloid style that became his hallmark, typified by the infamous headline, "LEPER RAPES VIRGIN, GIVES BIRTH TO MONSTER BABY". Purchases of the *Northern Territory News* in Darwin followed, and in 1960 the afternoon *Daily* and *Sunday Mirror* in the country's largest market, Sydney. Both Sydney titles deployed the full armoury of tabloid journalism becoming bywords for "titillation, sensationalism and vulgarity" with headlines like "Girl 13 raped 100 yards from home" and "We have schoolgirl's orgy diary". The substantial profits they generated helped finance further expansion topped up with income from an unlikely source.

Murdoch had no interest in music but saw that rock and roll was creating a new youth market around records and fashion. In September 1960, he acquired one of Australia's major record companies, Festival Records, founded in 1952. Under its manager, Alan Hely, Festival became the Australian distributor for leading independent labels based in Britain and the US and signed the Bee Gees and other local acts that became international stars, generating sustained profits that could be used for other ventures. As Hely, recalled, Murdoch would "ring at 3 am" and say, '[C]an you give me another million?'... if you had £10 million, they'd take £9 million." [16] Murdoch eventually sold Festival in 2005.

A substantial financial cushion was needed to support the continuing early losses from *The Australian*, the country's first nationally distributed title, that

Murdoch launched in 1964. Originally based in Canberra, the new seat of parliament, moving later to Sydney, it aimed to provide comprehensive political news and commentary for decision makers.

The strategy of controlling both the leading "quality" newspaper and the leading tabloid had been pioneered by Keith Murdoch's mentor Lord Northcliffe. Owning both *The Times* and the best-selling popular daily paper, the *Daily Mail*, had allowed Northcliffe to exercise political influence in two directions, orchestrating debate among the country's elite factions while simultaneously massaging popular opinion. Rupert Murdoch's ownership of the *Mirror* and *The Australian* replicated this strategy. It was a combination he was to repeat in Britain with his acquisition of both *The Sun* and *The Times*, and again in the United States with ownership of the *New York Post* and *The Wall Street Journal.*

In 1972, Murdoch extended his reach in Sydney, purchasing the *Daily* and *Sunday Telegraph*, and in 1987 defeated rival bids to purchase the Herald and Weekly Times Group in Melbourne, finally owning the company that his father had built up but never controlled.

2.2.2 Beyond Australia to Britain: Tabloid Tales and Privileged Conversations

The initial move to expand beyond Australia came in 1964 with the purchase of the *Dominion*, the major paper in Wellington, the seat of the New Zealand parliament, but News Corp's first major venture offshore centred on Britain where Murdoch had seen Lord Beaverbrook combine spectacular profits with political influence in a country in decline but still with a significant voice in global affairs.

In 1968, after an acrimonious contest for control with the Czech-born publisher Robert Maxwell, News Ltd acquired the *News of the World*, one of Britain's oldest titles. Launched in 1843 to capitalise on rising rates of working-class literacy under the slogan "All human life is there", it built its circulation around gossip, sensation, crimes, and scandals, often involving sexual deviance or excess, earning the nickname "News of the Screws". Lacking the funds to purchase outright, Murdoch transferred News Ltd assets to the *News of the World* in return for a new stock issue, giving him a majority of voting rights. Still Britain's leading Sunday paper, it was in decline. In 1954, it was selling 8.1 million copies. By 1968, that figure had dropped to 6.2 million. [17] Murdoch responded by intensifying the search for scoops. In 1969, the paper published an exclusive extract from the memoirs of Christine Keeler, whose affairs in 1962 with both the Secretary of State for War, John Profumo, and a Soviet naval attaché, Yevgeny Ivanov, had precipitated one of the major political scandals of the post-war years. The facts were already well known, and Keeler's account added nothing significant, but the paper trailed it as "the story the world has been waiting for … A story which in years to come will be retold in the nation's history books." [18] Following complaints, the *News of the World* was referred to the Press Council, the newspaper industry's self-regulatory body established in 1962 to pre-empt statutory oversight. The paper was accused of exploiting "sordid details" for commercial gain and paying a person engaged in "notorious misbehaviour", and duly censured.

The search for inside information on the lives of newsworthy individuals led eventually to the phone-hacking scandal at the *News of the World*, precipitating the paper's closure and an official Commission of Inquiry. It marked a watershed moment in News Corp's fortunes, which we will return to.

The *News of the World* was making a healthy profit, but there was a strong incentive to add a daily title so that the printing presses could be used seven days a week. In 1969, Murdoch filled that gap, purchasing *The Sun*, a middle-market broadsheet launched in 1964 in an effort to revive the fortunes of the *Daily Herald.*

Murdoch promised that "the new Sun will still be a paper that cares passionately about truth and beauty and justice", but the first issue's relaunch as a tabloid, carried the lead headline, "Horse dope sensation" and a serialisation of Jacqueline Susann's novel *The Love Machine*, which made it abundantly clear that *The Sun* would employ the tabloid techniques that had successfully boosted sales of the Sydney *Daily Mirror*. Within a week, it had pushed the boundaries of acceptability for a national daily with a photo of a topless model on page three, a feature that became the paper's signature. It appeared daily from 1975, with "Page Three" and "Page 3" becoming registered trademarks.

The new *Sun* retained the old *Herald* slogan "Forward with the People", but radically redefined it. The *Herald* had first appeared as a strike bulletin issued by the London Society of Compositors during their 1911 struggle for a 48-hour week. It continued publishing after the strike, weathering a series of financial crises to achieve stability from 1930 onwards under the joint ownership of the Trade Union Congress and Odhams, publishers of the popular Sunday title *The People.* It was the voice of the trade union and labour movements, and, by 1933, Britain's best-selling daily paper with a circulation of 2 million. By 1964, that figure had declined to 1.26 million. This was still almost five times more than *The Times* [19] but the *Herald*'s ageing working-class readership was increasingly unattractive to advertisers, creating a shortfall in income that its initial 1964 relaunch as *The Sun* was unable to stem.

Murdoch's new tabloid, *The Sun*, declared itself "the people's newspaper", promising that "the *Sun* is on the side of the people ... We are not going to bow to the Establishment in any of its privileged enclaves. Ever." [20] The new *Sun*'s "people" were no longer addressed primarily as workers but as decent, patriotic, citizens talked down to by politicians, bureaucrats, intellectuals, and progressives who denigrated their cultural tastes and core values. Capitalist enterprise was celebrated for creating expanded consumer choice. It was a right-wing populist platform. It tapped into the gathering reconstruction of the political landscape that crystalised a decade later with Margaret

Thatcher's electoral victory in 1979 and the neoliberal liquidation of the post-war social contract.

The mass national readerships of *The Sun* and the *News of the World* provided a formidable platform for orchestrating public opinion, but Murdoch's time with Beaverbrook, and his father's career, had demonstrated the importance of privileged access to networks of influence in shaping a positive business and political environment.

The obvious point of entry was *The Times*, which his father's mentor, Lord Northcliffe, had successfully operated alongside the mass market *Daily Mail.* With an established reputation as the county's primary newspaper of record, it remained widely read and respected in elite circles.

The Canadian press owner Roy Thompson had bought the *Sunday Times* in 1959, adding *The Times* in 1966 to form Times Newspapers Ltd. Launching a colour magazine in 1962 and an award-winning Insight investigative team in 1963 boosted the *Sunday Times*' readership. By 1967, it sold 1.5 million copies, over half a million more than its main rival, *The Observer.* The profits subsidised losses from *The Times.* In November 1978, production on both titles was suspended when the print unions objected to plans to allow journalists to input copy directly, with the loss of traditional typesetting jobs. The dispute lasted a year with no resolution. In August 1980, faced with a strike for increased pay by journalists, the Thompson family decided to sell, announcing that both papers would close in March 1981 if no sale was agreed.

After a contentious bidding process, in which Prime Minister Margaret Thatcher played a crucial but disputed role in securing his exemption from automatic referral to the Monopolies and Mergers Commission (in circumstances explored in Chapter 5), Murdoch acquired both titles.

The year-long stoppage at *The Times* titles underlined the print unions' ability to shut down the presses through their monopoly control of the typesetting process essential to production. Murdoch's determination to dismantle their control by computerising production and introducing direct copy inputting led to a year-long strike (examined in Chapter 3) at his new purpose-built site at Wapping. Once again, Margaret Thatcher intervened to guarantee the enhanced policing needed to ensure that lorries transporting printed copies could pass through the picket lines.

The strike ended in mass redundancies and the end of traditional typesetting. In a public lecture in 2007, Murdoch claimed that "our victory" helped to create "what is now the world's most vibrant newspaper market", [21] neglecting to mention that two of his own post-Wapping initiatives, *Today* and *The London Paper*, had failed.

Today was launched by the regional newspaper owner, Eddie Shah, in March 1986 as a mid-market national daily. Within months, it was bailed out by the metals conglomerate Lonrho, publishers of the *Observer*, who set a deadline of June 1987 for disposal. With electronic production and pioneering full-colour printing, it posed a threat to the new *Sun.* In response Murdoch made a successful bid just before the Lonrho deadline expired. Once again, his offer should have been referred to the Monopolies Commission, but using the same tactics of brinkmanship that had secured Times Newspapers, he threatened to withdraw if it was not approved within 24 hours. Fearing that the paper might otherwise close, the Secretary of State for Trade and Industry waved it through. Readership increased but remained well below its established mid-market competitors, the *Daily Mail* and *Daily Express*, and in November 1995, *Today* ceased publication. Two other closures followed.

In September 2009, News Corp's free *London Paper,* launched in 2006 targeting the capital's cosmopolitan youth, was cancelled. A freesheet did not fit with Rupert Murdoch's newfound insistence that News Corp's mission was "to increase our revenue from *all* our content" (italics in the original). [22] In a series of initiatives examined in Chapter 3, this drive centred on efforts to exploit the commercial potential of the internet.

In July 2011, in an attempt to limit the reputational damage from the phone-hacking scandal (which we will return to later in this chapter), the *News of the World* was summarily shut, replaced in February 2012 by the *Sun on Sunday*, leaving News Corp's British newspaper interests monopolised by the daily and Sunday editions of *The Times* and *The Sun.*

2.2.3 ***The United States: New York, New York***

Building a major presence in the US, the largest English-language market and the pivotal Western power, was an essential third step in establishing News Corp as a leading global force in news and print. In 1973, Murdoch bought two papers in San Antonio Texas, the *News* and the *Express.* The *News* adopted the tried and tested tabloid formula with extensive coverage of sports and sensational headlines, including "Handless Body Found" and "Uncle Tortures Pets with Hot Fork".

The American newspaper market, like Australia's, was overwhelmingly local and city-based. The tabloid *National Inquirer* sold at supermarket checkouts was one of the few nationally distributed titles. In 1974, Murdoch launched a rival tabloid, *The National Star*, renamed *The Star* in 1976, aimed at working-class women. Both the *News* and *The Star* made money, but both were later sold, primarily to service debts, *The Star* in 1987 for $400 million and the San Antonio titles in 1992.

In the early 1980s, he acquired titles in two major cities, the *Boston Herald* in 1982 and the *Chicago Sun Times* in 1983, but his major initiatives were centred on New York.

Murdoch had moved to the city in 1973. In 1976, he bought the *New York Post*, the city's only afternoon daily, and in 1977, The New York Magazine Company, publishers of *The Village Voice* and *New York* magazine which combined the "new" subjective narrative journalism typified by Tom Wolfe with extensive coverage of the city's social scene typified by the rising real-estate magnate, Donald Trump. His incursions into the New York market were not universally welcomed. *Time* magazine depicted him as King Kong with a cover story headed "Aussie Press Lord Terrified Gotham".

The *Post* had a venerable history counting Alexander Hamilton, one of the republic's founding fathers, among its initial investors. Over the post-war period, it had established a reputation for socially responsible and investigative journalism with coverage of slum clearances and Senator McCarthy's infamous communist witch hunt. Under Murdoch, it became much more of a tabloid with a "Page Six" gossip column alongside stories of celebrities and crime news often with sensationalised headlines, most famously "Headless Body in Topless Bar", reporting a decapitation during a robbery at a strip club. In 1987, following his purchase of Metromedia's chain of television stations, which included one in New York, Murdoch was forced to sell the *Post* to comply with regulations barring ownership of a television station and newspaper in the same city.

Mismanaged by its new owners and bankrupt, the *Post* was put up for sale again in 1993. Political interests, including the New York mayor, Mario Cuomo, approached Murdoch to ask if he would resume ownership. He agreed providing that the Federal Communication Commission (FCC) granted him a permanent exemption from the cross-ownership rule. Supporters successfully deployed the same argument used earlier to secure the takeover of *Times Newspapers*, that Murdoch was the only viable purchaser and refusing him would lead inevitably to the closure of an iconic newspaper. [23]

News Corp's last major move in the US newspaper market came in 2007 when the company acquired *The Wall Street Journal* as part of the wider purchase of the Dow Jones financial news and data services. Following the precedent established with the *Times*, an independent committee was established to police the paper's editorial independence.

Murdoch had become an increasingly enthusiastic supporter of Ronald Reagan's neoliberal policies, receiving a presidential plaque thanking him for his newspapers' support after Reagan's inauguration in 1981. In 1995, he established a mouthpiece in Washington, *The Weekly Standard*, providing a platform for right-of-centre ideas and arguments widely read in Republican political circles. It was sold in 2009. Following the familiar pattern of owning both a broadsheet addressing elites and a popular tabloid, this left the two New York titles, the *Post* and *The Wall Street Journal*, as News Corp's only major investments in the US newspaper market.

2.2.4 Investing in Magazines

In the early 1980s, Murdoch began to build a significant presence in the magazine market. In 1984, News Group Magazines headed by the earlier acquisitions of *The Village Voice* and *New York* added *New Woman*, acquired the Ziff-Davis travel and trade publications for $350 million, and entered into a joint venture with the French publisher Hachette for 50 per cent of the American and British editions of the fashion magazine, *Elle*. Then, in October 1988, in the "largest takeover in American magazine history", [24] Murdoch acquired Walter Annenberg's Triangle Publications. Annenberg, a prominent Republican supporter and donor, had known Murdoch socially from his time in London as American Ambassador and admired the militant anti-union campaign Murdoch had pursued at Wapping. The deal delivered the bible of the betting industry, *The Daily Racing Form*, the best-selling magazine for teenage girls, *Seventeen*, and the property Murdoch most wanted, *TV Guide*, ranked third by advertising revenues and offering a national platform for his Fox television network.

Observers were surprised that Murdoch accepted Annenberg's $3 billion asking price without quibbling since it added to his accumulated debts and, together with other liabilities, precipitated a major repayment crisis, which we will return to later in this chapter.

2.2.5 Acquiring Book Publishers

In 1981, Murdoch launched a hostile bid for control of William Collins, the venerable Glasgow-based company with rights to sell the Bible in Britain and overseas markets. He failed but secured 41.7 per cent of the voting stock. In 1987, he purchased the New York publisher Harper Row for $300 million, valuing the company at 50 times its annual profits. Under a prior agreement, Collins took up the option of purchasing a half share, creating one of the largest English-language publishing companies. Murdoch, however, wanted full control and in 1988 launched a second, and successful, bid for Collins. In 1989, the companies merged to form HarperCollins.

In 1988, building on Collins' Bible business, Murdoch acquired Michigan-based Zondervan, publishers of the New International Version (NIV) of the Old and New Testaments and a leading force in promoting Evangelical Christianity, addressing a right-of-centre constituency that later became one of Donald Trump's core bases of support. News Corp's stake in Christian publishing was extended in 2011 with the purchase of Thomas Nelson, originally a Scottish concern but by then based in the US, with a list that included Billy Graham and other leading evangelical figures.

The Christian division sat somewhat uneasily alongside the other major niche publishing market that New Corp cultivated: romantic fiction and erotica.

In 1999, HarperCollins purchased the leading paperback publisher, Avon Books, from the Hearst Corporation. Avon had begun publishing romantic fiction in 1972 with titles like *Sweet Savage Love*. In 2014, Harper's romantic list was boosted by the acquisition of Harlequin, which included the hugely successful London-based imprint Mills and Boon with around a hundred titles a month. Mills and Boon had launched their sexually explicit imprint, Blaze, in 2001, followed in 2006 by Avon's erotica imprint, Avon Red.

In April 2021, News Corp consolidated its market position, paying $460 million for Houghton Mifflin Harcourt. It was a major acquisition that added 7,000 titles to the HarperCollins back catalogue. They included George Orwell's *1984* and *Animal Farm* and Tolkien's *Lord of the Rings*.

2.3 Diversification: Moving into Broadcasting

The story of News Corp's holdings in broadcast services has unfolded in four acts.

Act One saw initial forays into commercial terrestrial television in Australia and Britain circumscribed by ownership regulations and eventually abandoned.

Act Two saw relaxations in regulations combine with favourable treatment from governments to allow News Corp to secure monopoly control of subscription television in Australia (Foxtel) and New Zealand (Sky) and direct satellite services in Britain (BSkyB).

Act Three saw a major move into the US market with the purchase of the 20th Century Fox film studio, acquisition of television stations in major cities to create a fourth broadcasting network, and the launch of the Fox cable channels.

Act Four saw a concerted push to globalise operations employing satellite distribution to enter the newly liberalised television markets in Continental Europe, Latin America, Japan, India, and China.

In the final act, a series of divestitures, including the Fox film studios, and the Sky and Asian satellite systems, left Foxtel in Australia and the Fox network in the United States as the only significant remaining stakes in broadcasting.

2.3.1 Restricted Entry: Commercial Television in Australia and Britain

Early television services were available at the point of use to any household with an aerial able to receive signals relayed from networks of ground-based (terrestrial) transmitters. Public service channels were funded out of taxation while commercial services were funded by companies paying to place advertisements ("commercials") in and around programmes. For a small fee, homes without clear over-air reception could purchase access from cable companies who collected signals on large antennae and relayed them over networks of twisted copper (coaxial) wires, later replaced by higher-capacity fibre optic connections.

In the first phase of television's expansion, commercial networks were subject to strong regulation. There were variable combinations of limits on the number of stations any one company could own, on cross-ownership with newspapers, and on foreign investors. Cable operators were restricted to relaying programming from terrestrial channels and barred from offering additional services.

In Australia and Britain, Murdoch found his early attempts to diversify into commercial television restricted by regulation, but his penchant for entering markets through the back door and failing to honour undertakings established patterns that would be repeated.

2.3.2 Britain

In 1955, Britain became the first major country in Europe to introduce commercial television, creating a duopoly split between the public service BBC and the companies that made up the new Independent Television (ITV) system. They competed for viewers but not for revenues. The BBC was funded by a compulsory government-issued licence fee on television set ownership. The ITV companies enjoyed monopoly rights to television advertising in their franchise region. Until the 1984 Cable and Broadcasting Act, cable companies were confined to relaying terrestrial transmissions, confirming the ITV companies as the primary arena of commercial opportunity.

Non-nationals were permitted to invest in ITV companies but not to assume control. In November 1970, News International acquired a 7.5 per cent share in London Weekend Television (LWT), the ITV franchise holder for the capital from Friday evenings to Monday mornings. In return for injecting £500,000 of new capital, Murdoch was given a seat of the board on condition that he did not intervene in programming. He broke the agreement and lobbied to become Chief Executive. The regulator, the Independent Television Authority (ITA), concerned that the influence Murdoch exerted through his British newspaper holdings was being extended into television, ordered that an independent candidate be appointed. The channel moved into profit, but Murdoch resented the ITA's ruling, seeing it as another instance of Establishment antagonism. In March 1980, News International sold its last bloc of LWT shares and looked for another way into the British television market. This came a decade later in 1990 with the capture of Britain's direct satellite broadcasting market and the launch of BSkyB.

The ambition to own a major free-to-air channel persisted, however. In 1994, BSkyB had been part of a consortium bidding to operate Britain's last terrestrial network, Channel 5. The bid failed but BSkyB's interest in Channel 5 continued.

In December 2002, the New Labour government introduced a Communications Bill relaxing cross-ownership regulations. In a provision critics dubbed the "Murdoch clause", the prohibition on companies with more than 20 per cent of the national newspaper market was retained for the ITV companies but lifted for Channel 5. In a further concession, the ban on ownership by companies based outside the EU was also abolished. Introducing the measure, the minister, Tessa Jowell, argued that the "possibility of ownership" from "American Australian, or other markets ... will free the industry from unnecessary interference, give it freedom to grow and diversify ... and gain access to new sources of investment". [25]

The original Channel Five franchise was awarded to a group that included CLT (Compagnie Luxembourgeoise de Telediffusion) and Pearson, owners of Thames Television, the ITV weekday franchise for London. In 2005, the channel was acquired by the German global media conglomerate Bertelsmann but sold in 2010 to the British press concern Northern and Shell, publishers of the mid-market national daily the *Daily Express* and the tabloid *Daily Star.* In 2014, it was put up for sale again. BSkyB submitted a joint bid with Discovery Communications, but Northern and Shell opted to sell to the US media conglomerate Viacom. Ironically, BSkyB was running all of Viacom's UK advertising at the time.

In December 2020, News Corp re-entered the British broadcast television market when the regulator, Ofcom, granted the company's British subsidiary, News UK, a licence to establish a new television channel. A full-service channel was seen as economically unviable and the operation, dubbed News UK, was envisaged as a streaming-only service limited to the evenings. Watching British television while isolated during the COVID pandemic, however, Rupert Murdoch reputedly became convinced there was a market niche for a right-of-centre channel.

In September 2021, plans for a full linear channel were revived under the title Talk TV, trading on the "Talk" brand promoted by the British radio stations. The decision was given added impetus by the launch of GB News in June 2021. Funded jointly by the investment fund Legatum and the hedge fund manager Sir Paul Marshall, a prominent donor to the Brexit campaign, GB News was aimed at the same market niche. Both channels set out to establish a British version of Fox News with platforms for explicitly right-of-centre political comment.

Talk TV's schedule pivoted around the weekday prime-time programme presented by the controversial tabloid journalist Piers Morgan, a former editor of Murdoch's *News of the World* and the *Daily Mirror*, where a judge summing up in a 2023 court case found him to have been complicit in phone hacking, Morgan's disparaging comments on Meghan Markle, the Duchess of Sussex, on his ITV morning show, *Good Morning Britain*, generated over 57,000 complaints, the largest number ever received by the broadcast regulator Ofcom.

Morgan's Talk TV programme, *Piers Morgan Uncensored*, opened with two interviews with the former US President, Donald Trump. A week later, the initial audience of 317,000 had dropped by 80 per cent to 62,000. Overall, the channel's ratings have remained consistently low. In May 2022, it was reaching 1.9 million viewers as against GB News's 2.19 million and 8.94 million for Murdoch's former channel Sky News. [26] By December 2023, GB News was pulling even further ahead, reaching 2.87 million viewers as against Talk TV's 2 million.

Although ambitions to replicate the success of Fox News have proved overly optimistic, both GB News and Talk TV have consistently challenged the impartiality rules governing British broadcasting, with mounting concerns over serving politicians presenting programmes and overtly biased language. In 2023, Talk TV paid substantial damages to a migrant charity for labelling its organisers as "human traffickers". [27]

In February 2024, Piers Morgan announced that he was leaving Talk TV and moving *Uncensored* to his YouTube channel. In March, Talk TV followed suit, confirming that it was closing its linear channel and moving entirely online

2.3.3 *Australia*

Introduced in 1956, Australian television followed Britain with a public service organisation, the Australian Broadcasting Corporation (ABC), modelled on the BBC, operating alongside advertising-supported channels. The commercial system eventually crystallised around three networks, Seven, 10, and Nine, based in the major metropolitan centres. Until 1987, however, operators were only permitted to own two stations.

The first franchises, for two stations each in Sydney and Melbourne, went to the major newspaper owners. In Sydney, Channel 7 was controlled by the Fairfax family and Channel 9 by the Television Corporation, owned by Frank Packer.

In 1958, franchises for Adelaide were advertised, and Southern Television Corporation, in which News Ltd had a 60 per cent stake, was awarded Channel 9.

The largest returns were generated in the two major urban centres, Sydney and Melbourne. Refused a franchise for Sydney, Murdoch threated to transmit into the city from Wollongong, 60 miles to the south, using his recently acquired stake in the town's Channel 4 and drawing on the exclusive deal he had signed with ABC, one of the three major US networks, giving him exclusive Australian rights to their programmes for five years. To pre-empt unwelcome competition, Packer offered Murdoch a quarter share in his company in return for access to ABC's programmes. Murdoch accepted but the episode convinced him of the need to control both content and carriage.

In 1967, he sold his holding back to Packer and in 1979 re-entered the Sydney market, increasing his stake in the city's Channel 10 to 48.2 per cent, giving him effective control. To comply with the two-station rule, he sold his Wollongong station and assured the newly installed oversight body, the Australian Broadcast Tribunal, that he would not trade his Adelaide station for one in Melbourne.

In 1963, the franchise for the third channel in Melbourne (Channel 0, later Channel 10) was awarded to Austarama Television, a subsidiary of the Ansett Transportation group. Once again, Murdoch entered the market through the back door, gaining control of Channel 10 when he joined with Peter Abeles' TNT transport group to acquire Ansett Transportation in 1979. The Ansett assets included Australia's second airline, generating substantial dividends that helped finance News Corp's expansion in America. After years of extracting maximum returns for minimal outlay, Murdoch sold his stake in 2000, leaving the Ansett air fleet ranked the second oldest among the 50 world-class airlines.

In 1987, regulations were introduced barring ownership of both a commercial television channel and a newspaper published at least four times a week in any one area. Having acquired the Herald press group, Murdoch opted to consolidate his press holdings and in February 1987 sold his Australian television assets.

2.3.4 Market Captures: Subscription Television

2.3.4.1 Australia: Foxtel

The 1992 liberalisation of Australian television under the Broadcasting Services Act opened the commercial market to competition from subscription (pay-TV) services offering sports and films not available on the free-to-air channels. Regulation was relaxed, permitting greater foreign ownership and tie-ups between broadcasters and telecommunications companies aimed at accelerating the construction of high-capacity fibre optic cables and communication satellites that could be used for telephony and internet connections as well as broadcast signals.

The first franchise, with exclusive rights to deliver pay-TV over satellite until 1997, was awarded to the Galaxy consortium headed by US cable operators (Century Communications and TCI) and investment companies (CVC and Guiness Peat). It launched on 1 January 1995, followed later that year by three competitors; Austar, Optus Vision, and Foxtel, a joint venture between the Australian telecommunications group Telstra and News Corp's Fox division. Fox was responsible for programming and Telstra for transmission over its hybrid coaxial-fibre cable network.

Despite launching late, Murdoch was determined to dominate the emerging sector. Galaxy offered attractive programming with a premier sports stream and exclusive rights to selected Hollywood films (Showtime and Encore) and popular US television (TV1), but the prohibitive costs of building the satellite and microwave systems required by its franchise opened question marks about its financial viability that Murdoch allegedly exploited. A case brought in the New York Supreme Court by Galaxy's US bondholders, who lost almost $800 million, claimed that the company's collapse had been accelerated by a series of hostile moves by Murdoch. These allegedly included providing prospective investors with "misleading and disparaging information" and a highly critical piece in *The Australian* predicting losses until 2009. In May 1998, Galaxy was declared insolvent and ceased trading. Two weeks later, Foxtel acquired its subscribers from the liquidator.

Foxtel's main rival in the major metropolitan pay-TV markets was Optus Vision, a joint venture between Optus, the principal competitor to Telstra in the Australian telecommunications market, and the US cable operator Continental Cablevision. Foxtel proposed a merger in October 1995 and again in July 1997 but was blocked both times by the regulator concerned with a reduction in competition.

By 2002, however, wasteful competition, marked by a refusal to share channels and infrastructure and sluggish take-up saw the industry's debts approaching $4 billion, siphoning money away from upgrading the telecommunications infrastructure.

As Optus Chief Executive Chris Anderson noted, "Subscription television costs have long been an economic burden on Optus", hindering the development of telephone and broadband internet services. [28] These costs were offloaded in November 2002 when Optus and Foxtel signed a Binding Content Agreement. Foxtel assumed Optus' financial obligations under its film and content arrangements and agreed to provide additional sports channels; Optus undertook to resell Foxtel subscription channels on its cable network until 2010 and to lease substantial capacity to Foxtel on its Optus C1 satellite.

The arrangement strengthened Optus' position in the telecoms market, allowing them to concentrate on developing "triple play" packages of telephone, internet, and television services. Foxtel secured guaranteed access to satellite distribution and became the main content provider for Australian subscription services.

Where Foxtel and Optus focused on metropolitan markets, the fourth pay-TV operator, Austar, served areas outside major population centres. Its reach into regional and rural areas added subscribers and its MyStar set-top box and personal video recorder, launched in 2008, enabling users to watch and record digital satellite television was a path-breaking innovation which News Corp later built on with its own set-top boxes. Foxtel acquired Austar in May 2012, assuming effective monopoly control over Australian pay-TV services.

In December 2016, News Corp Australia extended its presence in Australian broadcasting acquiring Australian News Channel Pty Ltd (ANC) originally launched in 1996 as a joint venture between BSkyB and the Australian networks, Seven Media Group and Nine Entertainment Co. Comcast's buyout of Sky ended direct links but the 'Sky' brand remains active with Sky News Australia distributed on Foxtel's pay platform, offering rolling news during the day and conservative commentators, modelled on Fox News, in prime time. In 2019, a partnership with YouTube, Microsoft News, Facebook and Taboola, made Sky content available across major digital platforms.

2.3.4.2 Britain: BSkyB

In Britain, Murdoch's entry into the pay-TV market pivoted on gaining monopoly control over direct satellite broadcasting.

In 1982, the BBC was allocated two of the five direct broadcasting by satellite (DBS) channels assigned to Britain by the 1977 World Administrative Radio Conference. The Corporation failed to raise the required financing, additional investors baulked at the costs, and the project lapsed.

In June 1983, News International purchased 65 per cent of Satellite Television Limited which had begun beaming programming across Europe in April 1982. Using the low-powered OTS satellite made direct home reception difficult, so the service relied on cable operators. In 1983, transmissions were extended to Britain, and early in 1984 the service was renamed Sky Channel. It operated at a loss, £10 million in 1987, but established News International as a serious player in the nascent DBS market.

In 1986, the Independent Broadcasting Authority (IBA) advertised commercial licences for three of Britain's allocated DBS channels. News International joined the bid mounted by the Direct Broadcasting Limited consortium which included major general companies, Sears and British and Commonwealth Shipping, but no communication corporations.

The franchise went to British Satellite Broadcasting (BSB), a consortium centred around established British media interests. Murdoch applied to have his satellite service included in the consortium but failed to secure regulatory approval. In June 1988, he announced that Sky Television would launch a British service of four direct-to-home channels, including the first 24-hour news channel.

Sky had three competitive advantages. First, it was not required to build its own dedicated satellites and could piggyback on the new European Astra satellite, whose signals could be picked up on relatively small dishes. Second, utilising the established PAL transmission system avoided the uncertainties attached to the new D-MAC system. Third, it enjoyed saturation cross-promotion in News International's newspapers. Sky went on air in February 1989, 13 months before BSB debuted in March 1990.

The initial costs of competition to both companies were huge, however, and a merger was announced. The terms of the tie-up, which contravened the newly introduced cross-ownership rules, were highly contentious. Despite vocal opposition, the deal went ahead, and was allowed to stand, granting Murdoch de facto monopoly control of British satellite broadcasting. We will return to the details of this case in Chapter 5 when we examine Murdoch's political relations and influence.

In 1993, the merged company BSkyB launched an expanded multi-channel service, moved to an entirely subscription-based business model, and began generating operating profits. In December 1994, the company was floated on the condition that News Corp reduced its 50 per cent shareholding to below 40 per cent.

To entice viewers to subscribe, BSkyB needed to offer exclusive access to programming not available elsewhere. Recent movies were part of the package, but as Rupert Murdoch told the 1996 News Corporation annual meeting, sport "absolutely overpowers" all other offerings "as a battering ram and a lead offering in all our pay television operations" around the world. [29]

BSkyB pioneered this strategy with its successful 1992 five-year deal for exclusive rights to games played in football's Premier League, the breakaway consortium of England's top-tier clubs, launched the previous year. The bid of US$4.9 million was six times the value previously paid for football rights by the free-to-air commercial broadcaster, ITV. It placed access to one of the cornerstones of English sport behind a paywall while offering a roster of games by iconic teams for broadcasting in global markets. In 1998, BSkyB attempted to strengthen its stake in the beautiful game, offering US$1.2 billion to acquire Manchester United, one of the world's most famous football clubs and England's richest. "Excluding money from television rights, it generated more income on a single game day than twenty-two of England's ninety-two professional and semi-professional clubs generated in an entire year." [30] The British Monopolies and Mergers Commission ruled against the bid on the grounds that it gave BSkyB a seat on both sides of table and an unfair advantage when future rights were being negotiated.

2.3.4.3 New Zealand: Sky

The New Zealand government had been an early and enthusiastic pioneer of marketisation, and in 1997, the Commerce Commission granted Murdoch, already a major presence in the nation's newspaper market, permission to become the lead shareholder in the country's pay-TV operation, coincidently named Sky.

Originally launched in 1987 as Sky Media Limited, beaming sports programming to pubs and clubs, in 1997 it secured UHF spectrum in the government auction and launched a direct broadcasting by satellite service. Following his initial investment, Murdoch moved to "take full advantage of New Zealand's weak regulatory arrangements". [31] In 2003, he used money from the sale of his print holdings to increase his stake and in 2005 avoided having to buy out other shareholders by merging Sky with his New Zealand operating company, Independent News Ltd (INL), to create Sky Network TV with a 43.65 per cent holding. Since the subscription cable service offered by Telstra-Clear, the main competitor in the pay-TV market, was largely a repackaged version of its channels, Sky effectively enjoyed a digital monopoly in the pay-TV market.

Sky also received significant government support in developing its programming. There was no effort to challenge its refusal to pay fees to retransmit channels carried on free-to-air platforms, and at the government's behest, two digital channels, financed from public money, the archive channel Heartland and the children's channel Kidzone, were placed exclusively on the Sky platform. News Corp sold its stake in Sky in February 2013.

Sky News Australia, operated by News Corp Australia since 2016, is available in New Zealand.

2.3.5 Investing in Radio

News Corp has invested in radio in both Britain and Australia.

2.3.5.1 Britain

News Corp had been involved in British commercial radio through its 30 per cent stake in the Wireless Group founded by former *Sun* editor, Kelvin MacKenzie, but withdrew when Wireless was sold in 2005. When the company came up for sale in June 2016, News Corp took full control and re-entered the sector with three major national channels: Talk Radio, Talk Sport, and Virgin Radio.

The declared intention was to maximise synergies by reactivating the relation with *The Sun* and "increasing engagement for both businesses through cross-promotion of our brands and the use of our respective talent". [32]

In June 2020, in a second synergistic move News Corp sought to capitalise on the journalistic resources of *The Times* and *The Sunday Times*, launching Times Radio as a 24-hour news and comments channel.

2.3.5.2 Australia

ARN, Australia's premier radio network for the 25–54 age group, sees News Corp Australia holding a 13.29 per cent stake in its ownership. In June 2023, ARN strengthened its position by acquiring a 14.8 per cent equity stake in its main competitor, Southern Cross Media Group. In 2005, shortly after leaving News Corp, Lachlan Murdoch established Illyria as a personal investment vehicle. By 2009, he acquired a 50 per cent share in Nova Entertainment, eventually gaining full ownership in 2012. Nova operates a national radio network and stations in Sydney, Melbourne, Adelaide (FIVEaa), and the Central Coast (Star 104.5). It also manages a podcast network (NEPN), Red Room live music platform, music services for Coles grocery stores, and an events company, eXp.

While Nova isn't formally economically linked to News Corp, it maintains relations by operating Smooth TV on Foxtel and leveraging News Corp outlets, including Sky News, for podcast content and presenters. Lachlan Murdoch's dual leadership roles in News Corp and Fox Corp add significance to his outside interests.

2.4 Americanisation: Building the Fox Brand

Murdoch recognised that in a global cultural market dominated by American film and television, any company aiming to be a major player needed a strong presence in US entertainment. As he told his biographer:

> A really integrated media company has to be in the production of entertainment. I went to entertainment [as] part of a broad strategy to get into the heart of the media industry … I know you can't really talk about one global economy, but there really is. There are certain things that are common. Hollywood studios still have the pre-eminent position. [33]

2.4.1 Investing in Hollywood: 20th Century Fox

Murdoch's initial move to break into Hollywood came in 1983 with the acquisition of 6.7 per cent of Warner Bros, one of the six major studios that dominated American film production, but he was bought out by owners concerned to retain control. A second chance came in 1985 when another studio, 20th Century Fox, came up for sale.

In 1981, Fox had been acquired by two oil men, Marvin Davis and Marc Rich. When Rich was charged with tax evasion and racketeering, his 50 per cent share had been seized by the American government. In 1985, Davis was permitted to place it on the market. Murdoch purchased it, acquiring Davis's half share soon afterwards to take full control, retaining the Fox name.

The film production division had a number of box office successes. They included the first- and third-highest grossing movies of all time, *Avatar* (2009) and *Titanic* (1997), with worldwide earnings of $2.84 billion and $2.20 billion, the *X-Men* and *Fantastic Four* superhero franchises, and distribution revenues from the revived *Star Wars* series. Mainstream production was supplemented by an animation studio responsible for the successful *Ice Age* series and the Searchlight studio funding low-budget, independent films including *The Full Monty* (1997), a dark comedy of English deindustrialisation, nominated for four Oscars and earning a $250 million return on a production budget of $3.5 million.

Building an "integrated media company" offered multiple opportunities to cross-promote other News Corp interests. Reports of the imminent alien invasion of Earth in the 20th Century Fox disaster movie *Independence Day* (1996) appear on screens prominently bearing the Sky News logo.

2.4.2 Satellite Broadcasting: Aborted Take-Off

Delivering programming directly to domestic dish receivers using satellites with nationwide coverage by-passed the regulatory limits placed on terrestrial station ownership and evaded cable operators' control over what would be carried over their systems. As Murdoch noted, "In a landscape of increasing [cable] consolidation it is essential to ensure our content continues to reach consumers and its long-term viability is greatly enhanced by owning a platform." [34]

In April 1983, his American holding company, News America Corp, acquired a controlling interest in Inter-American Satellite Television and signed a contract with Satellite Business Systems to lease transponders on their medium-powered KU-band satellite. A new division, Skyband Inc., planned to offer five premium subscription channels to homes not served by cable. However, since reception required a dish six to eight feet in diameter, the service was only likely to attract subscriptions from apartment blocks where Hughes Aerospace was planning a rival trial. In November 1983, Skyband was scrapped.

News Corp re-entered the market at the end of the 1990s to find control over satellite broadcasting in the United States concentrated in the hands of two companies, EchoStar and DirecTV, a subsidiary of Hughes Electronics owned by General Motors.

In December 2000, Murdoch's Sky Global Networks opened talks with Hughes to acquire DirectTV, but in May 2001, EchoStar countered with a merger proposal. News Corp successfully lobbied the US Justice Department to block the deal on competition grounds, forcing EchoStar to abandon its planned takeover. In April 2003, other potential bidders having withdrawn, News Corp's revised £4.1 billion bid for Hughes Electronics was accepted. Ignoring concerns from cable operators that Fox "would raise its programming prices … and pull programming to direct customers to Direct TV", [35] it was approved by both the FCC and the Department of Justice.

The bid was mounted in collaboration with John Malone of Liberty Media, America's largest cable operator, who had designs of his own on DirecTV. At the time, Malone was the largest investor in News Corp outside the Murdoch family. In 2004, he began exchanging his non-voting stock for voting shares, posing a threat to Murdoch's unchallenged control. In 2006, Malone agreed to relinquish his 16.3 per cent holding in return for News Corp's 38.5 per cent interest in DirecTV, effectively acquiring ownership through the back door and ending News Corp's US satellite distribution ambitions. In 2015, in a move confirming the increasing integration of telephone, internet, and television services, DirecTV was acquired by the major US telecommunications operator, AT&T.

2.4.3 Terrestrial Broadcasting: Building a Fourth Network

From 1949 onwards, American commercial television had been dominated by three companies: ABC, CBS, and NBC, each with a nationwide network made up of directly owned and operated stations and affiliated stations relying on them for most of their programming.

In 1981, President Reagan appointed Mark Fowler as Chair of the FCC, a position he held until 1987. Fowler championed radical deregulation. As he told an industry gathering:

> Deregulation … is the right direction for our nation's communications system. … The primary task that we have set for ourselves now is to get out of the way of … entrepreneurs who believe that they've got a product or service people want. [36]

Fowler's vocal support for competition signalled a permanent shift in the regulatory environment, paving the way for Murdoch to build a fourth network.

The Fox network launched in 1985 when six television stations purchased from Metromedia were added to the Fox studios to create a vertically integrated production and distribution system. The stations, based in key metropolitan markets, New York, Chicago, Washington, Los Angeles, Houston, and

Dallas, reached 22 per cent of American homes. To comply with FCC rules barring foreign ownership of broadcast stations, Murdoch applied for US citizenship. His submission was still pending when the Metromedia purchase was finalised. This should have disqualified him, but in a notable concession, the acquisition was waved through. However, the regulation barring ownership of a newspaper and broadcast station in the same city forced him to sell two of his major press titles, the *Chicago Sun Times* and the *New York Post*. In 1987, he added a Boston station.

In 1994, New World transferred its 12 stations to Fox. The deal included four NBC affiliates and breached the 25 per cent limit on foreign ownership. The FCC upheld NBC's objection but, eager to see a fourth TV network expand competition, urged Murdoch to seek a waiver on the limit, which was granted. Fox acquired New World outright in 1997 and in August 2000 added ten more stations purchased from Chris-Craft, establishing the network in all ten top markets with duopolies in two of the largest, New York and Los Angeles.

Its position as the largest terrestrial network conferred enormous bargaining power. As the CEO of Fox Television Studios noted, "we will be able to buy any show that's put out by any studio. You are just going to have to deal with us." [37]

This consolidation was the end product of a gradual expansion designed to bypass regulatory restrictions.

Fox network debuted on air in October 1986 with a late-night talk show. In 1987, it moved into prime time. The initial entry, a sitcom and comedy show on Sunday nights, was followed by a Saturday line-up of comedies and movies. The Monday night schedule, added in 1989, included two programmes that significantly boosted the network's ratings: the iconic animation *The Simpsons* and the tabloid crime show *America's Most Wanted.* Prime-time programming on Thursday and Friday nights was added in 1990, followed by Tuesdays and Wednesdays in 1993, establishing Fox as a prime-time presence on every night of the week. Following the strategy of acquiring key sports rights that had boosted BSkyB's ratings in the UK, in December 1993 Fox outbid CBS to secure a four-year contract with the National Football League (NFL) to televise American football games from the National Football Conference and the 1997 Super Bowl.

The gradualist approach to expansion had allowed Fox to bypass the FCC's Financial Interest and Syndication (Fin-Syn) separating programme production from distribution. The rules barred networks from having a financial interest in or leasing broadcast rights to programmes they had not produced themselves "in house". Introduced in the 1970s, they effectively transferred majority control of the $5 billion-a-year syndication market to the Hollywood studios who produced the majority of programming. [38] Since Fox broadcast less than the 15 hours or more of prime-time programming that defined a full network, it was permitted to retain its lucrative syndication business. In 1983, under increasing pressure from the networks, the FCC proposed to relax the

Fin-Syn provisions, but after concerted lobbying from the Hollywood studios, supported by the former film actor, President Ronald Reagan, the revisions were shelved.

By 1990, Fox was on the verge of exceeding the programme limit. It petitioned the FCC to waive the Fin-Syn provisions, arguing that they unduly restricted competition by discouraging it from offering a full menu of programmes. The FCC responded in 1991 by relaxing restrictions, but in 1992, Fox joined the networks to petition the Seventh Circuit court to abolish the rules altogether, arguing that they were invalidated by the increased viewer choice provided by cable services and videocassettes and the network's declining audience share, from 90 per cent to 65 per cent. Fox's decision to limit its prime-time offering was cited as key evidence that the rules restricted programme choice. By November 1995, following further court cases, the Fin-Syn provisions had virtually disappeared.

With the removal of the regulatory wall separating programme production from distribution, News Corp's strategy of building a vertically integrated corporation that combined a major network with a Hollywood studio became the industry norm. In 1995, The Walt Disney Corporation purchased ABC. In 1999, Viacom, owners of Paramount Pictures, acquired CBS, and in 2004, NBC's parent company General Electric took an 80 per cent share in Universal Studios.

Fox was also in the vanguard of a major shift in the television programming market, adding sales of formats to finished productions. Government support for national production in emerging markets, combined with popular preferences for local programming, placed limits on sales of imported programming. The solution was to develop a "pie and crust" strategy, selling a basic programme shell cooked to a pre-set recipe that could be filled with localised content. It proved particularly attractive to channels in newly liberalised television systems looking for programme ideas that had demonstrated their commercial value in established markets.

The profit potential had been demonstrated by the success of the reality singing contest *American Idol* in boosting Fox's own ratings. Based on an original British format *Pop Idol*, owned by Fremantle, a joint venture between two major media conglomerates, Bertelsmann and Pearson, it debuted in 2002 and ran for 15 seasons, becoming the most-watched US television programme of the 2000s. Fox entered the format market through Rupert Murdoch's daughter Elisabeth who had left her senior management role at BSkyB in 2001 to set up her own independent production company, Shine. BSkyB took a 5 per cent shareholding (later increased to 13%) and agreed to purchase an agreed amount of Shine programming for two years. Specialising initially in factual programming, Shine built up stakes in drama production (Kudos), entertainment (Princess Productions), and children's programmes, and acquired operating bases in the US (Reveille Productions) and Europe. News Corp acquired the Shine Group in 2011.

One of the leading players in the format market at the time was the Dutch company Endemol, launched in 1994. Its suite of successful reality programmes led by *Big Brother* and *Deal or No Deal* had sold to multiple global markets. Taken over by Silvio Berlusconi's holding company Mediaset in 2007, in 2012 Endemol had been bought out by the American private equity firm Apollo Global Management. In 2014, Fox entered into a joint venture with Apollo to combine the Shine and Endemol groups, creating the world's largest consortium of independent production companies trading in both formats and finished programmes.

Following the merger, Elizabeth Murdoch resigned as Chair of the Shine Group, declined a seat on the News Corp Board, and launched her own production company, Sister.

2.4.4 Cable Programming: The Rise of Fox News

By the mid-1990s, cable services were reaching the majority of US homes. In 1994, Fox launched a series of cable channels alongside its terrestrial network. The initial general entertainment channel FX and the movie channel FXM were joined in 1996 by Fox Sports Net and the Fox News Channel.

CNN (Cable News Network), launched in 1980, was for 15 years the only 24-hour news service. Having earlier failed to acquire the channel, Rupert Murdoch launched Fox News as a direct competitor, hiring Roger Ailes to direct the channel. As a media consultant, Ailes had placed appeals to the "silent majority" at the heart of Richard Nixon's presidential campaign. He saw Fox News mobilising the same "left behind" constituency, employing the opinionated formats alongside news that he had successfully developed in *The Rush Limbaugh* show, built around the right-wing talk radio celebrity (1992–1996) and NBC's vox-pop cable channel *America's Talking* (1994–1996).

Both ventures took full advantage of the extended space for more overtly partisan presentation opened up in 1987 by the abolition of the FCC's fairness doctrine, introduced in 1949, and required that broadcasters covering contentious issues present contrasting views.

In a fiercely competitive multi-channel market, Fox News's "flashy presentation and expressive anchoring" broke with the established templates of news reporting, carving out a distinctive niche and forging a new hybrid of politics with entertainment. [39] Building on the model established by News Corp's tabloid newspapers, it combined a dynamic visual style, pioneering the scrolling summary of headlines at the bottom of the screen, with a right-of-centre populism projected by programme anchors who performed the role of "authentic blue collar everyman" [40] claiming to speak for "decent ordinary working people" discarded and despised by a privileged political and cultural metropolitan elite. As one early observer noted, "Fox is about … us versus them. Insiders versus outsiders. Phonies versus non phonies … established media against insurgent media." [41]

Solidly Republican-supporting from the outset, Fox News migrated steadily to the party's right wing. Its anchors actively promoted the opposition to President Obama's stimulus and healthcare reforms organised by the Tea Party faction and publicised false claims that Obama was Muslim not Christian and, being born outside the United States, was disqualified from being President. These campaigns fed an undertow of popular racism that combined white supremacism with the demonisation of migrants and Islam. When asked, 68 per cent of viewers identifying Fox News as their most trusted media source agreed that the "values of Islam are at odds with American values", compared to 37 per cent of CNN viewers [42].

Dismissing CNN and other "mainstream" news outlets as "fake news" and selecting Fox News as his preferred media platform was central to the populist platform Donald Trump promoted during his presidential campaign and subsequent term in office, generating a powerful symbiotic relationship.

Over time, Trump's relations with Fox soured as his behaviour became more erratic, culminating in his accusation that Biden had "stolen" the 2020 Presidential Election by rigging votes. By then, Fox News "available in nearly ninety million homes … had been the most watched television news channel for nineteen consecutive years … routinely notching up the top ten programs in the genre". [43]

Fox News' promotion of Trump's claims, knowing them to be false, has caused major reputational damage, which we will return to later in this chapter when we review the crises the company has experienced.

But first, we need to follow News Corp's attempts to move beyond its core English-language markets and build a global television network using satellite systems to beam programming into Germany and Italy, Latin America, Japan, India, and China.

2.5 Globalisation: Satellite Ventures

In 2000, the push to globalise was announced in a new division, Sky Global Networks. Despite the technological promise of borderless distribution, initiatives consistently confronted political realities as dominant national players defended their market shares, governments imposed restrictions. and audiences expressed a marked preference for localised programming.

2.5.1 European Union: Germany and Italy

News Corp's initial foray into the German pay-TV market was a disaster. BSkyB had acquired a 22 per cent stake in Premiere, the digital satellite platform launched in 1996, majority owned by the Kirch Group. In May 2002, faced with mounting debt, Kirch filed for bankruptcy. BSkyB activated an option in the shareholder agreement requiring its \$1.4 billion investment to be returned. Kirch was unable to pay, forcing BSkyB to write off the entire amount and giving Murdoch what he later admitted was a "black eye".

In 2003, Murdoch entered one of Europe's other major television markets, Italy, acquiring two loss-making satellite platforms, Tilapia, owned by the French operator Canal+, and Stream TV, operated by the Italian telecommunications company Telecom Italia, to create Sky Italia. He was immediately confronted with the entrenched power of Silvio Berlusconi who had exploited a loophole in the Italian media law to break the public service broadcasting monopoly and establish a nationwide commercial network, diversified into newspapers and advertising, and used his media assets to support his successful bids to become the country's prime minister. He was elected for a second time in 2001. In 2004, he moved to expand beyond free-to-air commercial television, where he had established a dominant position, launching a pay-TV service in direct competition with Murdoch. Sports programming was central to Sky Italia's appeal, but a European Commission ruling had blocked it from acquiring exclusive access to relay soccer matches across all means of delivering television. Berlusconi exploited this restriction by purchasing the digital terrestrial rights to the games of Italy's leading soccer teams, capitalising on the substantial subsidies for the set-top boxes needed for viewing as part of the government push to move viewers from analogue to digital television by the end of 2006.

Berlusconi's rights coup came as a complete surprise to Sky Italia executives and underlined the need to cultivate political contacts and networks in new markets. As a News Corp executive regretfully noted, its people in Italy "were not as integrated into the society as they might have been". [44]

Following his re-election for a third term as prime minister in 2008, Berlusconi renewed his assault on Murdoch's revenues, doubling the value-added tax levied on satellite television and reducing the hourly amount of advertising permitted from 18 per cent to 12 per cent. Sky Italia steadily gained ground, however, and by October 2011 had five million paying subscribers and a potential audience of over 15 million viewers. [45] In November 2011, Berlusconi lost his parliamentary majority and resigned.

In 2008, News Corp had re-entered the German market. Following Kirch's bankruptcy, Premiere was taken over by the private equity firm Permira, and in 2005 the restructured network was floated on the stock market, promoted as Germany's "foremost pay-TV business". In 2008, News Corp acquired an initial 14.6 per cent share, increased its stake to 54.5 per cent, and in 2009 relaunched the service as Sky Deutschland.

In July 2014, in an effort to raise funds for a projected $80 billion renewed takeover bid for Time Warner Inc., Murdoch's audio-visual division 21st Century Fox agreed to sell its full ownership of Sky Italia and its stake in Sky Deutschland to BSkyB, who then bought out the remaining minority shareholders. 'British' was dropped from the company name and the newly consolidated pan-European satellite service rebranded as Sky.

2.5.2 Latin America

Murdoch has always preferred to exercise full control over the companies he invests in, but in entering national and regional satellite markets elsewhere, he has had to seek alliances with established local players, either voluntarily or in response to government pressure.

Television in Latin America was dominated by two major players – Mexico's Grupo Televisa in the Spanish-speaking market and Brazil's Globo in the Portuguese market. In 1995, News Corp announced that it was forming a joint venture with both corporations to launch a direct satellite service across Central and South America. The three main partners each had a 30 per cent share with the remaining 10 per cent held by the cable operator Tele-Communications. The project, named Sky Latin America, faced competition from a rival consortium launched in 1994 by DirecTV, then still owned by Hughes Electronics, in partnership with the Venezuela-based Grupo Cisneros. Originally named Galaxy, the group was rebranded as DirecTV Latin America in 2000.

Following News Corp's 2003 acquisition of DirecTV, it absorbed Sky's Mexican and Brazilian operations in 2005 but retained the Sky brand name. In 2006, as noted earlier, Murdoch was forced to sell DirecTV, ending his Latin American satellite ambitions. In 2015, following DirecTV's purchase by AT&T, DirecTV Latin America (renamed Vrio Corp in 2018) held 93 per cent of Sky Brazil and 41 per cent of Sky Mexico, with Globo and Televisa retaining the respective balances. In July 2021, AT&T sold Vrio's operations, except its stake in Sky Mexico, to Grupo Werthein, an Argentinian diversified conglomerate.

2.5.3 Japan

In 1997, DirecTV had entered the Japanese satellite television market with a minority stake in a joint venture majority controlled by two major electronics companies, Matsushita and Mitsubishi. It faced competition from PerfecTV, launched the year before and backed by a consortium of Japanese trading and financial corporations. Murdoch's Sky platform, JSkyB, eventually launched in 1999, was a relatively late arrival. In stark contrast to DirectTV's collaborative strategy, Murdoch aimed to obtain local programming through a pre-emptive acquisition of 21.4 per cent of Asahi National Broadcasting. This evoked angry comparisons with the arrival in 1853 of the American "Black Ships" that had forced Japan to open its economy. [46] Faced with strong opposition from Asahi shareholders, Murdoch reduced his holding and fell back on offering News Corp channels, including Fox News and Sky Sports. When this failed to enthuse audiences, in April 1988 he accepted an offer to participate in PerfecTV which by then had built a roster of 100 channels and nearly half a million subscribers. The new enterprise was named SkyPerfecTV, but with only 8.1 per cent of the stock, Murdoch's holding was eclipsed by the 9.9 per cent held by each of the three leading Japanese investors, Sony Broadcast Media, Fuji Television Network, and Itochu Corporation. Increased competition forced DirecTV out of the Japanese satellite television market in 2000, confirming SkyPerfectTV's prominence. Increasingly frustrated at being unable to increase its stake and its influence on the direction of the company, however, in August 2003 News Corp transferred its holding to the three leading Japanese investors.

In a pattern repeated in China, News Corp had contributed valuable technological, professional, and programming know-how but been unable to secure a significant position in the market. As the president of SkyPerfecTV noted, in a farewell address touched with irony, "We are grateful for News Corporation's support in the establishment and consolidation of the pay television industry in Japan." [47]

2.5.4 China

Murdoch first entered the Greater China market in 1983 through Hong Kong, administered by Britain until its return to China in 1997. The initial foothold provided by an 18 per cent stake in the magazine publisher Asia Magazines Ltd was strengthened in 1986 with the acquisition of the territory's leading English-language newspaper, the *South China Morning Post.* Murdoch's first visit to the mainland in spring 1985 confirmed the huge potential of the world's largest market, embracing consumerism under the impact of the post-Mao economic reforms with a newly liberalised and commercialised television system playing a leading role.

By 1985, there were 202 television stations in operation, reaching 68.8 per cent of the population and taking 11 per cent of national advertising spend. By 1990, 80 per cent of households were regular viewers, the number of stations had expanded to 509, and the medium's share of advertising had doubled to 22 per cent. [48] This rapid expansion posed a problem for the Chinese government. Building a strong domestic production base required access to Western expertise in popular commercial programming while avoiding importing "polluting" cultural values or compromising the Communist Party's control over the broadcasting system. Murdoch's failure to accommodate this political reality placed major limits on his Chinese ambitions.

In 1996, he entered into a joint venture to launch a Chinese-language channel, Phoenix, in partnership with Liu Changle's Today's Asia company. With a background in the People's Liberation Army and strong political connections, Liu delivered official approval, a guarantee reinforced by the minority stake in Phoenix held by China's national broadcaster, China Central Television (CCTV). The channel's mix of politically uncontentious dramas, talk shows, and pop music was widely viewed and approved in elite circles and seen as a template for acceptable popular programming. But as one of his senior executives noted, "Murdoch was never happy with the Phoenix arrangement, which gave him neither majority ownership nor editorial control," [49] His wider ambitions lay elsewhere.

In July 1992, Richard Li, the son of Li Ka-shing, head of Hong Kong's leading conglomerate, Hutchison Whampoa, put his Satellite Television for the Asian Region (STAR) operation on the market. News Corp purchased an initial 63.6 per cent stake for £525 million and in 1993 acquired the balance. With a footprint covering the whole of China and India, the world's two largest emerging economies, and the ability to beam directly into homes, buying STAR appeared to be major coup. It initially offered an English-language, pan-Asian platform aimed at upscale households across the continent, but it was soon obvious that services would have to take account of national differences. [50] The Chinese service offered a Mandarin channel alongside pop music on MTV Asia, entertainment on Star Plus, Prime Time Sports, and the BBC's World Service Television.

In September 1993, however, Murdoch made a major political misjudgement. Addressing a grand dinner in London, he claimed:

> Advances in the technology of telecommunications have proved an unambiguous threat to totalitarian regimes everywhere. Fax machines enable dissidents to bypass state-controlled print media … and satellite broadcasting makes it possible for information-hungry residents of many closed societies to bypass state-controlled television channels. [51]

Fax machines had helped organise the pro-democracy protests in Tiananmen Square in 1989. Chinese premier Li Peng, who had ordered the troops in, took Murdoch's remarks as a personal insult and "premeditated and calculated threat to Chinese sovereignty". [52] "In a calculated response, Chinese leaders banned private ownership of satellite dishes, prohibited newspaper advertising of foreign satellite services and selectively showcased the prosecution of violators." [53]

Murdoch was caught by surprise. As he later admitted, "I just didn't pick it up – not in the context of China. I was really thinking of the Soviet Union, the Berlin Wall coming down." [54] For the head of a corporation with global ambitions, this Western-centric perspective on the emerging international political order was a major blind spot.

Recognising his mistake, Murdoch made a series of concessions to repair relations. In 1994, STAR removed the BBC service, with its repeated references to Tiananmen. In 1995, HarperCollins published Deng Rong's biography of her father Deng Xiaoping. In 1996, News International paid for the website launched by the Communist Party's official newspaper, *The People's Daily.* The following year, HarperCollins cancelled the contract to publish the memoirs of the last British governor of Hong Kong, Chris Patten.

Access to the Chinese market, when it came, was on non-negotiable terms dictated by the Chinese government intent on globalising its own cultural reach. In October 2001, the Phoenix Chinese channel was given permission to broadcast into the Pearl River Delta region on condition that BSkyB in Britain carried CCTV's newly launched English-language service, Channel 9. In December, STAR was allowed to relay its new Chinese-language entertainment channel, Xing Kong Wei Shi, over the Guangdong Cable Television network, providing Fox channels in Los Angeles and San Francisco carried Channel 9.

Despite this thaw in relations with Chinese officialdom, Murdoch remained distrusted, a sense reinforced by his failure to play by Chinese rules in his business dealings.

In 2004, in a drive to attract investments and expertise, foreign concerns were permitted to acquire minority stakes in Chinese broadcasting companies. Murdoch invested in a satellite system based in Qinghai but neglected to seek official permission before distributing his STAR Mandarin channel. Its mix of US-style game shows and reality television was widely condemned as "spiritual pollution". In February 2005, the broadcast regulator SARFT announced:

> We must control the contents of all products of joint ventures in a practical manner, understand the political inclination and background of foreign joint venture parties, and in this way, prevent harmful foreign ideology and culture from entering the realm of our television program production. [55]

Murdoch continued to evade the rules, pressuring cable operators to distribute STAR programmes and disguise subscription payments. SARFT responded in July 2005, banning local television stations from renting channels to foreign operators or cooperating with them on running channels. The *People's Daily* pointedly announced that "Qinghai satellite TV has ceased its cooperation with the News Corporation held by Rupert Murdoch". [56]

It was now clear that STAR would never be allowed to become a major player in the Chinese market, and in 2010 News Corporation began divesting its holding. By 2014, it had withdrawn from China completely. Its presence did leave a legacy, however.

News Corp's involvement in Phoenix gave CCTV and rising regional channels "a Murdoch-financed course in his trade secrets", [57] while STAR's Xing Kong Wei Shi channel demonstrated the commercial value of localised versions of the reality television formats popularised by Fox and other major Western producers. SARFT's regulatory censure of STAR in 2005 coincided with the unprecedented ratings success of Hunan Satellite Television's *Super Girls* singing contest based on the *Pop Idol* format that had been Fox's television's most successful programme in the US.

Murdoch's limited entry in China placed a premium on success in the other major emerging Asian market, India.

2.5.5 India

In 1991, as part of a more general liberalisation of the Indian economy Doordarshan's state monopoly over television services ended and the market was opened to domestic commercial operators and foreign investors. As in China, however, overseas companies were subject to strict regulatory limits and under pressure to form partnerships with national concerns.

The first private channel, Zee, launched in 1992 by Subhash Chandra, beamed Hindi programming into India using transponder space purchased from Richard Li in Hong Kong. Chandra had allowed Murdoch to invest in his Asia Today holding company on the condition that STAR did not offer competing channels in India's most spoken language, Hindi. STAR's five English channels reached an educated urban elite that made up less than 5 per cent of the population. In an effort to extend his reach, Murdoch acquired Zee in 1993. In 2000, Zee bought back its shares, freeing Murdoch to relaunch his flagship Star channel as an all-Hindi service. Centred around original soaps and popular programming, it rapidly overtook Zee.

In further localising moves, STAR diversified into other major Indian languages, acquiring a majority stake in the Tamil service Vijay TV in 2001, starting a Bengali channel in 2008, and in 2009 joining with Asianet TV to launch STAR Jupiter with channels in Malayalam, Telugu, and Kannada. By the end of that year, News Corp claimed to be reaching half of India's 20 major language groups.

STAR's programming drew on Bollywood conventions but also relied heavily on localising Western entertainment formats. The huge success of the Indian version of the British game show *Who Wants to Be a Millionaire?* – broadcast in 2000 and hosted by the Bollywood star Amitabh Bachchan – established Star Plus as the country's most popular channel and, with Danny Boyle's 2008 film *Slumdog Millionaire*, winner of eight Academy Awards, came to represent the "glocalisation" of international television. This process was replicated in the "Murdochisation" of Indian news where Star News's "obsessive interest is glamour, crime and celebrity culture" is embedded within an ideological frame which "in the name of defending the national interest may in fact be propagating dominant neoliberal ideology". [58]

In 2001, in an effort to bypass cable distribution, Murdoch's investment arm, Network Digital Distribution Services (NDDS), established a joint venture with the Tata Group, one of India's leading industrial conglomerates, to develop a Sky-branded direct-to-home (DTH) satellite service, Tata Sky. It launched in August 2006. Murdoch's stake was pegged at 20 per cent by India's regulations limiting broadcaster investments in DTH, but in 2010 NDDS increased its share to 30 per cent via a 49 per cent stake in Tata's investment arm, TS Investments, which had acquired a 20 per cent stake in Tata Sky. By 2015, Tata Sky had a 21.5 per cent share of India's DTH market, the world's largest, with 94.61 million subscribers.

In 2019, Tata Sky was sold and later rebranded as Tata Play, underlining the domination of national ownership. The Tata disposal was part of a wider sale of 21st Century Fox's film and television holdings to the Disney Corporation. It marked a major shift in the scale and focus of News Corp's operations following earlier disposals and retrenchments as the corporation responded to internal crises and changes in the business environment.

2.6 Crises and Restructurings

Reviewing the institutional career of News Corp, alongside Bertelsmann and Time Warner, Scott Fitzgerald was struck by "how often uncertainty, failure and crisis have marked their strategies and operations". [59] There have been three major restructurings in News Corp's institutional career: in 1991 in response to the debt repayment crisis, in 2011 in the aftermath of the phone-hacking scandal, and in 2018 with the sale of the Fox film interests and BSkyB. More recently, it has faced substantial reputational damage from lawsuits lodged against Fox News for continuing to promote Donald Trump's "stolen election" claims, knowing them to be false.

2.6.1 1991 The Debt Crisis

By August 1990, the $3 billion purchase of Triangle magazines coupled with the costs of launching Sky Television, upgrading newspaper presses, and consolidating the HarperCollins publishing division, had boosted News Corp's total debt to $8.7 billion, spread across 147 different banks, much of it in short-term loans due for repayment. After months of tense negotiations overseen by Citibank, the banks agreed to reschedule deadlines and extend a $600 million credit line, but there was a price to pay.

Eighteen per cent of News Corp's international workforce were laid off. A series of share sales raised $575 million but reduced the Murdoch family's holding from 46 per cent to 39.5 per cent. A similar sum was raised by selling a 55 per cent share in the Australian magazine and printing operations. The 49 per cent share in the *South China Morning Post* was disposed of, together with most of the US magazine properties. The half share in *Elle* had already been sold in September 1988. In 1991, the *Daily Racing Form* and *Seventeen* were bought by K-III Communications Corp, and other titles in the magazine division, including *New Woman*, were sold. *TV Guide* was retained but, faced with falling revenues, was merged with the TV listings channel controlled by John Malone's Liberty Media to create an interactive portal, Gemstar TV-Guide. When this failed, the print edition of *TV Guide* was relaunched in 2005 as a celebrity-focused entertainment magazine. In 2008, Murdoch severed his final ties, selling his 41 per cent stake in Gemstar.

2.6.2 2011 The Phone-Hacking Crisis

As mentioned earlier, in January 2007 Clive Goodman, the royal reporter for Murdoch's British Sunday tabloid, the *News of the World*, was convicted of illegally obtaining voicemail messages of members of the royal family. The company insisted that he was a lone operator, but successive payments to others claiming to have been hacked suggested that the practice was widespread, a conclusion supported by investigative articles in *The Guardian* in July 2009.

In April 2011, News International admitted liability in eight cases of hacking and paid compensation. When *The Guardian* revealed in July 2011, that the phone of the murdered schoolgirl Milly Dowler had been hacked, the backlash became impossible to contain.

There were immediate economic costs. In an attempt to limit the damage, on 7 July 2011 Rupert Murdoch announced the immediate closure of the *News of the World*, still a substantial profit centre. A week later, continuing political reaction forced him to withdraw his bid to take full control of BSkyB. This was a major blow since up until then approval had seemed almost certain. In August, in New York, the centre of Murdoch's US newspaper interests, the state cancelled a contract to monitor student performance.

Over the longer term, substantial sums have continued to be paid to a succession of hacking claimants in out-of-court settlements By July 2021, ten years after the first cases, the total from payments and legal fees had reached £1 billion. [60]

Closing the *News of the World* was not sufficient to limit the immediate reputational damage. Mounting public pressure prompted a public inquiry into the "culture, practices and ethics of the press" chaired by Lord Justice Leveson and hearings on phone hacking held by the House of Commons Culture, Media and Sport Committee. Rupert Murdoch was called to testify to both, together with senior managers and editors and leading politicians who recounted their contacts and dealings with Murdoch over the years.

Appearing before the House of Commons Committee, Murdoch appeared contrite, admitting that "This is the humblest [sic] day of my life" and claiming that "At no time do I remember being as sickened as when I heard what the Dowler family had to endure". [61] At the same time, he avoided taking responsibility. Explaining his failure to investigate early allegations of wrongdoing, he claimed:

> The *News of the World* is less than 1% of our company. I employ 53,000 people around the world … Perhaps I am spread watching and employing people whom I trust to run those divisions. [62]
>
> Perhaps I lost sight of, maybe because it was so small in the general frame of our company. [63]

The Committee rejected this explanation and delivered a damning verdict arguing that "Rupert Murdoch … exhibited wilful blindness to what was going on in his companies and publications" and "therefore is not a fit person to exercise stewardship of a major international company". [64]

2.6.3 2012 Separation: News Corp and Fox Corp

The scandal prompted a major reorganisation of the company's structure with the erection of a Chinese wall separating the print and entertainment interests.

Table 2.1 Major Interests of 'New' News Corporation and Fox Corporation [65]

'New' News Corp	*New cable and entertainment company (later Fox Corporation)*
Dow Jones	Fox Broadcasting
The Wall Street Journal	Twentieth Century Fox Film
Dow Jones Newswires	Twentieth Century Fox Television
HarperCollins	Fox Sports
The New York Post	Fox International Channels
The Daily	Fox News Channel
The Australian	Fox Business Network
The Herald-Sun	FX, Star
The Daily Telegraph	National Geographic Channels
The Courier-Mail	Shine Group
The Times, The Sunday Times	Fox Television Stations
The Sun	BSkyB
marketing services group	Sky Italia
digital education group	Sky Deutschland
Wireless Generation	

A company statement issued in June 2012 announced the division of News Corporation into two distinct publicly traded companies with Rupert Murdoch as Chair and CEO of both. News Corp's cable and television assets, filmed entertainment, and direct satellite broadcasting businesses were assigned to the newly named 21st Century Fox. The second company, New News Corp, assumed responsibility for the newspaper interests, together with the book publishing, education, and integrated marketing services divisions and Dow Jones financial information services. The main businesses grouped within each company are shown in Table 2.1.

The statement announcing the division deployed standard corporate puffery. It presented a defensive move designed to limit the migration of reputational damage as a major new opportunity to develop "distinct strategic priorities and industry-specific opportunities" and enable "enhanced strategic alignment and increased operational flexibility with respect to an unparalleled portfolio of assets, brands and franchises". [66]

2.6.4 2018 Retrenchment: Selling 21st Century Fox and BSkyB

The rapid rise of video streaming services led by Netflix, which debuted in 2007, placed established film and television companies under increasing pressure, prompting a search for consolidation. In 2014, Murdoch attempted to boost 21st Century Fox's competitive position with a $80 billion offer for Time Warner. The bid, 60 per cent in shares and 40 per cent in cash, was rejected as under-valuing the company and offering only non-voting shares. Its failure further weakened Fox's ability to compete effectively with the streaming platforms and reduced the long-term value of the entertainment holdings. By 2017, shares in 21st Century Fox were down 30 per cent from their peak in December 2014.

In November 2017, 21st Century Fox became a takeover target itself when the Walt Disney Company, aiming to strengthen its production capacity and back catalogue prior to entering the streaming market, opened negotiations to acquire the Fox film, cable, and direct satellite broadcasting divisions. That same month, Comcast, owners of the Universal film studios and NBC television network, entered the bidding but dropped out in December, leaving Fox and Disney to announce a $52.4 billion deal.

In June 2018, AT&T's bid to acquire Warner cleared the last major regulatory hurdle reinforcing the logic of consolidation. Comcast re-entered the contest for 21st Century Fox with a $65 billion all-cash bid. Disney countered with an increased offer of $71.3 billion. In July, Comcast dropped its bid but retained its interest in acquiring Sky, opening the way for Disney and Fox shareholders to approve the merger.

The Justice Department raised antitrust concerns but approved the acquisition, providing Disney, as owners of the ESPN national sport channels, sold Fox's regional sports networks. In 2019, they were acquired by the Sinclair Broadcasting Group.

Disney acquired most of Fox's film and television assets. They included the 20th Century Fox film studio; the 20th Century Fox Television production arm; the Shine-Endemol independent production companies; a 73 per cent stake in National Geographic partners; a 30 per cent stake in the streaming service Hulu, giving Disney majority control with 60 per cent; a 39 per cent stake in Sky; and a stake in the Star India satellite broadcasters.

In addition to production and distribution facilities, the deal gave Disney a substantial back catalogue of past film and television productions and the rights to successful film and television franchises including *Avatar*, the original *Star Wars* film, *The Simpsons*, and the reincorporation of the *X-Men* and *Fantastic Four* comic book characters into Disney's Marvel Universe.

The deal was a major coup for Murdoch. Disney paid $71 billion for a company Murdoch had bought for $575 million in 1985, paid $19.8 billion in cash, and assumed responsibility for $19.2 billion in debt. The Murdoch Family Trust's 17 per cent share in 21st Century Fox netted nearly $12 billion available for distribution in equal shares to Rupert Murdoch's six children as the Trust's beneficiaries.

In January 2020, Disney, concerned that the "Fox" name was too closely associated with the right-wing stance of Fox News, dropped it from all the divisions they had acquired. In October 2020, the Endemol-Shine Group was sold to Banijay.

The other major Fox asset in contention was the 39 per cent holding in the Sky satellite service. In 2016, Murdoch's own attempt to purchase the remaining 61 per cent was blocked by concerns over its possible impact on news plurality, and in September 2018 Comcast outbid Disney to acquire 21st Century's holding for £12 billion.

2.6.5 2021 The "Stolen" Election Crisis

As noted earlier, for much of his presidency, Fox was Donald Trump's preferred television platform. The channel's hosts and guests repeatedly endorsed his views, creating tensions with the news desk's journalistic commitments.

On election night, 3 November 2020, Fox News journalists, using a proprietary statistical model, were the first to call the crucial swing state of Arizona for the Democrats. Trump's son-in-law Jared Kushner, a personal friend of Rupert Murdoch, called him to complain, but Murdoch insisted that "the numbers are numbers". [67] On 7 November, Fox projected that Trump had lost the election.

The following day, a guest on the channel's *Sunday Morning Futures* Show claimed that there was "a massive and coordinated effort … to delegitimize and destroy votes for Donald Trump and manufacture votes for Joe Biden". Two companies operating voting machines, Dominion Voting Systems and Smartmatic, were accused of malpractice. Both filed lawsuits against Fox News for damaging their businesses. Internal Fox documents obtained by Dominion demonstrate beyond doubt that everyone associated with the channel knew from the outset that the claims of vote rigging were false. As Rupert Murdoch confirmed when questioned under oath:

> Q: It is fair to say you seriously doubted any claim of massive election fraud?
>
> A: Oh, yes … we thought everything was on the up-and-up. I think that was shown when we announced Arizona. [68]

On 12 November, President Trump, released a flurry of tweets vilifying Fox for calling the election for Biden and encouraging viewers to switch to Newsmax and other rival right-wing channels. By 15 November, the Fox prime-time audience had fallen by 37 per cent.

To repair the damage, Fox News actively promoted Trump's accusation that the election had been "stolen". As Rupert Murdoch later explained, he did not want to antagonise Trump since "He had a very large following, and they were mostly viewers of Fox, so it would have been stupid". [69]

When challenged under oath, he conceded that Fox presenters had repeatedly endorsed claims they knew to be false:

> Q: You are aware now that Fox did more than simply host these guests and give them a platform; correct?
>
> A: I think you've shown me some material in support of that.

Q: In fact, you are now aware that Fox endorsed at times this false notion of a stolen election?

A: Not Fox, but maybe Lou Dobbs, maybe Maria, as commentators. [70]

The attempt to deny managerial responsibility and shift the blame to presenters is contradicted by Murdoch's multiple phone calls and emails to Fox News CEO, Suzanne Scott, with "suggestions" on how to cover the conspiracy claims, [71] his regular attendance at editorial meetings and his later "long talk" with Scott on the direction Fox should take "in response to falling ratings and the viewer backlash". [72] He later admitted that he had the power to stop programmes hosting Rudi Giuliani and other Trump supporters promoting claims of election rigging but deliberately chose not to exercise it.

Q: And you could have said to the hosts "Stop putting Rudy Giuliani on the air?"

A: I could have. But I didn't. [73]

On 20 November, Dominion sent a letter to Fox demanding that they retract the false allegation of vote rigging. Fox News hosts continued to endorse them, one labelling Dominion as an "organized criminal enterprise" financed by Cuba. [74] In marked contrast, on 17 November *The Wall Street Journal* had published an editorial headed "Rage Against the Voting Machine", stating that there was no evidence of election fraud, pointing once again to the tension within News Corp, between reporting directed at decision makers and populist comment.

Fox News' promotion of the "stolen election" narrative paid commercial dividends when Trump agreed to appear on *Sunday Morning Futures* on 29 November.

Reviewing the evidence, the Dominion deposition concluded that "Fox took a small flame and turned it into a forest fire. As the dominant media company among those viewers dissatisfied with the election results, Fox gave these fictions a prominence they otherwise would never have had." [75]

On 18 April 2023, with the trial jury already sworn in, in a last-minute bid to avoid testifying in open court and incurring additional reputational damage, Fox agreed to pay Dominion $787.5 million. In a statement, untouched by irony, Fox presented the settlement as reflecting its "continued commitment to the highest journalistic standards". [76]

At the time of writing, the case against Fox lodged by Smartmatic is still active.

There are echoes here of Marx's famous adage that history repeats itself, the first time as tragedy, the second time as farce. Reporting on the results of the 2000 Presidential Election, Fox News was the first to place George W. Bush in the "win" column for the key state of Florida. The other main news outlets followed soon after. The recommendation came from the Fox team analysing exit poll data. It was headed by John Ellis, Bush's first cousin. [77] The Florida vote was highly controversial, with debate again centring on faulty voting machines. The outcome was only finally decided by a Supreme Court ruling to cancel a recount and endorse a Bush victory by 537 votes. By creating the impression that Bush had "won" the White House on the night, Fox's false call arguably helped predispose the final decision in his favour. Bush's Democratic opponent, Al Gore, was a dedicated campaigner for concerted action on climate change.

In August 2022, Lachlan Murdoch launched a case against the Australian independent news site Crikey. He accused the publication of defamation for an opinion piece analysing the violent assault on the Capitol building by Trump supporters intent on preventing the formal ratification of Biden's election victory. It was headlined "Trump is a confirmed unhinged traitor. And Murdoch is his unindicted co-conspirator", a phrase referring to President Nixon's role in Watergate. Crikey argued that no one would read the words literally as suggesting that Murdoch was guilty of treason or personally responsible for the riot. Rather, they were a statement of the author's "opinion based on his knowledge of the extensive reportage of Fox News' involvement in the events leading up to Jan 6" and the Murdochs' role in guiding "Fox's editorial strategy and programming". [78]

Citing evidence of Lachlan Murdoch's "guiding role" in Dominion's deposition, the lawyer representing Crikey argued that because "He permitted this lie [of the 'stolen election'] to be broadcast we say that gives rise to culpability where this lie is the motivation for the insurrection". [79] In April 2023, Lachlan Murdoch withdrew the case. The tensions surrounding Fox News' relations with Donald Trump remained.

In November 2021, Fox News' most popular presenter, Tucker Carlson, presented a three-part documentary series on Fox Nation, the channel's pay streaming service. Entitled *Patriot Purge*, it borrowed from conspiracy theories to present the Capitol siege as a "false flag" operation masterminded by President Trump's enemies. In February 2023, Carlson was given the chance to reach the general Fox News audience when the Republican Speaker of the House, Kevin McCarthy, granted him exclusive rights to over 40,000 hours of previously confidential security footage of the siege. Carlson used the material to present Trump in a positive light and downplay the violence of his supporters.

In April 2023, days after the Dominion settlement, in a sign of continuing tensions at the channel and anxieties over further reputational damage, Carlson was taken off air, although he remained under contract. In June 2023, after Trump had been charged with illegally retaining classified documents, a banner running along the bottom of a split screen showing President Biden and Trump speaking, broadcast in Carlson's former time slot, read, "Wannabe dictator speaks at White House after having his political rival arrested." Carlson's former producer was held responsible and dismissed.

References

[1] William Shawcross (1993) *Rupert Murdoch: Ringmaster of the Information Circus*, London. Pan Books, p. 33.
[2] Ellis Ashmead-Bartlett (1928) *The Uncensored Dardanelles*. London. Hutchinson & Co, p. 239.
[3] Rupert Murdoch (2007) 'Text of Murdoch Letter to Bancrofts', *Wall Street Journal*, 14 May. Available at www.wsj.com/articles/SB117916921467602256
[4] Richard Tofel (2011) 'Bancroft Family Members Express Regret at Selling Wall Street Journal to Murdoch', ProPublica, 13 July. Available at www.propublica.org/article/bancroft-family-members-express-regrets-at-selling-wall-street-journal-to-m#:~:text=A%20number%20of%20key%20members,the%20time%20of%20the%20deal
[5] Rupert Murdoch oral evidence, Tuesday 19 July 2011, Q385, pp. 36–7. House of Commons Culture, Media and Sport Committee (2012) *News International and Phone-Hacking Eleventh Report of Session 2010–12: Volume II Oral and Written Evidence*. HC 903-II London: Stationery Office.
[6] Mark Barker (2016) 'The Myth of Keith Murdoch's Gallipoli Letter', *Inside Story*, 27 June. Available at https://insidestory.org.au/the-myth-of-keith-murdochs-gallipoli-letter
[7] Mark Barker, 2016, op. cit.
[8] Mark Barker, 2016, op. cit.
[9] Peter Putnis (2011) 'Keith Murdoch: wartime journalist, 1915–1918', *Australian Journalism Review*, Vol. 33, No. 2, p. 63.
[10] Tom Roberts (2020) 'Murdoch begins: The story of Rupert Murdoch's father Keith', *The Irish Times*, 1 February. Available at www.irishtimes.com/culture/books/murdoch-begins-the-story-of-rupert-murdoch-s-father-keith-1.4157453
[11] Tom Roberts, 2020, op. cit.
[12] Roy Greenslade (2020) 'A Very Bloody Liar', *British Journalism Review*, Vol. 31, No. 2, p. 76.
[13] Sally Young (2019) 'The secret history of News Corp: a media empire built on spreading propaganda', *The Conversation*, 16 May. Available at https://theconversation.com/the-secret-history-of-news-corp-a-media-empire-built-on-spreading-propaganda-116992
[14] William Shawcross, 1993, op. cit., p. 77.
[15] Benedetta Brevini and Michael Ward (2021) '*Who Controls Our Media? Exposing the impact of media concentration on our democracy*'. Sydney: GetUp. Available at www.getup.org.au/campaigns/abc-media-campaigns/share-the-media-diversity-report/who-controls-our-media-the-new-report-commissioned-by-getup
[16] David Higgins (2005) 'A long way to the bottom', *Sydney Morning Herald*, 10 November. Available at www.smh.com.au/entertainment/music.a-long-way-to-the-bottom-2051110-gdmeu1.html
[17] George Munster (1987) *Rupert Murdoch: A Paper Prince*. Ringwood, Victoria: Penguin Books Australia, p. 125.
[18] George Munster, 1987, op. cit., p. 127.
[19] James Curran and Jean Seaton (1981) *Power Without Responsibility: The Press and Broadcasting in Britain*. London. Fontana, p. 69.
[20] Paul Laity (1996) 'The Sun Says', *London Review of Books*, Vol. 18, No. 12. Available at www.lrb.co.uk/the-paper/v18/n12/paul-laity/the-sun-says

[21] Rupert Murdoch (2008) *A Golden Age of Freedom* Sydney. ABC Books, pp. 52–3.

[22] Ciar Byrne and Ben Dowell (2009) 'Why Murdoch closed the London Paper', *The Guardian*, 24 August. Available at www.theguardian.com/media/2009/aug/24/thelondonpaper-rupert-murdoch-news-international

[23] Rachel L. Seeman (2009) *A Case Study of Cross-Ownership Waivers: Framing Newspaper Coverage of Rupert Murdoch's Requests to the Keep the New York Post*. MA Thesis. Department of Communications, Miami University, pp. 41–3.

[24] See Richard Belfield, Cristopher Hird and Sharon Kelly (1994) *Murdoch: The Great Escape*. London. Sphere.

[25] Hansard (2002) Tessa Jowell introducing the Communications Bill. House of Commons Debate, 3 December, Vol. 395, paras 783 and 793. Available at https://api.parliament.uk/historic-hansard/commons/2002/dec/03/communications-bill

[26] Aisha Majid (2022) 'Talk TV ratings three weeks in: New channel a distant fourth for TV viewers', *Press Gazette*, 25 July. Available at https://pressgazette.co.uk/publishers/broadcast/talktv-ratings-piers-morgan

[27] Mark Henderson (2023) 'Migrants Organise charity receives substantial damages and apology from Talk TV's Mike Graham and News UK libel claims', *Doughty Street Chambers*, 14 June. Available at www.doughtystreet.co.uk/news/migrants-organise-charity-receives-substantial-damages-and-apology-talktvs-mike-graham-and

[28] Optus Media Centre (2002) 'Breakthrough agreement in subscription television', 5 March. Available at www.optus.com.au/about/media-centre/media-releases/2002/03/breakthrough-agreement-in-subscription-television

[29] Quoted in Barry Crane (1998) 'Murdoch's Big Play', *Macleans*, 19 October, p. 56.

[30] Craig Robertson (2004) 'A Sporting Gesture? BskyB, Manchester United, Global Media, and Sport', *Television and New Media*, Vol. 5, No. 4, p. 299.

[31] Peter A. Thompson (2012) 'The Murdoch empire in New Zealand', *Global Media and Communication*, Vol. 8, No. 1, pp. 21–5.

[32] Mark Sweney (2016) 'Rupert Murdoch's News Corp buys Talk Sport owner in £220m deal', *The Guardian*, 30 June. Available at www.theguardian.com/media/2016/jun/30/rupert-murdochs-news-corp-buys-talksport-owner-in-220m-deal

[33] William Shawcross, op. cit., p. 312.

[34] Teather, David (2003) 'DirecTV succumbs to Murdoch', *The Guardian*, 10 April. Available at https://www.theguardian.com/media/2003/apr/10/newscorporation.citynews1

[35] Geoffrey Drake (2021) 'Old Man and the Sky: The Brazilian Antitrust Implications for Rupert Murdoch's Expansion of the Sky Global Satellite Network', *Vanderbilt Journal of Transnational Law*, Vol. 37, p. 1150.

[36] Mark S. Fowler (1987) 'The Federal Communications Commission 1981–1987: What the Chairman Said', *Hastings Communication and Entertainment Law Journal*, Vol. 10, No. 2, pp. 428–31.

[37] Quoted in Tom Johnson (2000) 'Murdoch Buys Chris-Craft', CNN Money, 14 August. Available at https://money.cnn.com/2000/08/14/deals/newscorp/index.htm

[38] Christopher J. Pepe (1994) 'The Rise and Fall of the FCC's Financial Interest and Syndication Rules'. Available at https://digitalcommons.law.villanova.edu/mslj/vol1/iss1/5

[39] Reece Peck (2022) 'Comparing Populist Media: From Fox News to the Young Turks, From Cable to YouTube, From Right to Left', *Television and New Media*, Vol. 24, No. 6. Available at https://doi.org/10.1177/15274764221114349

[40] Reece Peck, 2022, op. cit., p. 4.

[41] Quoted in Michael Wolff (2002) 'One Nation Under Fox', *New York Magazine*, 9 December, p. 22. Available at https://nymag.com/nymetro/news/media/columns/medialife/n_8080
[42] Daniel Cox, E.J. Dionne Jr., Robert P. Jones, and William A. Galston (2011) 'What it Means to Be American', PRRI, 6 September, p. 9. Available at www.prri.org/research/what-it-means-to-be-american
[43] *US Dominion Inc v. Fox News Network.* Complaint in the Superior Court of the State of Delaware. Available at www.documentcloud.org/documents/20527880-dominion-v-fox-news-complaint para 26, p. 16.
[44] The Economist (2005) 'Warring Moguls', 20 January. Available at www.economist.com/business/2005/01/20/warring-moguls
[45] Paulo Gerbaudo (2012) 'Murdoch vs Berlusconi: The Battle for the control of Italian media', *Global Media and Communication,* Vol. 8, No. 1 pp. 7–11.
[46] JungBong Choi (2010) 'Banishment of Murdoch's Sky in Japan: A Tale of David and Goliath' in *Television, Japan and Globalisation.* Ann Arbor: University of Michigan Centre for Japanese Studies, p. 11.
[47] Quoted in Choi, 2010, op. cit., p. 18.
[48] Shu-Yun Ma (1996) 'The Role of Power Struggle and Economic Change in the "Heshang Phenomenon" in China', *Modern Asian Studies*, Vol. 30, No. 1, Table 1, p. 40.
[49] Bruce Dover (2008) *Rupert Murdoch's China Adventures.* North Clarendon, VT: Tuttle Publishing, p. 175.
[50] Michael Curtin (2005) 'Murdoch's dilemma, or "What's the Price of TV in China?"', *Media, Culture and Society*, Vol. 27, No. 2, p. 160.
[51] Quoted in Bruce Dover, 2008, op. cit., p. 25.
[52] Jack Shafer (2008) 'The Political Re-Education of Rupert Murdoch', The Slate, 12 February. Available at https://slate.com/news-and-politics/2008/02/the-political-re-education-of-rupert-murdoch-at-the-feet-of-his-chinese-masters.html
[53] Michael Curtin, 2005, op. cit., p. 159.
[54] Quoted in Bruce Dover, 2008, op. cit., p. 28.
[55] Quoted in Bruce Dover, 2008, op. cit., p. 214.
[56] Quoted in Bruce Dover, 2008, op. cit., p. 224.
[57] Stephen Kotkin (2008) 'How Murdoch got lost in China', *The New York Times,* 4 May. Available at www.nytimes.com/2008/05/04/business/media/04shelf.html
[58] Daya Kishan Thussu (2007) 'The "Murdochization" of news? The case of Star TV in India', *Media, Culture and Society*, Vol. 29, No. 4, p. 599.
[59] Scott W. Fitzgerald (2012) *Corporations and Cultural Industries: Time Warner, Bertelsmann, and News Corporation.* Lanham, MD: Lexington Books, p. 400.
[60] William Turvill (2021) 'News of the World claims ten years on: How hacking scandal cost Murdoch's UK tabloid business £1bn', *Press Gazette*, 8 July. Available at https://pressgazette.co.uk/news/phone-hacking-scandal-total-costs
[61] House of Commons Culture, Media and Sport Committee (2012b) *News International and Phone-Hacking Volume II Oral and written evidence.* House of Commons, 27 April, HC 903-II, answer to question 418.
[62] House of Commons Culture, Media and Sport Committee, 2012b, op. cit., answer to question 167.

[63] House of Commons Culture, Media and Sports committee (2012b), op. cit, answer to question 274.
[64] House of Commons Culture, Media and Sport Committee (2012a) *News International and Phone-Hacking Eleventh Report: Volume 1*, House of Commons, 1 May. HC 903-I, p. 115.
[65] News Corporation (2012) News Corporation Announces Intent to Pursue Separation of Businesses to Enhance Strategic Alignment and Increase Operational Flexibility. Press release 28 June. Available at https://newscorp.com/2012/06/28/news-corporation-announces-intent-to-pursue-separation-of-businesses-to-enhance-strategic-alignment-and-increase-operational-flexibility
[66] News Corp (2012) 'Separation Would Create Two Category-Leading Public Companies', 28 June. Available at https://newscorp.com/2012/06/28/news-corporation-announces-intent-to-pursue-separation-of-businesses-to-enhance-strategic-alignment-and-increase-operational-flexibility
[67] US Dominion Inc (2023) Dominion's Combined Opposition to Fox News Network LLC's and Fox Corporation's Rule 56 motions for Summary Judgment. In the Superior Court of the State of Delaware. Redacted Public Version Filed February 27. p. 12.
[68] US Dominion Inc, 2023, op. cit, pp. 12–13.
[69] *US Dominion Inc v Fox News Network*. Complaint in The Superior Court of the State of Delaware. Available at www.documentcloud.org/documents/20527880-dominion-v-fox-news-complaint, para 55, p. 28.
[70] US Dominion Inc, op. cit., p. 28.
[71] US Dominion Inc, op. cit., p. 10.
[72] US Dominion Inc, op. cit., p. 12.
[73] US Dominion Inc, op. cit., p. 30.
[74] *Dominion Inc v Fox News Network*, op. cit., para 89, p. 49.
[75] *Dominion Inc v Fox News Network*, op. cit., p. 3.
[76] Sam Levine and Kira Lerner (2023) 'Fox and Dominion settle for $787.5m in defamation lawsuit over US election lies', *The Guardian*, 19 April. Available at www.theguardian.com/us-news/2023/apr/18/fox-dominion-settle-us-defamation-lawsuit#:~:text=Fox%20and%20the%20voting%20equipment,to%20steal%20the%202020%20election.
[77] Howard Kurtz (2000) 'Bush Cousin Made Florida Vote Call for Fox News', *The Washington Post*, 13 November. Available at www.washingtonpost.com/archive/lifestyle/2000/11/14/bush-cousin-made-florida-vote-call-for-fox-news/68c8b308-d61e-460f-a4d8-f98371aeab5f
[78] Amanda Meade (2022) 'Lachlan Murdoch defamation case: Crikey article was "self-evidently hyperbolic", publisher argues', *The Guardian*, 22 September. Available at www.theguardian.com/media/2022/sep/22/lachlan-murdoch-defamation-case-crikey-article-was-self-evidently-hyperbolic-publisher-argues
[79] Australian Associated Press (2023) 'Lachlan Murdoch "culpable" for January 6 insurrection because of Fox News "lies", Australian defamation case hears', *The Guardian*, 4 April. Available at www.theguardian.com/media/2023/apr/04/lachlan-murdoch-culpable-for-january-6-insurrection-because-of-fox-news-lies-australian-defamation-case-hears

3 Digital Disruptions: From Media to Data

News Corp's emergence as a global media giant has coincided with a fundamental shift in the technological base of communication. Moving from analogue to digital systems has altered the organisation of production, the terms of competition, and the opportunities for profit generation in fundamental ways. This chapter charts the company's responses to this transition.

3.1 Rationalising Production, Displacing Labour

Cutting production costs by replacing human labour with machines has been a central corporate strategy since the beginning of industrialisation. The development of easy-to-use computer interfaces and digital networks opened new opportunities.

3.1.1 Computerising Typesetting: From Hot Metal to Direct Input

When Rupert Murdoch acquired *The Times* and *Sunday Times*, pages were still typeset using the hot metal process developed in the 1880s. Linotype machine operators entered text on a 90-character keyboard to assemble moulds into which molten metal was poured and cast for printing. It was a "closed shop" only open to workers approved by the union. Their ability to stop the presses gave them enormous bargaining power in securing wages and conditions.

Having witnessed the printers' strike that had closed *The Times* under its former owners, Murdoch was determined to shed staff and reduce costs by moving to computerised typesetting, allowing journalists to input copy directly. There were precedents.

The first significant clash erupted in December 1962 when a strike by the International Typographical Union closed every New York newspaper for over 100 days. The dispute ended in compromise, but by 1978 the city's leading title, *The New York Times*, had shifted completely to computerisation. [1]

DOI: 10.4324/9781003255086-3

Dismantling trade union power was central to Margaret Thatcher's political project in Britain. Observing the aggressive policing employed to break the year-long miner's strike in 1984–1985, Murdoch knew he could count on her full support in his battle with the print unions.

National newspapers were traditionally produced in Fleet Street in the heart of London. Murdoch had built a new production facility at Wapping, in the old docklands area. It was presented to union representatives as the site of a new title, the *London Post*, and negotiations on staffing began. Under the newly introduced anti-trade union legislation, the cheapest way to lay off workers while avoiding redundancy payments was to dismiss them while participating in a strike. In January 1986, management refused to sign up to the substantial concessions on staffing levels and work practices agreed by the unions and a strike was called, opening the way for Murdoch to implement his carefully planned Project 800. Journalists were bussed into the new plant, where state-of-the-art machinery had been secretly installed, passing picketing strikers, massed police, and a wall of razor wire. Clashes, often violent, continued for 13 months, but production of News International's four national titles continued uninterrupted with copies transported by vehicles operated by Murdoch's co-investor in Ansett Transport, TNT. Almost 5,500 employees were sacked. Cost savings from direct copy inputting and non-unionised labour pushed profits up from £39.1 million in 1985 to £675 million in 1990. [2]

3.1.2 Automating Content Creation: Deploying Artificial Intelligence

The recent explosive growth of generative artificial intelligence (AI) poses a fundamental challenge to established media companies. Tapping into vast stores of data accumulated by trawling the internet, AI systems generate professional-looking text and imagery from voice or written commands. The most widely used, ChatGPT, was released in December 2022 by the US-based company, Open AI, supported financially by Microsoft.

Enthusiasts argue that deploying AI for routine, otherwise time-consuming support tasks, such as searching and summarising official documents and transcribing verbal exchanges, allows reporters to spend more time on developing stories. But AI can also substitute for journalists. News Corp's local newspapers in Australia, many serving small communities, are providing a testing ground for automating content creation. Between 2008 and 2018, the sector as a whole saw 106 titles close, leaving 21 local government areas without a single newspaper [3] and communities as "news deserts" with no regular targeted coverage of local events and decisions. In May 2020, News Corp Australia added to this total announcing that 112 of its local and regional titles would cease printing, with 76 becoming digital only and 36 closing altogether. The year 2021 saw access to local coverage curtailed again, with 20 regional papers incorporated into major city titles and placed behind paywalls.

In a major innovation, the company launched 75 digital-only "hyperlocal" sites. They are concentrated in areas defined as "progressive communities with active sporting, political, business and tourism interests", criteria that exclude areas of deprivation and marginalisation. Stories produced by single staff reporters are supplemented by weather, traffic, and other local information generated by the AI program operated by the company's Data Local unit which generates 3,000 articles a week for distribution across the company's titles. Their AI origins are not disclosed on the sites they appear on.

The move was announced at a conference in Taipei in June 2023 by News Australia Investment's Executive Director, Michael Miller, prompting editorial staff to write to him asking why they only found out from an article in *The Guardian* and how else the company planned to use AI.

We will return to the wider implications of AI for News Corp's operations later in this chapter.

3.2 Retrieving Revenues: Paywalls and Payments

The search cost savings from displacing labour have been largely prompted by rapidly declining press revenues as advertising migrates to digital platforms.

The business model developed by the leading platforms offered users free access in return for granting the platforms monopoly rights to collect, analyse, and sell the personal data they generated as they interacted with the site. The resulting fine-grained consumer profiles promised advertisers unprecedented precision in targeting appeals. Advertising deserted established media.

In 2017, the Australian Competition and Consumer Commission launched an inquiry into the impact of digital platforms on traditional media businesses. The findings confirmed the picture already familiar from Britain and the United States. Between 2003 and 2018, print's share of total Australian advertising fell from 55 per cent to 11 per cent, while the share going to online platforms rose from less than 1 per cent to 53 per cent with $47 in every $100 spent going to Google and $24 to Facebook. [4]

News Corp has responded to this seismic shift in two ways: placing titles behind paywalls and charging readers a subscription to access content, and launching a concerted campaign to compel the digital majors to pay for the news content carried on their platforms.

3.2.1 Shifting to Subscription

In 2000, Google, the leading web search engine, launched its online news aggregator, Google News, assembling stories from a range of sources and hosting advertising. Neither Google nor its users paid for the news items carried. The income newspapers generated from ads on their own websites was far less than the sums they were losing. As Google's Chief Executive, Eric Schmidt, noted, "they're replacing analogue dollars with digital cents". [5]

Speaking at a seminar convened by the Federal Trade Commission in December 2009, Murdoch dismissed the aggregators as pirates who "think they have a right to take our news content and use it for their own purposes without contributing a penny to its production … Their wholesale misappropriation of our stories is not 'fair use'. To be impolite, its theft." [6]

In response, he announced a "new business model", moving from advertising to subscription, "charging consumers for the news we provide on our Internet sites" and extending the paywall introduced at the *Wall Street Journal* to all "newspapers in the News Corporation stable". [7]

Addressing the Royal Television Society earlier that year, Schmidt had argued that paywalls might operate successfully for titles offering premium content but were unlikely to work for those aimed at "general public consumption" since there were too many freely accessible alternatives. [8]

He was proved right. *The Sun*'s pay wall, faced with continued competition from popular advertising-supported titles, was abandoned in 2015, but as Table 3.1 confirms, News Corp's broadsheet press titles have built viable subscriber bases.

In 2022, *The Wall Street Journal* was ranked the second most successful English-language news provider, with 3.17 million subscribers, but some way behind the market leader, *The New York Times*, whose recent acquisition of *The Athletic* (ranked fourth) will further strengthen its position. News Corp's other Dow Jones publications were ranked 11th and News Corp Australia and *The Times* titles seventh and 17th respectively.

3.2.2 Charging the Pipers

The concentrated market power of the digital majors, led by Google and Facebook, has attracted increasing political scrutiny and calls for regulation.

Table 3.1 Top English-Language Subscription News Providers 2022 [9]

Rank	*News source*	*Subcription*
1	The New York Times	8.83 million
2	The Wall Street Journal (WSJ)	3.17 million
3	The Athletic	2.68 million*
4	The Washington Post	2.5 million
7	News Corp Australia	1.01 million
9	The Guardian	1 million
10	Financial Times	1 million
11	Dow Jones (excluding WSJ)	972,000
13	The Economist (Nikkei)	626,200
17	The Times/Sunday Times/TLS	489,000

Figures for *The Washington Post* are for the year to October 2021; for *The Economist* and *The Guardian* for the year to March 2022. All other figures are for the year to December 2022.

* The Athletic was acquired by *The New York Times* in January 2022.

In December 2020, the Australian parliament introduced the News Media and Digital Platforms Mandatory Bargaining Code requiring digital platforms to pay for news content. To qualify, news organisations must be registered by the Australian Communication and Media Authority and generate revenues over AU$15,000 a year. This excludes many small local and alternative outlets, so that far from enhancing choice and diversity, the Code has reinforced the dominance of the major media companies. [10] Estimates suggest that Australia's three major news providers, led by News Corporation which campaigned intensely for the Code, "will together gain around 90 per cent of Facebook and Google's total contributions". [11] In February 2021, News Corp secured significant payments for making content from its global titles available on Google's News Showcase.

These moves underline, once again, the central role of changing regulatory regimes in shaping News Corp's development. The initial deregulatory wave allowed it to dominate the daily press market in Britain and Australia. The belated regulatory backlash against the leading digital platforms has enabled it to capitalise on its position by guaranteeing a substantial additional source of income.

3.3 Capitalising on Content

3.3.1 Mobilising Social Media

Thirty-three per cent of those questioned by the Australian Competition and Consumer Commission inquiry claimed to obtain their news from social media. [12] Later international research found the figure for young people to be even higher, [13] promoting concerted attempts to reach them on the sites they use most often.

In April 2022, *The Australian* launched a youth-oriented online section, *The Oz*, offering celebrity, lifestyle, and sports content alongside news. With accounts on Instagram and TikTok, it took on some of the worst features of social media tabloidisation. In July 2022, it carried a graphic account of the alleged sexual activities of a member of the royal family based on unsubstantiated gossip from an Instagram account. In January 2023, faced with low take-up, the site was closed.

The Sun's daily edition on Snapchat's Discovery Section, launched in April 2016 and strongly focused on celebrity culture, has been more successful. Targeted firmly at young people and configured for smart phones, it was, as Derek Brown, *The Sun*'s Head of Strategy, explained, "for people who don't read the paper or go to our site". [14] Advertising revenue is shared between the two companies.

As Table 3.2 shows, in October 2022 *The Sun* was generating 2 million monthly engagements (measured by the number of likes and reposts) on Snapchat and 1.2 million on TikTok, both popular with young people.

Table 3.2 User Engagements with News Posts on Leading Social Media Sites for Selected Months 2022–2023 [15]

News Organisation	*TikTok*	*Instagram*	*Snapchat*
Fox News		8.2 million	
New York Post	471,000		34,500
The Wall Street Journal		4.5 million	
The Sun	1.2 million		2 million

Tik Tok figures are for January 2023. Instagram figures are for June 2023. Snapchat figures are for October 2022

News Corp has also has a substantial presence on the longer-established global social media sites YouTube and Facebook.

As Table 3.3 shows, in 2022 Fox News was the fifth most-visited English-language news source on YouTube and *The Wall Street Journal* the tenth. *The Sun*, with 3.1 million subscribers, featured at 21st and Sky News Australia at 24th.

As Table 3.4 demonstrates, Fox News (ranked 13th) also features in the leading Facebook news sources by "engagements" measured by the number of "likes", comments, and shares. The Sun, ranked 25th, falls far short of its two main British tabloid rivals, the *Daily Mail* and the *Daily Mirror*.

Table 3.3 Twenty-Five Largest English-Language News Sources on YouTube (Ranked by Number of Subscribers, June 2022) [16]

Rank	*News source*	*Subscribers*	*Average views per video*
1	CNN	14 million	76,350
2	ABC News (US)	13.2 million	163,930
3	BBC News	12.5 million	231,410
4	Vox	10.7 million	2,089,000
5	Fox News	9.6 million	142,210
10	The Wall Street Journal	6.4 million	51,460
21	The Sun	3.1 million	209,090
24	Sky News Australia	2.6 million	26,550

Table 3.4 Top 25 News Sources on Facebook (March 2022) [17]

Rank	*News Source*	*Engagements*
1	dailymail.co.uk	32.7 million
3	mirror.co.uk	23.1 million
4	bbc.co.uk	19.6 million
6	cnn.com	13.7 million
13	foxnews.com	10.8 million
13	thesun.co.uk	7.7 million

3.3.2 Token Returns: Blockchain

News Corp's drive to maximise digital returns from content production has prompted moves into blockchain technology.

Blockchain databases provide permanent, unalterable, and transparent records of data and transactions, making it possible to securely hold or exchange anything of value in digital form. Their best publicised application has been for storing Bitcoin and other digital currencies. These are fungible tokens. Every Bitcoin is interchangeable with every other Bitcoin at the same value. Non-fungible tokens (NFTs), such as digital works of art, are unique, one-of-a-kind artefacts whose value depends on how much a buyer is willing to pay.

In May 2021, Fox Entertainment announced the creation of a new division, Blockchain Creative Labs (BCL), to develop and sell NFTs using blockchain technology to confirm their authenticity as unique objects, verify ownership, and track transactions. In August 2021, Fox invested $100 million in seed money and took a minority stake in start-up Eluvio to provide the underlying platform technology for managing and monetising the process.

The potential was demonstrated in late 2021 with the launch of MaskVerse, allowing viewers to buy, sell, and trade digital collectables based on the Fox television show, *The Masked Singer*. More than 300,000 fans opened digital wallets to collect the NFTs. The aim is to build on this base with a new business model for content distribution based on direct relations between producers and viewers. In addition to NFTs that allow fans to own a unique piece of their favourite shows, dedicated NFT collectors may be given privileged access to online meetings with cast members and the chance to appear as an "extra" in the programme. [18]

3.3.3 Monetising Interaction: Online Sports Gambling

News Corp has had a long-standing involvement in betting services through stakes in the interactive wagering services caried on the TVG (Television Games Network) cable and satellite channel in the United States, Foxtel in Australia, and BSkyB in the United Kingdom. [19] Following the deregulation of the UK gambling industry in 2005, Sky Betting and Gaming became a major player, generating very substantial profits by the time it was sold for $4.7 billion in April 2018.

Online sports betting has been boosted by recent deregulation. In May 2018, the US Supreme Court legalised sports gambling. The Amended Australian Interactive Gambling Act of 2017 confirmed permission for sport betting, providing bets are placed before the start of the event. During COVID-19 lockdowns, with physical locations largely closed, wagering moved online. A significant proportion stayed there after restrictions were lifted. News Corp has moved to capitalise on these expanded opportunities with two joint ventures.

Fox Corp already had relations with Flutter Entertainment, the leading global online gambling company, through the 50/50 joint venture Fox Bet and Fox's equity stake in Flutter. In December 2020, Fox purchased additional shares to support Flutter's acquisition of a 37.2 per cent stake in the leading fantasy sports concern, FanDuel, with an option for Fox to acquire an 18.5 per cent equity stake in Fan Duel.

In April 2022, News Corp announced a ten-year deal with the Las Vagas digital sports gambling concern, Tekkorp, to launch a new company, NTD, offering online betting on racing and sports in Australia and New Zealand. Tekkorp provides the technology, and News Corp promotes the services across its major metropolitan titles and news sites and Foxtel's sports streaming service Kayo. The aim is to attract younger "punters" more interested in betting on sports than horse racing. As Tekkorp's President Robin Chhabra noted, "News Corp have significant skin in the game … this isn't just levering their media presence. They have a presence on the board." [20]

3.4 Internet Ventures: Serial Failures

The launch of the World Wide Web and Mosaic browser in 1993 transformed the internet from a restricted network to an open public resource, but News Corp's attempts to establish an independent presence in key web services have been marked by successive failures.

News Corp entered the digital services market early, purchasing Delphi Internet Services, the first commercial operator offering full internet access, for $15 million in 1993. By 1995, Delphi's text-only service was facing increasing competition from rivals led by AOL offering easy-to-use point-and-click interfaces. The plan to build a comprehensive digital platform to promote News Corp's print and broadcast content never materialised. More immediately promising initiatives were marginalised. The executives Rupert Murdoch hired from IBM to oversee expansion clashed with the company's original founders and ignored their suggestions. Proposals to boost subscriptions with a free email service were disregarded, leaving Hotmail and other entrants to colonise a valuable market. Paid Delphi subscriptions declined from a peak of 500,000 to 125,000, and in 1996 NewsCorp sold the company back to its original investors. [21]

The years between 1995 and 2000 saw money poured into a variety of internet ventures as investors searched for ways to capitalise on the Web's increasing centrality to social life. Overly optimistic speculation was followed by a crash as start-ups failed or lost most of their value.

Fox re-entered the digital marketplace after the dot-com bubble had burst. As Rupert Murdoch noted, "We have tens of billions of asset value in our news, sports and general entertainment businesses … [O]ur priority now in truth our mandate is to perfect a plan that will monetize them across the world of the internet." [22]

In 2005, a new corporate division, Fox Interactive Media, was launched with a budget of up to $2 billion to purchase web businesses. In August 2005, the company entered into talks to acquire a controlling interest in Blinkx, a multi-media search engine that assembled internet video and audio clips into folders and linked users to other related material. Searches were confined to organisations that Blinkx had agreements with, however, and did not cover the whole of the Web. News Corp's interest was not pursued, and in 2006 Blinkx technology was adopted by Microsoft and incorporated into its MSM service.

Other acquisitions and investments covered a wide range of areas. They included: the sports site Scout Media; the photo sharing site Photobucket; the online job listings network Simply Hired; and IGN Entertainment, the hub for a variety of sites; the film review site Rotten Tomatoes; the male lifestyle site Ask Men; the popular IGN gaming site; and, for a brief period, UGO, an independent gaming community. These sites appealed particularly to young men, a demographic traditional media found it hard to reach.

In 2007, Rupert Murdoch reaffirmed his faith in the digital future in the annual Boyer Lectures, hosted by Australia's public service broadcaster, the ABC. Under the title *A Golden Age of Freedom*, he championed digital technologies as forces of creative destruction "ushering in a new golden age" of unprecedented individual choices with "the news and entertainment industry right in the centre of the maelstrom". [23]

The company's initial ventures were short-lived. Photobucket was sold in 2009, Rotten Tomatoes in 2010, and IGN Entertainment in 2013, when plans to establish it as the hub of a new consumer division were abandoned. News Corp's most significant online investment and its most significant failure was the mishandling of the social media site MySpace.

MySpace was launched in August 2003. By 2005, it was the world's fastest-growing social network with 20 million unique monthly visitors in the United States. In July 2005, News Corp won a bidding war with Viacom, acquiring the site for $580 million. Within a year, it had tripled in value and, in June 2006, overtook Google as the most-visited website. By September 2007, it accounted for 11 per cent of the time Americans spent online and was projected to generate $800 million in revenues, up from $23 million when Murdoch first acquired it. [24] It moved rapidly beyond the US, establishing a presence in a number of countries. But there were three problems.

From the outset, the horizontal logic of peer-to-peer networking and user-generated content was in tension with the vertical logic of distribution. News Corp used MySpace to promote its own productions and generate additional income by licensing professionally produced and emerging content. It operated its own record label. MySpace TV carried News Corp clips alongside material from major media companies, promotional videos, and user-generated content.

Second, the site was oversaturated with advertising. In 2006, Google agreed to pay $250 million a year to 2010 to place search-based and keyword-targeted ads. This income covered the costs of the initial purchase but led to the site becoming saturated with promotion. On one typical day in 2007, it carried a total of 7.3 billion ads. [25]

Third, users could remain anonymous and assume any identity. Imposing few limits on who or what appeared opened the site to sexual predators and pornography. In 2006, an inquiry by the Attorney General of Connecticut raising questions about children's exposure to pornography attracted an avalanche of negative publicity.

In July 2011, MySpace was sold to the advertising network Specific Media for $35 million, leaving Facebook, launched in 2004, as the dominant social networking site. Responding to questions, Rupert Murdoch admitted that "we screwed up in every way possible, leaned lots of valuable expensive lessons". [26]

Lessons learned have not prevented later failures.

Addressing the G8 meeting in Paris in 2011, Murdoch presented schools as "the last holdout from the digital revolution", arguing that "the same digital technologies that transformed every other aspect of modern life can transform education", adding, "my company is determined to try – in a big way". [27] In an earlier speech to business leaders, he had speculated that 10 per cent of News Corporation's business might be "made up of educational revenues in the next five years". [28] He was encouraged by moves to overhaul schooling on both sides of the Atlantic.

Between 2010 and 2014, the British Secretary for State for Education, Michael Gove, set out to transfer control over schools from local councils to private consortia and reduce staff payrolls by encouraging digital delivery. An editorial writer on *The Times* before entering parliament, he had close ties with Murdoch and hosted him when he visited London to discuss investing in the new private academies.

In 2010, News Corp acquired the US educational technology firm Wireless Generation. Renamed Amplify, the new division aimed to produce a tablet computer as the exclusive point of access for its suite of curriculum resources in US schools. From the outset, Amplify ran into problems.

News Corp had sold its US educational publishing division, responsible for elementary and high school textbooks, in 2005 to focus on general consumer books, severing the company's relations with teachers and principals.

The major educational publishers were designing materials for downloading on to the standard devices manufactured by Apple, Microsoft, and Google, giving schools flexibility of choice. Amplify's insistence that users purchased their dedicated tablet was an expensive mistake. Early tablets had faults. Some had cracked screens and had to be recalled. Marketing underestimated the strength of the trusted relations that major educational publishers had established with schools. There was widespread suspicion that News Corp would use their proprietary tablets as a platform for promoting their media interests.

By early 2015, News Corp had spent an estimated $1 billion dollars on developing the system but only 20 schools had adopted it. The division was sold for an undisclosed price, to a consortium controlled by Emerson Collective, the philanthropic foundation headed by Lauren Powell Jobs, the widow of Steve Jobs, founder of Apple. By 2018, 950,000 American students were using its science resources, confirming the potential of the market and the scale of News Corp's failure.

Later digital ventures have also failed. In 2015, NewsCorp paid $90 million in cash for Unruly, specialists in video advertising. In 2019, the company was sold to one of the sector's global leaders, Tremor International, for £1, a 6.91 per cent stake, and Tremor's exclusive right to sell video on News Corp's digital publications. Two years later, under Tremor's management News Corp's stake was worth £74 million, suggesting that strategic investments and partnership in areas where News Corp lacked prior experience were more likely to pay dividends that outright ownership.

In January 2020, two months before settling its dispute with Google over payment for its news content, News Corp launched Knewz, a rival news aggregator. Its promise to present the "latest news from the widest variety of sources free of narrow-minded nonsense" was challenged by research showing a marked skew towards News Corp's *New York Post* and Fox News and the right-wing *Daily Mail*. [29] It closed in July 2021, having failed to make a profit. It was acquired by the Empire Media Group and is operating successfully at the time of writing.

3.5 Confronting Artificial Intelligence

In June 2023, News Corp joined with other media companies in publishing "Principles for the Development and Governance of Generative AI". The document addresses three main concerns: first, fair compensation for using media companies' intellectual property in training AI systems; second, protecting content creators from the unlicensed use of their output; and, third, not creating "or risk creating unfair market or competition outcomes" by allowing the digital platforms to restrict market entry. [30]

Individual media companies have responded to the explosive growth of AI in various ways. Bloomberg and *The Guardian* have blocked ChatGPT for using their content to train its chatbot. *The New York Times* has gone further, bringing a case for compensation before the Manhattan federal court, arguing that Open AI has enjoyed "a free-ride on *The Times*' massive investment in its journalism by using it to build substantive profits without permission or payment". [31] In response, Open AI claims to be committed to "providing new ways for news providers to connect with readers" by "displaying real-time content with attribution". [32] This option has been taken up by the Springer group in Germany with ChatGPT paying for permission to respond to user queries with summaries of current articles from Springer titles, including *Politico* and *Business Insider*, with due attribution and links to the original source.

The press release accompanying News Corp's Annual 2023 Report hailed the "momentum gathering pace in the age of generative AI" as "a remarkable opportunity to create new streams of revenues". [33]

At the time of writing, News Corp has not announced details of its AI strategy, but recent remarks point to a Springer-like arrangement rather than litigation.

It remains to be seen how much revenue this will generate. What we know for sure is that News Corp, along with other news organisations, are closely monitoring a significant risk posed by potential disruptions in search traffic stemming from the introduction of AI-driven updates to search engines, such as the upcoming integration of generative AI into Google's search platform. This imminent evolution aims to provide users with succinct information directly in response to their queries, alongside the customary array of linked pages. This transition may *de facto* lead a substantial reduction in search traffic for publishers, with huge losses of users and therefore revenues. Unlike most news organisations, however, News Corp commands a core digital resource: data vital to decision making in key economic sectors.

Anne Dias, former Fox Corporation board member, writing on the website of Aragon Global Management, the company she heads, has argued that:

> AI will do for data what electricity did for energy. It will allow us to quantify and analyse all kinds of things in real time that used to be intuitive, inexact, or plain unknowable. This will create considerable value for companies that can leverage it. [34]

Whether News Corp can be one of those companies is central to its future viability.

3.6 From Media to Data

Analysis of stocks traded on the Nasdaq electronic exchange during the dot-com boom showed wide variations in returns. Only 14.7 per cent of communications companies were paying out dividends compared to three-quarters (75.3%) of financials and over half (53.6%) of real-estate concerns. [35]

These figures underline the centrality of the FIRE economy (finance, insurance, and real estate) in contemporary capitalism. A series of acquisitions has seen News Corp emerge as a major provider of data services to these sectors.

Alongside *The Wall Street Journal*, News Corp's purchase of Dow Jones delivered a suite of online financial services. They include: the website MarketWatch, aimed at active investors; Factiva, a content aggregator drawing on news and information sources from over 200 countries; Dow Jones Newswires distributing real-time financial information; and Dow Jones Risk and Compliance providing data on regulatory and reputational risks.

News Corp has also built a major presence in the digital real-estate market. It currently holds a controlling 61.6 per cent stake in the REA Group, the dominant force in online advertising for residential, commercial, and rental properties across Australia and Asia. In November 2014, it entered the US real-estate market, purchasing an 80 per cent interest in Move, the county's leading provider of digital real-estate services. In April 2021, it paid $244 million to add the mortgage broking company, Mortgage Choice, to the REA Group's property advertising portfolio.

Recent acquisitions have extended Dow Jones online data services to two other key sectors: energy and chemicals. In August 2021, News Corp acquired the major global oil and gas data reporting site, Oil Price Information Service (OPIS), followed in June 2002 by the purchase of Base Chemicals, a specialist in energy, renewables, and chemicals. Introducing the acquisition, New Corp's CEO pointed to the value of user data from Dow Jones subscription publications in shaping priorities, noting that "we see strong cross-sell and upsell potential using the potent Wall Street Journal, Investor's Business Daily and Market Watch audiences as a premium pool for customer leads". [36]

More generally, the consumer data collected from News Corp's press and television subscription sites offers marketers and advertisers a valuable resource for refining appeals.

Exploiting these resources is not without problems. Data has been widely hailed as the "new oil", but realising value requires crude oil to be refined. Both the data storage and cloud computing capacities required to run AI applications are concentrated in the hands of the major digital platforms who will demand a share of revenues.

Introducing News Corp's 2022 Annual Report the company's Chief Executive Robert Thompson stressed that:

> The News Corporation of nine years ago is not the News Corporation of now. The provenance and the principle endure but the business is fundamentally transformed. [37]

The next chapter details the economics of the transformation from media to data.

References

[1] See Scott Sherman (2012) 'The Long Goodbye', *Vanity Fair*, 30 November. Available at http://scottgsherman.com/writingsonthepress/thelonggoodbye.php

[2] John Pilger (1998) *Hidden Agendas*. London: Vintage, p. 466.

[3] Australian Competition and Consumer Commission (2019) *Digital Platforms Inquiry: Final Report.* Canberra, Australian Capital Territory, p. 18.

[4] Australian Competition and Consumer Commission, op. cit., p. 122.

[5] Charles Arthur (2010) 'Eric Schmidt talks about threats to Google, paywalls and the future', *The Guardian*, 2 July.

[6] Rupert Murdoch (2009) 'From Town Crier to Bloggers: How Will Journalism Survive in the Internet Age', Federal Trade Commission Workshop, 1 December, pp. 11–12.

[7] Ruper Murdoch, op. cit., p. 11.

[8] Oliver Luft (2009) 'Google boss: Paid-for-online news won't work Rupert', Press Gazette, 18 September. Available at https://pressgazette.co.uk/publishers/nationals/google-boss-paid-for-online-news-wont-work-rupert

[9] Aisha Majid (2023) 'Mail Joins 100k Club exclusive ranking of world's top paywall news publishers', Press Gazette, 6 April. Available at https://pressgazette.co.uk/paywalls/digital-news-subscriptions-ranking-2023

[10] Benedetta Brevini (2021) 'Private Deals Between Digital and Media Lords to Save Journalism: The Case of the Australian News Media Bargaining Code', *The Political Economy of Communication*, Vol. 9, No. 1, p. 85.

[11] 'Who Controls Our Media? Exposing the impact of media concentration on our democracy'. Sydney: GetUp. Available at www.getup.org.au/campaigns/abc-media-campaigns/share-the-media-diversity-report/who-controls-our-media-the-new-report-commissioned-by-getup, p. 37.

[12] Australian Competition and Consumer Commission, op. cit., p. 55.

[13] Kirsten Eddy (2022) 'The Changing News Habits and Attitudes of Younger Audiences', in Nic Newman et al., *Reuters Institute Digital News Report 2022*. Reuters Institute, Oxford University, Section 2.3, p. 43.

[14] Digiday (2016) 'The Sun launches on Snapchat Discover, plans a dozen pieces of content daily', 26 April. Available at https://digiday.com/media/the-sun-snapchat-discover

[15] Aisha Majid (2023) 'Tik Tok: Who are the news publishers with the biggest following and fastest growth?', Press Gazette, 12 January. Available at https://pressgazette.co.uk/media-audience-and-business-data/tiktok-who-are-the-news-publishers-with-the-biggest-followings-and-fastest-growth

Aisha Majid (2023) 'News publishers' Instagram growth from 2021–2023', Press Gazette, 3 July. Available at https://pressgazette.co.uk/media-audience-and-business-data/media_metrics/ranked-news-publishers-instagram-growth-from-2021-to-2023

Aisha Majid (2022) 'How the Daily Mail's 35 strong Snapchat team connects with 15 million subscribers', Press Gazette, 7 October. Available at https://pressgazette.co.uk/news/daily-mail-snapchat

[16] Bron Maher (2022) 'Revealed: The biggest English-language news outlets on Youtube and their most popular videos', Press Gazette, 29 June. Available at https://pressgazette.co.uk/media-audience-and-business-data/biggest-news-youtube

[17] Aisha Majid (2022) 'Ukraine coverage helps Daily Mail become top news provider on Facebook'. Press Gazette, 17 November. Available at https://pressgazette.co.uk/news/biggest-publisher-facebook-daily-mail/#:~:text=Ukraine%20coverage%20helps%20Daily%20Mail%20become%20top%20news%20publisher%20on%20Facebook&text=The%20Daily%20Mail%20was%20biggest,according%20to%20an%20independent%20ranking

[18] Todd Spangler (2022) 'Why Fox Is Investing Millions in NFTs and Blockchain Technology', *Variety*, 17 August. Available at https://variety.com/2022/digital/news/fox-nft-blockchain-1235342878

[19] Holly Kruse (2009) 'Betting on News Corporation: Interactive Media, Gambling, and Global Information Flows', Television *and New Media*, Vol. 10, No. 2, pp. 179–94.

[20] Robin Harrison (2022) 'Inside the deal to bring News Corp Australia into sports betting', IGB, 21 April. Available at https://igamingbusiness.com/sports-betting/online-sports-betting/news-corp-moves-into-betting

[21] Arlyn Tobias Gajilan (1999) 'They Coulda Been Contenders Once upon a time, Delphi was fighting it out with AOL. Then along came Rupert', *CNN Money*, 1 November. Available at https://money.cnn.com/magazines/fsb/fsb_archive/1999/11/01/270056/index.htm

[22] Quoted in Midnight_Son (2005) 'Rupert Murdoch to buy IGN?', Quarter to Three Forums, August. Available at https://forum.quartertothree.com/t/rupert-murdoch-to-buy-ign/20722

[23] Rupert Murdoch (2008) *A Golden Age of Freedom* Sydney. ABC Books, pp. 32–35.

[24] David Kirkpatrick (2007) 'As Facebook takes off, MySpace strikes back', *Fortune*, 19 September. Available at https://money.cnn.com/2007/09/18/technology/myspace_strikes.fortune/index.htm

[25] David Kirkpatrick, op. cit.

[26] Quoted in John C. Abell (2012) 'Murdoch on MySpace: "We Screwed Up in Every Way Possible"', Wired, 13 January. Available at www.wired.com/2012/01/murdoch-on-myspace

[27] Rupert Murdoch (2011) 'Education: The Last Frontier', Speech to the e-G8 Forum, Paris 24 May. Available at https://edu.blogs.com/files/blog—murdoch-education—the-last-frontier-may-2011.pdf

[28] David Leigh (2012) 'The schools crusade that links Michael Gove to Rupert Murdoch', *The Guardian*, 27 February. Available at www.theguardian.com/politics/2012/feb/26/schools-crusade-gove-murdoch

[29] Pete Brown (2020) 'Knewz vowed to diversify the news. Has it?', *Columbia Journalism Review*, 13 March. Available at www.cjr.org/tow_centre/knewz-murdoch-promotion-tool-coronavirus.php

[30] Digital Content Next (2023) 'CN's Principles for the Development and Governance of Generative AI', 5 June. Available at https://digitalcontentnext.org/blog/2023/06/05/dcns-principles-for-development-and-governance-of-generative-ai

[31] New York Times (2023) Deposition, Case 1.23-cv-11195, Document 1, United States District Court Southern District of New York, 27 December.

[32] OpenAI (2024) 'OpenAI and journalism', 8 January. Available at https://openai.com/blog/openai-and-journalism

[33] News Corp (2023) 'News Corp Reports First Quarter and Full Year Results for Fiscal 2023', 10 August. Available at https://newscorp.com/2023/08/10/news-corp-reports-fourth-quarter-and-full-year-results-for-fiscal-2023

[34] Aragon Global Management website. Available at www.aragonglobal.com/en/home/who-we-are/investment-philosophy

[35] Yuchao Fan (2022) 'Dissecting the dot-com bubble in the 1990s: NASDAQ', Table 2, p. 18. Available at https://arxiv.org/abs/2206.14130

[36] News Corp (2022) 'News Corp Completes Acquisition of Base Chemicals', Press Release, 1 June. Available at https://newscorp.com/2022/06/01/news-corp-completes-acquisition-of-base-chemicals/#:~:text=New%20York%2C%20NY%20(June%201,from%20S%26P%20Global%20Market%20Intelligence

[37] Robert Thompson, Chief Executive's Introduction to News Corporation Annual Report 2022.

4 Economic Profile: Holdings, Revenues, and Market Shares

This chapter, detailing News Corporation's economic organisation, is divided into three parts. Section 4.1 provides a comprehensive list of current holdings. Section 4.2 analyses the changing distribution of revenues and profits. Section 4.3 charts News Corp's market shares in key sectors.

4.1 Contemporary Corporate Structure and Holdings

This section lists the current holdings of both News Corporation and Fox Corporation.

4.1.1 News Corporation

4.1.1.1 Advertising and Marketing

News UK operates the influencer marketing agency The Fifth, and Studio PI, focused on recruiting creatives from marginalised groups.

In June 2022, News Corp Australia acquired full ownership of the Medium Rare Content Agency, building on its interests in producing digital social and video content established with previously purchased stakes in Visual Domain, Australia's largest full-service video company, and digital finance marketing group Stockhead.

4.1.1.2 Print

4.1.1.2.1 BOOK PUBLISHING

HarperCollins is one of the 'Big Five' English-language publishers with general and children's literature under the imprints grouped under the Harper and Houghton, Mifflin and Harcourt divisions together with romantic fiction (Avon and Harlequin) and Christian publishing (Thomas Nelson and Zondervan).

DOI: 10.4324/9781003255086-4

4.1.1.2.2 NEWSPAPERS

News Corp owns four national newspapers in Britain, *The Sun* and *The Sun on Sunday* and *The Times* and *Sunday Times*, two major titles in the United States, *The Wall Street Journal* and the *New York Post*, and is the leading newspaper publisher in Australia. It owns the country's only national newspaper *The Australian* and *The Weekend Australian*. It also owns daily newspapers in every major metropolitan centre except Perth, including *The Daily Telegraph* and *The Sunday Telegraph* (Sydney), the *Herald Sun* and *Sunday Herald Sun* (Melbourne), *The Advertiser* and *Sunday Mail* (Adelaide), *The Courier-Mail* and *The Sunday Mail* (Brisbane), and *The Mercury* and *Sunday Tasmanian* in Tasmania. Also it controls [1] leading regional publications based in Geelong (Victoria), Townsville, Gold Coast, and Cairns (Queensland), and Darwin (Northern Territory).

4.1.1.2.3 CONSUMER MAGAZINES

News Corp owns the *Times Literary Supplement* in Britain. News Corp Australia publishes a range of print and web titles in the areas of style, food, health, and family, including *Vogue Australia*, *GQ Australia*, *Vogue Living*, the leading food and recipe site Taste.com.au and the parenting site Kidspot.com.au

4.1.1.3 Broadcasting

4.1.1.3.1 RADIO

The Wireless Group in Britain operates five national commercial radio channels, TalkRadio, talkSPORT 1 and 2, Virgin Radio UK, and Times Radio, together with eight local stations in Ireland.

News Corp Australia holds a 13.29 per cent interest in Australian Radio Network (ARN) (formerly HT&E Limited – Here, There and Everywhere) Australia's leading radio network with listeners aged 25–54. In June 2023, ARN consolidated its position by acquiring a 14.8 per cent equity stake in its main rival, Southern Cross Media Group. [2]

Within days of leaving News Corp in 2005 to return to Australia, Lachlan Murdoch established a personal investment vehicle, Illyria. In 2009 he acquired a 50 per cent share in Nova Entertainment and the remaining shares in 2012. Nova operates a national radio network of broadcast and online services in Sydney, Melbourne, Adelaide (FIVEaa), and on the Central New South Wales Coast (Star 104.5).

Nova also operates a podcast network (NEPN), a live music platform, Red Room, music services to the Coles chain of grocery stores, and a live events company e.xp.

Nova is not formerly linked economically to News Corp but has relations through operating the Smooth TV channel on Foxtel and drawing on News Corp outlets, including Sky News for podcast material and presenters. Lachlan Murdoch's rejoining of the family company in 2014, coupled with his current position as the Chair of News Corporation (since 2023) and his potential succession, make his external interests noteworthy.

4.1.1.3.2 TELEVISION

The Wireless Group subsidiary operates the Talk TV news and comment channel in Britain. Originally launched as a linear broadcast service, faced with persistently low audience figures it moved entirely online in 2024.

News Corp has a major presence in Australian television through two subsidiaries providing pay-TV and streaming news, sports, and entertainment services to subscribers and commercial licensees over cable, satellite, and Internet connections.

The Foxtel Group, 65 per cent owned by News Corp (and 35% owned by Telstra Corporation Limited) is the country's largest Australian-based subscription television provider. It hosts 200 channels (including a number owned and operated) offering entertainment, movies, documentaries, children's programmes, news, and sports and recently launched aggregation services: Kayo Sports, BINGE (entertainment), and Flash (News). FOX SPORTS Australia provides live sports programming. Foxtel also offers "triple play" packages allowing subscribers to add broadband and telephone services.

Australian News Channel, licenced by Sky International to use the Sky trademarks and domain names operates a range of news channels in Australia, covering general news (Sky News Live and three Sky News Extra channels), weather (Sky News Weather), regional news (Sky News Regnal), and sports news (Fox Sports News), together with a New Zealand service (Sky News New Zealand) and the international Australian IPTV service.

4.1.1.4 Information Services

4.1.1.4.1 DOW JONES FINANCIAL AND INDUSTRY SERVICES

4.1.1.4.1.1 Consumer Financial Products

- *Barron's* investment news, analysis and company profiles.
- *MarketWatch* investment and financial news website.
- *Investor's Business Daily.*

4.1.1.4.1.2 Professional Financial Products *Factiva* global business information draws on 33,000 news and information sources from over 200 countries.

Dow Jones Risk and Compliance supplies data relevant to identifying regulatory, corporate and reputational risks from money-laundering, corruption, sanctions and other threats.

Dow Jones Newswires distributes real-time financial news, analysis and commentary.

4.1.1.4.1.3 Oil Price Information Services (OPIS) Provides data and analysis on prices and events related to energy commodities (oil, coal, natural gas, renewables), petrochemicals, metals, and through its Chemical Market Analysis business, base chemicals.

4.1.1.4.2 DIGITAL REAL ESTATE SERVICES

REA Group (61.4% interest) is the leading global digital business specialising in property, with operations in Australia, the US, and Asia.

Australian subsidiaries, including realestate.com.au and Flatmatescom.au, advertise domestic, rental, and commercial property and provide financial services, including mortgage advice and a digital loan application service (in conjunction with a division of National Australia Bank). *Move*, operating through Realtor.com, is the leading US provider of digital real-estate services, advertising properties and connecting buyers to lenders. REA has a major presence in India through Elara Technologies and in Southeast Asia through the region's largest digital property marketplace, Property Guru, with leading positions in Singapore, Malaysia, Thailand, and Vietnam.

4.1.1.4.3 HOME IMPROVEMENT SERVICES

News Corp Australia holds 28.5 per cent in Hipages Group Pty Ltd, the country's leading on-demand home improvement services marketplace.

4.1.1.4.4 DIGITAL SUPPORT SERVICES

News UK operates three subsidiaries, Zesty, Tibus, and Web Bureau, providing complementary services in web design, secure hosting, digital strategy, and marketing campaign management.

4.1.1.4.5 SOCIAL NEWS MONITORING

Digital News Agency Storyful, acquired by News Corp in 2013, collates, verifies, and contextualises eyewitness news footage and viral video from Twitter, Facebook, YouTube, and other social media platforms for inclusion in news reports and for corporations to monitor reputational risks and opportunities.

4.1.2 Fox Corporation

4.1.2.1 Television

4.1.2.1.1 PRODUCTION

FOX Studio Lot, with 15 sound stages, two broadcast studios, and editing suites, provides television and film production facilities to third parties.

Fox operates four subsidiaries producing popular programming.

Fox Alternative Entertainment's full-service studio makes unscripted programming. Bento Box Entertainment develops and produces animation programming. MarVista Entertainment and TMZ produce syndicated magazine programming and broadcast television specials. Studio Ramsay Global, co-owned with the celebrity chef, Gordon Ramsay, produces culinary and lifestyle programming.

4.1.2.1.2 DISTRIBUTION

FOX Television Stations own and operate 29 broadcast television stations delivering network content, local news, and syndicated programming in 18 local markets across the US, including 14 of the 15 largest with duopolies in the three biggest: New York, Chicago, and Los Angeles. It also operates the free live news streaming service LiveNOW.

MyNetwork TV distributes two hours of programming from syndicates, nighty on weekdays, to over 100 licenced stations including ten Fox stations.

The FOX Network reaches 99.9 per cent of television households, with prime-time sports and entertainment programming focused on comedy and unscripted productions, distributed to 18 owned and operated stations and 208 local affiliates. Sports coverage, which constitutes a significant proportion of the network's programming, is secured through long-term licensing agreements with professional and collegiate organisations responsible for overseeing a range of sports, including American football, basketball, soccer, and professional wrestling. Entertainment programming is made in-house and purchased from major studios and independent production companies.

TUBI, the leading AVOD (free advertising supported video on demand) streaming service, is available on 25 digital platforms in the US and selected international regions. It features FOX entertainment and sports programming, live local and national news, movies from every Hollywood studio, and content from over 350 other partners. Fox has recently introduced streaming channels based on Fox-produced entertainment programmes including *The Masked Singer* and *Global Gordon Ramsey.*

4.1.2.2 Cable Network Programming

The segment produces and licenses programming for distribution through multichannel video programming systems (MVPDs) and FOX-branded websites and apps. It operates two divisions.

FOX News Media Networks produces FOX News and FOX Business. FOX Sports Networks has three streams. FS1 and 2 carry live coverage of events across a range of sports including basketball, soccer, horseracing, rugby, and motor sports. The Big Ten Network features college football and athletics. FOX Deportes is a Spanish-language service.

The Outkick Media subsidiary operates a website offering sports news and analysis and producing commentary shows for Facebook, YouTube, and Twitter.

In April 2022, FOX Sports moved into staging events, launching USFL, a professional football league of eight teams playing during the spring season.

Betting Fox Corp has a partnership with Flutter to develop sports betting in the US. Flutter has an exclusive licence to use FOX trademarks. FOX Sports has an option to acquire 50 per cent of the Flutter majority-owned The Stars Group and 18.5 per cent of Fan Duel, Flutter's fantasy sports subsidiary.

A second partnership, NTD, with the Las Vegas-based digital concern, Tekkop, aims to develop online sports betting in Australia and New Zealand.

Blockchain Creative Labs aims to establish a leadership position in the third age of the Internet based on blockchain technologies and token-based economies by developing and monetising non-fungible collectable items generated by programming produced by Fox and external partners.

4.1.2.3 Financial Services

Credible (66% stake) provides personalised advice on financial products ranging from loans to mortgages and insurance.

4.2 Company Finances: Assets, Revenues, and Liabilities

The year 2023 was crucial for News Corp, as the company, after a recovery from COVID-related hurdles, reported a significant 75 per cent decline in its full-year earnings. It declared a net profit of US$187 million for the fiscal year, a substantial drop from the previous year's record of US$760 million. The decline is clearly due to reduced print and digital advertising revenues at News Corp Australia, which includes its flagship newspaper, *The Australian*, as well as decreased print advertising at its UK news division.

At the same time, in 2023 over 50 per cent of the company's revenue was generated from its digital platforms. After publication of the latest financial results, in August 2023, News Corp shares climbed 4.6 per cent despite the losses, as analysts and investors predicted a significant opportunity for New Corp offered by AI, for generating new revenue streams while simultaneously reducing operational costs across the entire organisation. Since 2023, the company has actively engaged in discussions with AI companies to establish the value of its content and the use of articles to train language models.

4.2.1 News Corporation

Figure 4.1 below shows News Corporation balance sheet 2013–2023. [3]

Since the splitting of the company in 2013 assets have had an average value of $15.9 billion (Figure 4.1), up to 16.9 billion in 2023.

Liabilities averaged $5.2 billion (Figure 4.1) and reached $8.0 billion in 2023. [4] Equity has declined by almost one-third since 2013, from $12.7 billion to $8.9 billion in 2023.

As Figure 4.2 shows, in 2022/23 revenues totalled $9.9 billion, a recovery from the COVID-related declines in 2020 and 2021, and is the third largest revenue since 2013. In the period up to June 2022, the company achieved its highest net income since 2013, $760 million (while in 2021 it was $389 million). [5] This has been reversed in 2023 by its 75 per cent decline in the current year, down to a net income of US$187 million.

A significant contributor to News Corporation's losses was impairment charges as well as equity losses of affiliates.

The grey columns in Figure 4.2 display the figures for EBITDA. These calculate earnings after subtracting operating, selling, general, and administrative expenses "before interest, taxes, depreciation and amortization". [6] They are routinely used by investment analysts in assessing companies' financial performance. Note the difference between EBITDA and net income, due to the exclusion of interest, tax, depreciation, and amortisation costs.

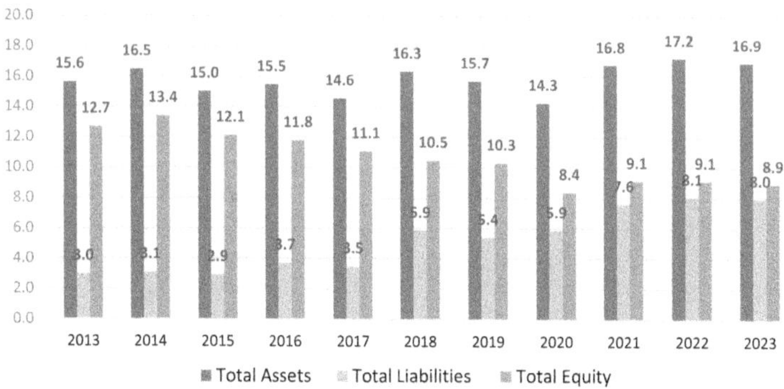

Figure 4.1 News Corp Balance Sheet 2013–2023 [7]

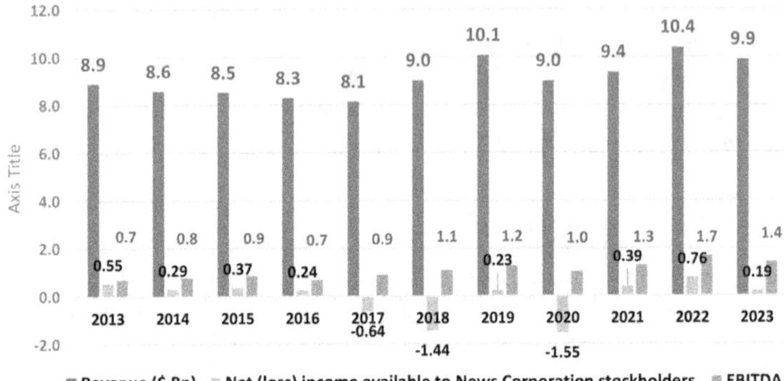

Figure 4.2 News Corp Revenue and Net Income 2013–2023 [8]

Between 2013 and 2023, News Corp total EBITDA grew by 106 per cent or almost $1 billion, from $688 million in 2013 to $1.273 billion in 2021, to $1.669 billion in 2022. [9] This trend, however, was completely reversed in 2023, driven by lower Total Segment EBITDA at $1.4 billion in 2023. [10]

These figures confirm the major shifts in News Corp's key sources of revenue, from newspapers to digital/information services and pay-TV detailed in the next section.

4.2.2 Fox Corporation

Figure 4.3 shows the Fox Corporation balance sheet for the years 2015–2023. Over the period, company assets have grown from US$9.8 billion to US$21.9 billion and liabilities from US$3.3 billion to US$11.4 billion. The major

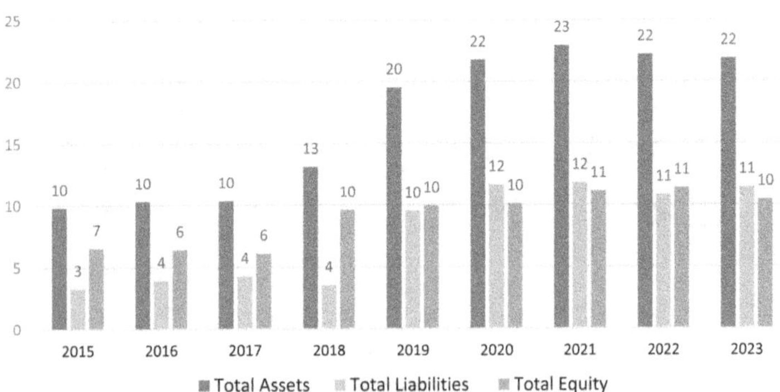

Figure 4.3 Fox Corporation Balance Sheet 2015–2023 [11]

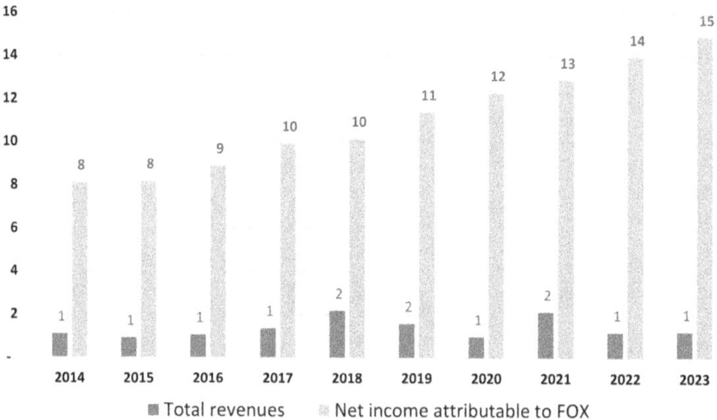

Figure 4.4 Fox Corporation Revenue and Net Income 2014–2023 (US$billion) [12]

reason for the change is the effect of the Disney acquisition and Fox achieving a $4.6 billion deferred tax asset in 2019 and a significant increase in cash (US$4.3 billion in 2023). On the liabilities side, Fox has over US$7 billion in borrowings in 2023.

Equity has grown from US$6.5 billion in 2015 to US$10.4 billion in 2023.

Fox Corporation's revenues, detailed in Figure 4.4, have risen by over 80 per cent between 2014 and 2023, from $8.1 billion to $14.9 billion, and the company has earned almost $14 billion in net income since 2014.

Net revenue declined in 2020 due to the impact of COVID. In 2021, it recovered to $2.15 billion, its second highest recorded figure, before declining to $1.2 billion in each of the last two years. [13]

4.2.3 Revenues by Operating Sector

4.2.3.1 News Corporation

As the tables and figures show, the relative contribution to revenues of News Corporation's various operating sectors has changed markedly since 2013.

The most significant shift is the sharp decline in the value of the 'News & Information/News Media' segment covering the newspaper interests and, until 2017, Dow Jones. In 2013, this segment contributed just over three-quarters (76%) of News Corp's total revenue of $9.9 billion. [14] By 2023, this had declined to less than a quarter (23%) with Dow Jones (which includes *The Wall Street Journal* and the consumer and professional financial services) now listed separately, contributing a further 22 per cent. [15]

Table 4.1 News Corp Revenues by Sector 2013–2023 (US$billion) [16]

Revenue by Sector	*2013*	*2014*	*2015*	*2016*	*2017*	*2018*	*2019*	*2020*	*2021*	*2022*	*2023*
	US$	*US$*	*US$*	*US$*	*US$*	*US$*	*US$*	*US$*	*US$*	*US$*	*US$*
News Media/ News and Information	6.7	6.2	5.7	5.3	3.6	3.6	3.4	2.8	2.2	2.4	2.3
Dow Jones*					1.5	1.5	1.6	1.6	1.7	2.0	2.2
Book Publishing	1.4	1.4	1.7	1.6	1.6	1.8	1.8	1.7	2.0	2.2	2.0
Digital Real Estate Services	0.3	0.4	0.6	0.8	0.9	1.1	1.2	1.1	1.4	1.7	1.5
Digital Education	0.1	0.1									
Subscription Video Services (Cable Network Programming)	0.3	0.5	0.5	0.5	0.5	1.0	2.2	1.9	2.1	2.0	1.9
Other	0.0	0.0	0.0	0.0	0.0	0.0	0.0	0.0	0.0	0.0	
Total Revenues	**8.9**	**8.6**	**8.5**	**8.3**	**8.1**	**9.0**	**10.1**	**9.0**	**9.4**	**10.4**	**9.9**

* Prior to 2017, Dow Jones revenue was reported in the 'News Media/News and Information' column.

Table 4.2 News Corp Revenues by Sector 2013 to 2023 (Percentage Share) [17]

Revenue % By Sector	*2013*	*2014*	*2015*	*2016*	*2017*	*2018*	*2019*	*2020*	*2021*	*2022*	*2023*
News Media/ News and Information	76	72	67	64	44	40	34	31	24	23	23%
Dow Jones*					18	17	15	18	18	19	22%
Book Publishing	15	17	20	20	20	19	17	18	21	21	20%
Digital Real Estate Services	4	5	7	10	12	13	12	12	15	17	16%
Digital Education	1	1	0	0	0	0	0	0	0	0	0%
Subscription Video Services (Cable Network Programming)	4	6	6	6	6	11	22	21	22	20	20%
Other	0	0	0	0	0	0	0	0	0	0	0%
Total Revenues	**100**	**100**	**100**	**100**	**82**	**100**	**100**	**100**	**100**	**100**	**100%**

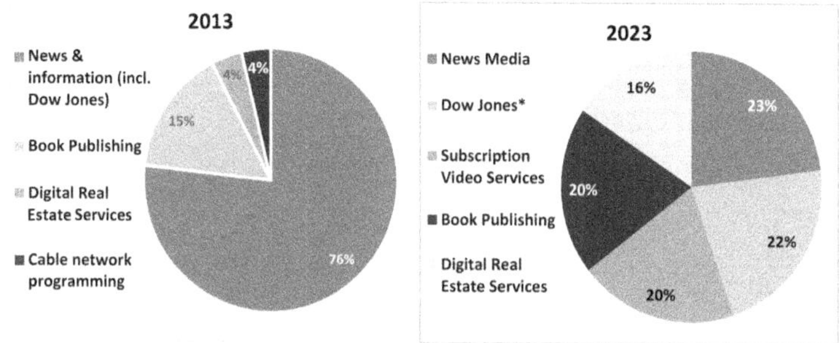

Figure 4.5 News Corp Revenues by Segment 2013 and 2023 [18]

The second major shift is the marked increase in the contribution coming from the subscription services operated by the Australian pay television interests, from 4 per cent ($300 million) in 2013 to 22 per cent ($2.2 billion) in 2021. The value of the subscription services contribution declined to $1.9 billion or 20 per cent in 2023.

The third significant change is the increased contribution to revenues from the digital real-estate interests, from 4 per cent in 2013 to 16 per cent in 2023.

Book publishing, already established as significant source of revenues by 2013, has also seen its contribution increase from 15 per cent in 2013 to 20 per cent in 2023.

These shifts are confirmed by the EBITDA data detailed in Table 4.3 and in Figure 4.6, which compares the relative contribution of different segments in 2013 and 2023.

The EBITDA calculations shown in Table 4.3 and Figure 4.6 underline the major change in News Corporation's sources of revenues with the News Media segment's earning contribution dropping from 68 per cent in 2013 to just 10 per cent in 2023. Even allowing for Dow Jones' inclusion in the earlier (2013) segment data, this is evidence of a major shift in sector income.

In marked contrast, subscription video's EBITDA share has grown from 5 per cent to 21 per cent. Dow Jones Financial Information Services contributes 30 per cent and Digital Real Estate, 28 per cent increasing from 14 per cent in 2013.

Taken together, the figures point to a fundamental transformation in News Corporation's operating base. Although its British, Australian, and US newspapers continue to play significant roles in the political cultures of all three countries, they are no longer the main source of revenues. The pivot of the company's financial viability has shifted to data services, the Australian pay-TV operation, and book publishing divisions.

Table 4.3 News Corp EBITDA by Sector 2013 to 2023 (US$billion) [19]

EBITDA by Segment	*2013*	*2014*	*2015*	*2016*	*2017*	*2018*	*2019*	*2020*	*2021*	*2022*	*2023*
News Media/ News and Information	0.8	0.7	0.6	0.2	0.4	0.2	0.2	0.1	0.1	0.2	0.2
Dow Jones*						0.2	0.2	0.2	0.3	0.4	0.5
Book Publishing	0.1	0.2	0.2	0.2	0.2	0.2	0.3	0.2	0.3	0.3	0.2
Digital Real Estate Services	0.2	0.2	0.2	0.3	0.3	0.4	0.4	0.3	0.5	0.6	0.5
Digital Education	(0.1)	(0.2)	(0.1)	–	–	–	–	–	–	–	–
Subscription Video Services (Cable Network Programming)	0.1	0.1	0.1	0.1	0.1	0.2	0.4	0.3	0.4	0.4	0.3
Other	(0.3)	(0.2)	(0.2)	(0.2)	(0.2)	(0.1)	(0.2)	(0.2)	(0.3)	(0.2)	(0.2)
EBITDA	**0.7**	**0.8**	**0.9**	**0.7**	**0.9**	**1.1**	**1.2**	**1.0**	**1.3**	**1.7**	**1.4**

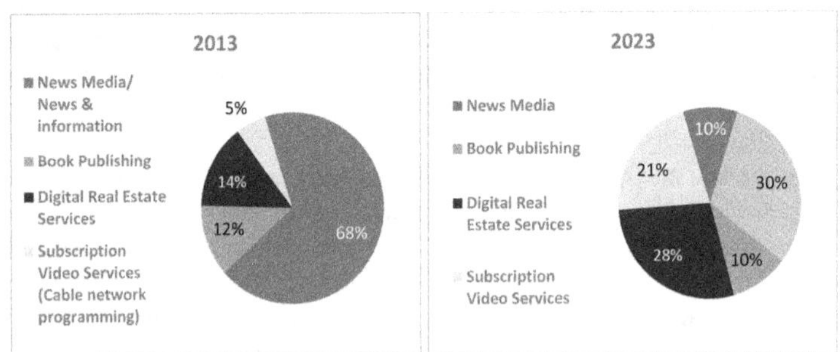

Figure 4.6 News Corp EBITDA Percentage by Segment 2013 and 2023 [20]

4.2.3.2 Fox Corporation

Table 4.4 below shows Fox Corporation revenue by segment from 2016 to 2023.

4.2.3.2.1 GEOGRAPHICAL DISTRIBUTION OF REVENUES

Almost all of Fox Corporation's revenues are generated by its television and cable interests in the United States. Conversely, Australia has overtaken the US as the leading revenue centre for News Corp, contributing 39 per cent of the 2023 total, closely followed by the US with 38 per cent. The growth of its Australian pay-TV operations has seen its overall share increase from 31 per cent in 2013. Over the same period, the UK's contribution, still heavily reliant on newspaper publishing, has fallen sharply, from 20 per cent to 12 per cent.

4.3 Market Shares

4.3.1 Book Publishing

General consumer book publishing is concentrated in five companies, the "Big Five". News Corp, Bertelsman, and Paramount Global are major multimedia conglomerates and two have other media interests. The Lagardere Group publishes *Paris Match* and *Elle*. Holtzbrinck publishes the German weekly newspaper, *Die Zeit*.

Penguin Random House and Hachette dominate the market, taking 64.8 per cent of total revenues in 2021 with News Corp taking just under a fifth (18.2%). In the major consumer market for paperbacks in 2021, the Big Five accounted for over three-quarters (77.4%) of best-selling titles in the US, over a quarter of which (27%) came from HarperCollins. [21]

Recent years have seen further moves to consolidation. In 2020, Bertelsmann's bid to purchase Simon & Schuster was rejected on competition grounds, but News Corp has strengthened its position purchasing Houghton Mifflin Harcourt.

4.3.2 Newspapers

4.3.2.1 United States

Both News Corp titles feature in the top five US newspapers ranked by print circulation with the *New York Post* outselling the nationally distributed *USA Today* and *The Wall Street Journal* selling over twice as many copies as its main broadsheet rival *The New York Times*.

Table 4.4 Fox Corporation Consolidated Statements of Operations (2016–2023) (US$billion) [22]

	2016	*2017*	*2018*	*2019*	*2020*	*2021*	*2022*	*2023*
By Segment								
Cable Network Programming								
Affiliate Fee	2.7	3.1	3.5	3.8	3.9	4.0	4.2	4.2
Advertising (Inc. Other: 2016)	1.1	1.1	1.1	1.2	1.2	1.3	1.5	1.4
Cable Network Programming – Other		0.2	0.4	0.4	0.5	0.4	0.4	0.5
Total Cable Network Programming	**3.8**	**4.3**	**5.0**	**5.4**	**5.5**	**5.7**	**6.1**	**6.0**
Television								
Advertising	3.8	4.1	3.5	3.9	4.2	4.1	4.4	5.2
Affiliate Fee	1.3	1.2	1.4	1.7	2.0	2.4	2.7	2.9
Television – Other		0.3	0.2	0.4	0.5	0.5	0.6	0.6
Total Television	**5.1**	**5.6**	**5.1**	**6.0**	**6.7**	**7.0**	**7.7**	**8.7**
Other (Corporate and Eliminations)	0.0	0.0	0.0	0.0	0.2	0.2	0.2	0.2
Total Revenues	**8.9**	**9.9**	**10.2**	**11.4**	**12.3**	**12.9**	**14.0**	**14.9**
Net Income Attributable to FOX	**1.1**	**1.4**	**2.2**	**1.6**	**1.0**	**2.2**	**1.2**	**1.2**

Table 4.5 News Corporation: Percentage of Revenues by Country and Region (2013–2023) [23]

Geographical Regions	*2013*	*2014*	*2015*	*2016*	*2017*	*2018*	*2019*	*2020*	*2021*	*2022*	*2023*
US	42	41	42	46	45	43	39	41	37	39	38
Canada	2	2	2	1	2	1	1	1	1	1	2
UK	20	21	19	18	16	16	13	13	14	13	12
Europe	3	3	4	4	4	4	4	3	4	4	5
Australia	31	31	27	28	28	32	40	39	42	40	39
Asia, Papua New Guinea, and New Zealand	2	2	5	2	4	4	4	3	3	3	3
Total	**100**	**100**	**100**	**100**	**100**	**100**	**100**	**100**	**100**	**100**	**100**

Table 4.6 "Big Five" English-Language Publishers Share of Revenues 2016 and 2021 [24]

Publisher	*Owned by*	*% Share of Total Revenues*	
		2016	*2021*
Penguin Random House	Bertelsmann	39.1	39.4
Hachette	Lagardere Group	26.3	25.4
HarperCollins	News Corp	17.1	18.2
Macmillan	Holtzbrinck	9.4	8.7
Simon & Schuster	Paramount Global	8.0	8.2
Total Sector Revenues in US$ Million		**9.549**	**12,056**

Table 4.7 Top Five US Newspapers (Ranked by Average Print Circulation in the Six Months to March 2023) [25]

Title	*Circulation in Thousands*	*% Change Year on Year*
The Wall Street Journal	609.6	–13
The New York Times	296.33	–10
The Washington Post	139.23	–12
New York Post	135.98	–07
USA Today	132.64	–17

4.3.2.2 UK

As Table 4.8 shows, the markets for popular dailies and Sundays are both more or less evenly divided between three companies: News Corp, The Daily Mail and General Trust, and Reach (publishers of the *Daily Express* and *Daily Mirror*). News Corp commands just under a third (32.04%) of the combined market but both *The Sun* and *The Sun on Sunday* have been displaced as market leaders by the *Daily Mail* and *The Mail on Sunday*.

The English broadsheet market is more concentrated, with News Corp commanding almost half (49.38%) of the combined daily and Sunday title circulation. *The Times* leads the daily market with a 36.8 per cent share while *The Sunday Times* dominates the weekend market with a 61.1 per cent share. The *Times* titles have also built a subscription base, but it is less than half the size of broadsheet rivals, *The Guardian* and the *Financial Times*, both with one million.

Table 4.8 UK National Newspaper Market Shares (Average Circulation April 2023) [26]

	Circulation	*Market Share*
Daily Tabloid and Mid-Market		
Daily Mail and General Trust	780,774	34.86%
Reach**	741,144	33.09%
News UK – The Sun*	717,714	32.04%
Daily Broadsheet Market		
The Times*	216,859	36.8%
The Daily Telegraph*	188,371	31.9%
Financial Times*	109,637	18.6%
The Guardian*	74,183	12.6%
Sunday Tabloid and Mid-Market		
Mail on Sunday	652,385	35.5%
Sun on Sunday	600,870	32.7%
Reach**	584,897	31.8%
Sunday Broadsheet Market		
Sunday Times	383,848	61.1%
Sunday Telegraph	147,161	23.5%
The Observer	96,424*	15.4%
News UK Share of Combined Tabloid Market		32.33%
News UK Share of Combined Broadsheet Market		49.38%

* These titles stopped releasing figures compiled by the Audit Bureau of Circulation in 2020. Figures shown here are therefore estimates.

** Reach publishes four daily titles – *Daily Mirror*, *Daily Express*, *Daily Star* and *The i* – and four Sunday titles – the Sunday editions of the *Mirror*, *Express*, and *Star* plus the *Sunday People*.

4.3.2.3 Australia

News Corporation publishes print and digital news nationally and in five Australian states. Owning 17 of the 31 main news outlets, [27] it dominates Australia's concentrated media sector, with 59 per cent of the main metropolitan titles, having increased from 25 per cent in 1984 and 57 per cent in 2011. [28] News Corporation also publishes another 70 regional and suburban metropolitan print and digital titles. Because of changes in the methods of calculating the publicly available data on newsprint and digital titles, it is not possible to compare with previously published analyses. However, as Table 4.9 below shows, News Corporation-owned titles dominate readership, accounting for half of the top ten Australian news titles in 2022.

Table 4.10, with a recent snapshot of online news access, shows News Corporation-owned news.com.au as the top Australian news website, with other news sites such as The Daily Telegraph and Herald Sun dominant in their local markets of Sydney and Melbourne, respectively.

Table 4.9 Australian Major News Titles 2022 Four-Weekly Average Audience [29]

	Unique Audience	*Owner*
Sydney Morning Herald	8.1 million	Nine Entertainment
The Age	5.6 million	Nine Entertainment
Herald Sun	4.3 million	News Corp
The Australian	4.3 million	News Corp
The West Australian & PerthNow	4.0 million	Seven West Media
Daily Telegraph	4.0 million	News Corp
The Australian Financial Review	3.6 million	Nine Entertainment
The Courier-Mail	3.0 million	News Corp
The Adelaide Advertiser	1.8 million	News Corp
The Saturday Paper	0.9 million	Schwartz Media

The recent data confirms the findings of the Australian Competition and Consumer Commission's 2018 report, which stated that "print news, now print/online news, is particularly concentrated, with News Corp and Fairfax controlling 57.6% and 30.6% of the newspaper publishing market respectively". [30]

4.3.3 Subscriptions and Websites

As Table 4.10 demonstrates, print circulation offers only a partial indicator of market position. Broadsheet titles have moved increasingly to subscription. As Table 3.1 in Chapter 3 has shown, in 2022 *The Wall Street Journal* was ranked the second most successful English-language news provider in building a subscription base (of 3.17 million) with News Corp's other Dow Jones publications ranked 11th.

News Corp's British broadsheet titles also feature in the top 20, ranked 17th.

For tabloid titles without paywalls, news organisations' websites operate as additional channels for access. Figures for June 2023 in Table 4.11 show News Corp's tabloid titles, *The Sun* and the *New York Post*, together with Fox News, in the top 20 most visited news websites globally.

Table 4.10 Australian Major Online News Titles August 2023 [31]

Position	*Website*	*Audience (1,000s)*	*Owner*
1	news.com.au	11,648	News Corp
2	ABC News	10,898	ABC
3	Nine.com	9,910	Nine Entertainment
4	7news.com.au	9,428	Seven West Media
5	Daily Mail Australia	8,821	DMG
6	The Guardian	7,698	Guardian Media Group
7	The Sydney Morning Herald	6,893	Nine Entertainment
8	The Age	4,911	Nine Entertainment
9	SBS News	4,224	SBS
10	Yahoo (Australia) News	4,172	

Table 4.11 Top 50 News Websites in the World by Global Visits June 2023 [32]

Global Rank	*Website*	*Global Visits*	*US Visits*	*Rank*
1	BBC	1.1 billion	153.7 million	6
3	CNN	708.4 million	458 million	1
4	New York Times	579.6 million	432.2 million	2
5	Daily Mail	409.6 million	121.7 million	11
8	Fox News	298.6 million	276.9 million	4
12	New York Post	177.0 million	153.1 million	6
13	The Sun	164.6 million	57 million	22

4.3.4 Broadcasting

4.3.4.1 Radio

4.3.4.1.1 UK

Britain's public service broadcaster, the BBC, continues to dominate radio news and comment, operating the top four channels measured by reach (average number of listeners tuning in at least once a week). The main challenge comes from LBC's channels, owned and operated by Britain's leading commercial radio network, Global Media & Entertainment.

The Wireless Group's most successful market entry is the sports channel Talk Sport, ranked sixth by audience reach, an increase of 29 per cent over the previous year, boosted by synergies generated by the launch of Talk TV. 'Shock jock' stations have not been a feature of the British radio landscape, but the 33 per cent yearly increase in reach achieved by the radio relay of the right-of-centre television channel GB News suggests a growing audience for populist radio commentary. In contrast, Times Radio saw a 2 per cent drop.

Table 4.12 UK Radio: News and Comment Stations Weekly Reach and Listening Hours (First Quarter of 2023) [33]

Rank	*Station*	*Weekly reach*	*Listening hours*
1	BBC Radio 2	14.5 milion	153 million
2	BBC Radio 4	9.4 million	112.7 million
3	BBC local radio	5.3 million	38.2 million
4	BBC Radio 5 Live (sports)	5.1 million	30.4 million
5	LBC brand UK	3.5 million	32.4 million
6	Talk Sport	3.3 million	19.2 million
11	Talk Radio	840,000	5.7 million
12	Times Radio	554,000	3.5 million

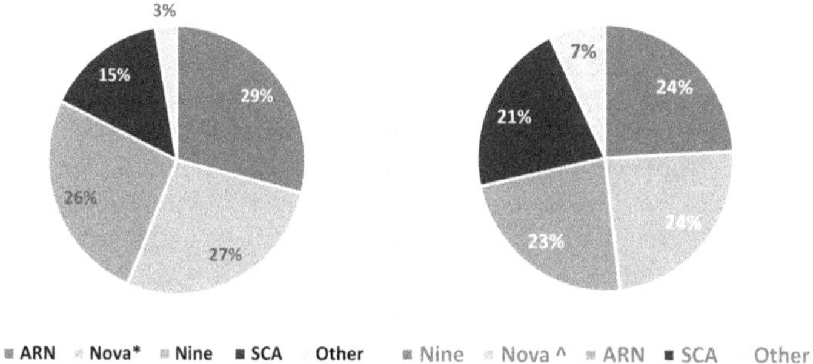

Figure 4.7 Sydney and Melbourne Commercial Radio Market Audience Share 2023 [34]

4.3.4.1.2 AUSTRALIA

News Corporation, Southern Cross Austero (SCA), and Nova Entertainment [35] dominate the Australian radio market. As noted, News Corp owns 13.29 per cent of ARN Media Limited, which holds 14 capital city radio licences and 42 regional radio licences. Additionally, Lachlan Murdoch, Chair of News Corporation (formalised in mid-November 2023 after the AGM) and Executive Chair, Fox Corporation, is chair of Nova Entertainment, which has nine metropolitan and one regional radio licence. Nova, ARN, and SCA also operate several radio joint ventures. [36]

The graphs above summarise audience ratings data for Australia's two major commercial radio markets, Sydney and Melbourne. News Corporation's ARN and associated entity Nova hold 47 per cent of Melbourne's commercial radio audience and 56 per cent of the audience in Sydney.

4.3.4.2 Television

4.3.4.2.1 USA

Although the three major networks continue to head the list of most-viewed broadcast services with the Fox 'fourth' network in fourth place, Table 4.13

Table 4.13 Most-Watched US Networks 2015 and 2022 (by Total Views in 1,000s) [37]

Rank	*Network*	*2015 views*	*2022 views*	*% change*
1	NBC	7,757	5,148	–33.6
2	CBS	9,419	5,144	–45.4
3	ABC	6,894	3,887	–43.4
4	Fox	5,198	3,233	–37.8
5	Fox News	1,775	2,309	+30.08

confirms their continuing decline and the consolidation of Fox News in fifth place overall with a 30 per cent increase in total views since 2015.

Fox News is the leading cable news service, outstripping its main competitors by some margin. In February 2023, it commanded 2.26 million viewers as against MSNBC's 1.165 million and CNN's 587,000. [38] CNN has a major presence on YouTube, however, with 14 million subscribers as against Fox News's 9.6 million (see Table 3.3 in Chapter 3). In March 2022, CNN also attracted the sixth largest number of active user engagements on Facebook, 13.7 million (see Table 3.4 in Chapter 3).

4.3.4.2.2 AUSTRALIA

News Corporation's Foxtel Group, [39] the "largest Australian-based subscription television provider", [40] overwhelmingly dominates Australia's audiovisual subscription market, operating subscription broadcaster Foxtel and Foxtel Now, Kayo, and BINGE streaming services nationwide. News Corporation subsidiary, the Australian News Channel, also owns Sky News, [41] which is broadcast and streamed on Foxtel.

Foxtel competes with free-to-air broadcasting and streaming services and "content providers that deliver video programming over the internet". [42]

Audience ratings data (see Table 4.14) shows that in 2022 Foxtel gained around 15 per cent of the prime-time free-to-air and subscription television audience and 17 per cent of the all-day audience, the same level as the Australian public service broadcaster, the ABC. [43] Foxtel further extends its broadcast presence with its Sky News service branded as Sky News Regional through channel delivery deals with regional free-to-air television networks in Victoria, New South Wales, Queensland, and South Australia. [44]

As Table 4.15 below shows, despite a decline in broadcast subscriptions, Foxtel now has 4.65 million paid subscribers. Over 3 million of these are streaming subscriptions, with Kayo, a sports service with 1.4 million subscribers, and BINGE, an entertainment service with almost 1.5 million subscribers. [45]

As shown in Table 4.15, an increase in paid streaming numbers for Kayo and BINGE of over 2.5 million since 2019 has not offset the revenue impact

Table 4.14 Australian Television (FTA and STV): Metropolitan City Audience Share ("Prime Time" and "All Day") [46]

	Prime Time	*All Day*
Seven West Media	23%	23%
Nine Entertainment	23%	23%
Network Ten	15%	12%
Subscription TV (News Corp Foxtel)	15%	17%
ABC	15%	17%
SBS	7%	6%

Table 4.15 News Corporation: Foxtel Group Paid Subscriptions (2019–2023) [47]

Foxtel Group subscribers	*2019*	*2020*	*2021*	*2022*	*2023*	*Change (2019–2023)*
Broadcast Subscribers	**(000s) Paid**	**(000s) Paid**	**(000s) Paid**	**(000s) Paid**	**(000s) Paid**	**(000s) Paid**
Residential	2,104	1,903	1,651	1,481	1,341	–763
Commercial	264	86	234	242	233	–31
Total Broadcast Subscriptions	**2,368**	**1,989**	**1,885**	**1,723**	**1,574**	–794
Streaming Subscribers (Total and Paid)						
Kayo	331	419	1,054	1,293	1401	1,070
BINGE		56	733	1,192	1487	1487
Foxtel Now	446	313	219	194	170	–276
Total Subscribers (Total & Paid)	**3,145**	**2,777**	**3,891**	**4,413**	**4,650**	1505

Table 4.16 News Corporation: Foxtel Group Revenues (2019–2023) [48]

Subscription Video Services	*2019*	*2020*	*2021*	*2022*	*2023*	*US$ m change*	*% Change*
	US$ m	*US$ m*	*US$ m*	*US$ m*	*US$ m*		
Circulation and Subscription	1926	1673	1825	1753	1671	(255)	–15%
Advertising	215	174	210	232	227	12	5%
Other	61	37	37	41	44	(17)	–39%
Total revenues	2202	1884	2072	2026	1942	(260)	–13%

of the net loss of almost 800,000 broadcast subscriptions. [49] The decline in broadcast subscriptions is the main reason there has been a drop in Foxtel's revenue.

Total Foxtel revenue was $1.942 billion in 2023. [50], [51] Table 4.16 shows that over the last five years, there has been a $260 million or 12 per cent decline in total revenues from $2.202 million in 2019. Subscription revenue dropped by $255 million from $1.926 billion in 2023 to $1.671 billion in 2023, with advertising revenue up $12 million to $227 million. [52]

4.3.4.2.3 UK

News Corp's sole television channel, Talk TV, was launched in April 2022 to contest the market for populist news and comment initiated by GB News, launched a year earlier in June 2021. Both channels remain, for the moment, minority niche services. In June 2023, Talk TV had a 0.17 per cent share of total television viewing and GB News 0.71 per cent. [53]

References

[1] For a full overview, please refer to page 54, Figure 7, 'Newspaper readership by title' in Benedetta Brevini and Michael Ward (2021) 'Who Controls Our Media? Exposing the Impact of Media Concentration on Our Democracy'. Sydney: GetUp. Available at www.getup.org.au/campaigns/abc-media-campaigns/share-the-media-diversity-report/who-controls-our-media-the-new-report-commissioned-by-getup
[2] As of 18 October 2023, ARN and partner Anchorage Capital Partners made a bid for 100 per cent of Southern Cross Media Group. While, in May 2024 Anchorage withdrew from the bid, ARN stated it is still committed to the bid (ARNMedia, Market Announcement, 13 May 2024, https://investors.arn.com.au/static-files/00103b07-335f-44e8-955d-0c925cdb3db7).
[3] News Corporation (2014) Form 10-K Delaware. News Corp. https://investors.newscorp.com/sec-filings?field_nir_sec_form_group_target_id%5B%5D=471&field_nir_sec_date_filed_value=2014#views-exposed-form-widget-sec-filings-table (multiple years, 2014; 2015; 2016; 2017; 2018; 2019; 2020; 2021; 2022; 2023).
[4] News Corp, 2014–2023.
[5] News Corp, 2014–2023.
[6] Dwayne Winseck, (2011) 'Financialization and the "crisis of the media"', in Dwayne Winseck and Dal Yong Jin (eds) *The Political Economies of Media: The Transformation of the Global Media Industries*. London: Bloomsbury Academic, pp. 142–166.
[7] News Corp, 2014–2023.
[8] News Corp, 2014–2023.
[9] News Corp, 2014–2023.
[10] News Corporation (2023) Form 10-K Delaware. News Corp.
[11] New Fox Corporation (2018) Form 10. Delaware. New Fox Corp, https://investor.foxcorporation.com/static-files/4d412985-43c5-4e55-a956-c973968a6fbe; Fox Corporation (2019) Form 10-K. Delaware. Fox Corp, https://investor.foxcorporation.com/static-files/4d412985-43c5-4e55-a956-c973968a6fbe (multiple years, 2019; 2020; 2021; 2022; 2023).
[12] New Fox Corp, 2018 and Fox Corp, 2019–2023.
[13] Fox Corporation, 2021 Form 10-K, Delaware, Fox Corp.
[14] News Corp, 2014.
[15] News Corp, 2023.
[16] News Corp, 2014–2023.
[17] News Corp, 2014–2023.
[18] News Corp, 2014–2023.
[19] News Corp, 2014–2023.
[20] News Corp, 2014–2023.
[21] Amy Watson (2023) 'Share of adult hardcover and paperback bestseller positions held by leading publishers in the United States from 2019 to 2021', Statista, 16 June. Available at www.statista.com/statistics/1234734/book-publishers-bestsellers-list-share
[22] New Fox Corp, 2018 and Fox Corp 2019–2023.
[23] News Corp, 2014–2023.

[24] Dimitrije Curcic (2022) 'The Big Five Publishers Statistics', 17 November. Available at https://wordsrated.com/the-big-five-publishers-statistics

[25] Aisha Majid (2023) 'Top 25 US newspaper circulations: Print circulations of largest titles fall 14% in year to September 2023', Press Gazette, 26 June. Available at https://pressgazette.co.uk/media-audience-and-business-data/media_metrics/top-25-us-newspaper-circulations-down-march-2023

[26] Bron Maher (2023) 'DMGT acquisition of Telegraph could give it 50% of daily newspaper market share', Press Gazette, 12 June. Available at https://pressgazette.co.uk/media_business/dmgt-daily-mail-telegraph-acquisition-market-share

[27] Benedetta Brevini and Michael Ward (2021) 'Who Controls Our Media? Exposing the Impact of Media Concentration on Our Democracy'. Sydney: GetUp.

[28] Franco Papandrea and Rod Tiffen (2016) 'Media Ownership and Concentration in Australia', in E. Noam (ed.). *Who Owns the World's Media? Media Concentration and Ownership Around the World*. New York: Oxford University Press, pp. 703–739.

[29] ThinkNewsBrands (2023) Total News Fact Pack. February 2023. Available at https://thinknewsbrands.com.au/resource/fundamentals-facts-and-stats-feb-2023

[30] ACCC (2018) 'Digital Platforms Inquiry: Preliminary Report'. ACCC. December 2018, p. 251.

[31] Ipsos iris Ranking report Top 10 News Category (excluding Weather & Aggregators) August' 23. Available at https://iris-au.ipsos.com/rankings/

[32] Aisha Majid (2023) 'Top 50 news websites in the world', Press Gazette, 17 July. Available at https://pressgazette.co.uk/media-audience-and-business-data/media_metrics/most-popular-websites-news-world-monthly-2

[33] Aisha Majid (2023) 'RAJARS: Talk Radio posts record reach after Talk TV launch but Times Radio down', *Press Gazette*, 18 May. Available at https://pressgazette.co.uk/media-audience-and-business-data/media_metrics/rajars-q1-2023-talkradio-bbc-sounds

[34] GFK (2023) 'Radio Audience Measurement: Survey Summary Reports'. www.gfk.com/press/radio-audience-measurement-survey-summary-reports

[35] GFK, (2023) Radio Audience Measurement: Survey Summary Reports. Survey 6 2023, www.gfk.com/press/radio-audience-measurement-survey-summary-reports

[36] ACMA, 2023, Lachlan Murdoch Media Interests, www.acma.gov.au/sites/default/files/2023-07/ACMA_LachlanMurdoch_3July2023.pdf

[37] Michael Schneider (2022) 'Most-Watched Television Networks: Ranking 2022's Winners and Losers', Variety, 29 December. Available at https://variety.com/2022/tv/news/most-watched-channels-2022-tv-network-ratings-1235475170

[38] Fox News (2023) 'Fox News Channel marks two consecutive years sweeping cable news in every category', 28 February 2023. Available at https://press.foxnews.com/2023/02/fox-news-channel-marks-two-consecutive-years-sweeping-cable-news-in-every-category

[39] News Corp, 2023, p. 5.

[40] News Corp, 2023, p. 35.

[41] News Corp, 2023, p. 5.

[42] News Corp, 2023, p. 5.

[43] Oztam (2022) 'Consolidated Metropolitan Total TV Share of All Viewing, 5 City Share Report – All Homes', https://oztam.com.au/documents/2022/OzTAM-20221218-D1MetTTVShrCons.pdf

[44] Sky News, 2023, Sky News Regional. www.skynews.com.au/sky-news-regional#:~:text=Sky%20News%20Regional%20is%20a,56%20and%20WIN%20Channel%2053.

[45] News Corp, 2023, p. 35.

[46] OzTam, 2022. Oztam 2022 Consolidated Metropolitan Total TV Share of All Viewing, 5 City Share Report – All Homes.

[47] News Corp, 2019; 2020; 2021; 2022; 2023.

[48] News Corp, 2019; 2020; 2021; 2022; 2023.

[49] News Corp, 2023, p. 46.

[50] In 2018, News Corp increased its ownership in Foxtel to 65 per cent while Australian telco Telstra reduced its ownership from 50 to 35 per cent.

[51] Foxtel revenue increased substantially in 2019 from 2018 (by over $1 billion) due to News Corporation's acquisition of a further 15 per cent of the company from Telstra, as noted above. If Foxtel's 2023 revenue is compared to the pre-purchase level of 2018, it has increased by almost 50 per cent. The period 2019 has been selected because it compares revenue on a like-for-like ownership basis.

[52] News Corp, 2019; 2020; 2021; 2022; 2023, p. 45.

[53] Barb (2023) 'Monthly viewing by channel service'. Available at www.barb.co.uk/monthly-viewing

5 Political Profile: Ownership, Control, Influence

This chapter examines the organisation and deployment of power both within and by News Corp. The first section – internal relations – reviews the company's shareholding structure and labour relations. The second – external relations – charts the web of connections linking News Corp to other key nodes of power and examines the company's influence on politics and policy in its three major English-language markets.

5.1 Shareholdings: Ownership and Control

5.1.1 The Dual Shareholding Structure

News Corp and Fox Corp are governed by dual shareholding structures. Holders of Class A preference shares are entitled to dividends but cannot vote on proposals affecting the companies' operations or future direction. Control over strategic decisions is vested exclusively in the owners of Class B voting shares. In June 2023, the Murdoch family trusts controlled 39.7 per cent of the voting shares in News Corporation and 43 per cent in Fox Corporation [1] (see Table 5.1). These substantial blocs have allowed Rupert Murdoch to maintain overall control with only around 14 per cent of the companies' total equity.

The dual structure goes back to 1993 when Murdoch asked the Australian Stock Exchange to waive its strict "one share, one vote" principle so the company could issue shares with differential voting rights for certain shareholders, primarily the Murdoch family trusts. [2] Widely condemned as an erosion of shareholders' rights, the proposal was withdrawn but revived with News Corporation's 2004 reincorporation in the US.

Investors objected to moving the company's domicile from Australia to the US and obtaining a primary listing on the New York Stock Exchange. They argued that the law in Delaware, the location selected for reincorporation, expressly favoured "managerial fiat", providing much weaker protections for minority shareholders than Australian corporate law, allowing the Murdoch family to consolidate its control more easily. They demanded the retention of

DOI: 10.4324/9781003255086-5

existing Australian shareholder rights. Concessions were secured from News Corp but were "later effectively subverted by a variety of means". [3] The two-class share structure was implemented and remains in place.

Dual shareholding structures are not unusual in the communication industries – both *The New York Times* and *Meta* operate on this basis – but they are controversial and have been challenged by investors wanting more influence. [4]

5.1.2 The Murdoch Family: Maintaining Control

Sir Keith Murdoch's will bound his estate into a family company, Cruden Investments, with super voting shares guaranteeing control divided between his wife, Elizabeth, and his four children, Rupert, Helen, Anne, and Janet. The company name came from his father's birthplace, Cruden Bay in Aberdeenshire, later adopted for the family's farm on the outskirts of Melbourne.

Despite Keith Murdoch's express instructions that his trustees "provide the fullest opportunity" for Rupert to have charge of the most valuable assets, the shares in Queensland Newspapers and HWT, the shares were sold while Murdoch was completing his Oxford University degree. The experience fostered a deep resentment and a "dogged determination to retain control of both the public and private companies". [5]

The majority of Cruden Investments' assets were held in family accounts controlled by the trustees of Keith Murdoch's estate. The other major holder, Kayarem, named after Rupert Murdoch's initials KRM, administered his personal interest, including his 34 per cent of the voting shares. [6] His sisters lent his early business ventures "unwavering support while pursuing different interests" [7] but there was always the possibility he would be outvoted. By 1986, holdings purchased from other members of the family had given him a 50.1 per cent share of Cruden's voting shares and effective control.

In 1990, with News Corp loaded with debt and open to attack, he moved to take further command of the family voting shares, consolidating both his immediate control and the legacy to hand on to his children.

Kayarem was renamed Karlholt in October 2004, with a prospectus describing it as "the ultimate holding company for the Cruden Group of Companies owned and controlled by the Murdoch Trusts". [8] In 2005, a week before News Corp's reincorporation in the US, Kayarem moved to Bermuda, a legal tax haven, avoiding an Australian tax bill of up to £500 million.

As part of the 1999 divorce settlement with his second wife Anna Torv, Murdoch agreed to unbreakable terms, giving their three children, James, Lachlan, and Elizabeth, together with Prudence, from his first marriage, votes in the family trust. His two children, Chloe and Grace, from his third marriage to Wendi Deng, are beneficiaries but have no voting rights.

The trust is currently governed by eight votes. Murdoch commands four and the children one each. Votes are decided by majority: "There is no deadlock provision; if anybody litigates, they are disinherited; and unanimous agreement is required to change the trust deeds or for any beneficiary to sell their stake of votes." [9] Under these arrangements, control of Cruden's voting rights in Fox and News Corp remains in Rupert Murdoch's hands. On his death, his votes will be distributed equally to the four children prompting speculation of clashes over the companies' future management and direction.

While Murdoch's control of substantial blocs of voting shares in both News Corp and Fox Corp gives him a dominant voice in decisions, neither gives him a majority. He needs the endorsement of other holders to counter challenges.

As noted earlier, in 2004 John Malone, the head of Liberty Media, exchanged his 22.3 per cent of non-voting equity for voting shares, thereby almost doubling his holding from 9.2 per cent to 17.2 per cent, which laid the ground for a possible takeover. Murdoch responded by introducing a "poison pill" protection, limiting Liberty to 18 per cent and extending it without shareholder approval in breach of the company charter. Shareholder objections were ignored again when an eventual deal was struck exchanging Malone's News Corp shares for News Corp's 38.4 per cent of the satellite operator DirectTV and gaining Murdoch an extra US$550 million in cash.

During the confrontation with Malone, Murdoch enjoyed the unreserved support of Prince Al-Waleed Bin Talal, a member of the Saudi royal family and holder of the second largest block of voting shares after the Murdoch family. He offered to sell his non-voting stock to boost his voting holding to a level sufficient to block any attempted takeover. He lent his full public support again at the time of the 2011 hacking scandal.

Al-Waleed's News Corp investment was held by his wholly owned Kingdom Holding Company, a diversified conglomerate whose interests include the Rotana Group, the Arab world's largest entertainment company spanning free-to-air television stations, music radio, film production, and the region's major record label. Investing in Rotana offered News Corp a ready-made point of entry into the Middle East and North Africa (MENA) market.

In May 2010, News Corp acquired an initial 9.09 per cent stake in Rotana, increased to 14.5 per cent in 2011 and 18.97 per cent in May 2012. The tie-up appeared to consolidate the partnership, but Al-Waleed was beginning to re-evaluate his own investment portfolio. In February 2015, he reduced his holding in News Corp to around 1 per cent but retained the stake in 21st Century Fox, declaring that "our investment constitutes a solid foundation for our long-standing relationship which we expect will endure". [10] By December 2015, however, the stake had fallen from 6.6 per cent to 4.98 per cent, and by the end of September 2017, it was zero. The sale coincided with a major shift in control over Saudi investments.

In October 2017, Al-Waleed was forcibly detained in the Ritz-Carlton hotel in Riyadh along with around 200 other princes and prominent businessmen and pressured to transfer money and assets as part of a concerted drive to centralise power in the hands of the new head of state, Crown Prince Muhammad bin Salman. In April 2022 the Public Investment Fund, the country's sovereign wealth vehicle, which bin Salman directs, purchased a 16.87 per cent stake in Kingdom Holdings, previously 95 per cent owned by Al-Waleed, with the clear intention of shaping the direction of future investments.

The career of Al-Waleed's stakes in News Corp offers another reminder of the central role played by shifting balances in national politics in globalised business.

5.1.3 Institutional Investors: Conditional Support

The shares held by companies managing assets on behalf of pension funds and other clients have increased markedly since the financial crash of 2008. Control is increasingly concentrated in the hands of three concerns: Vanguard, State Street, and BlackRock. Rather than seeking short-term gains by "actively" trying to outperform stock market indices, the "Big Three" purchase shares in firms included in a particular index and hold them "forever", relying on returns from tracking rises in the index. [11] By 2015, the "Big Three" together were the largest shareholder bloc in 88 per cent of the 500 US companies in the S&P index. [12]

Table 5.1 Major Holders of Shares in News Corp and Fox Corp (US Listing June 2023) [13]

Murdoch Family Trust	*News Corp*		*Fox Corp*	
	Non-voting %	*Voting %* 39.7	*Non-voting %*	*Voting%* 43.0
External shareholders				
T. Rowe Price Associates	18.3	2.5		
The Vanguard Group	13.7	2.1	10.9	6.6
Independent Franchise Partners	7.8	6.5	6.4	
SOF Ltd		5.1		
SSgA Funds Management Inc.	4.6	2.4	4.6	3.2
Yacktman Asset Management	4.4			3.7
Southeastern Asset Management	4.2	13.1		
Dodge and Cox	2.8		13.5	4.9
Burgundy Asset Management	2.7			
BlackRock*	2.4		5.4	
Metropolis Capital	2.3			
Ninety One UK Ltd			4.0	
Morgan Stanley Investment Management			2.8	
LSV Asset Management			2.6	
% held by the top two	32.00		24.40	
% held by the top five	48.76		40.79	
% held by the 'Big Three'	20.63	4.45	20.91	9.79

* The BlackRock listing for News Corp refers solely to BlackRock Fund Advisors. The listing for Fox Corporation also includes BlackRock Advisors LLC.

As Table 5.1 shows, asset management companies command major holdings in both News Corp and Fox Corp. The top five investors in each company account for 48.76 per cent and 40.79 per cent of the total non-voting shares and the top two for 32 per cent and 24.4 per cent. The 'Big Three', led by Vanguard, hold 20 per cent of both News Corp and Fox.

The largest stake in News Corp's non-voting stock, 18.3 per cent, is held by T. Rowe Price Associates. This, together with their 2.45 per cent holding of voting shares, opens privileged channels of access to information and potential influence. As the company's website explains to prospective clients:

> In U.S. equities ... our analysts have been developing and nurturing relationships with companies [giving] us unparalleled access to the key decision-makers where we can ask the right questions to make fully informed decisions ... It's made all the difference to our clients over the years, and it's still the difference today. [14]

Ownership of voting shares not controlled by the Murdoch family is less concentrated, but asset managers still have a notable presence. Southeastern Asset Management and Independent Franchise Partners account together for 19.6 per cent of News Corp and Vanguard and Dodge and Cox for 11.42 per cent of Fox Corp. Asset managers relying on tracking an index "generally vote in favour of management (rather than taking activist decisions against management) at annual general meetings". [15] This support is conditional on the company's continuing stability and profit prospects, however.

Institutional holders of voting shares may intervene if they see the value of their investment threatened. In November 2022, Irenic Capital Management, which currently owns 2.69 per cent of News Corp voting stock, publicly opposed the proposal to recombine News Corp and Fox, declaring that "walking away from a potential transaction is better than agreeing to a deal that fails to maximise News Corp's value". [16] They were joined by Independent Franchise Partners, with 6.54 per cent of News Corp's voting shares. The re-merger plan was abandoned in February 2023. Concerted challenges have also come from activist independent shareholders.

5.1.4 Activist Shareholders: Pressing for Change

By 2021, shareholder resolutions had been formally lodged in 11 of the 16 years since News Corp's move from Australia to the US in 2005.

The dual shareholding structure has been a constant focus of dispute, with activist shareholders demanding one share, one vote. Motions for change were put seven times between 2011 and 2021 with support steadily rising from 28.8 per cent to 49.5 per cent. "On every occasion if the Murdochs hadn't voted [the motion] would have received majority support". [17]

In September 2022, in an agreement with shareholders, a ceiling was placed on the potential accretion of voting power by the Trust and Murdoch family members, limiting their collective holding of voting shares to 44 per cent.

Activists have persistently questioned company decisions they see as benefitting the Murdoch family to the detriment of shareholders.

Not all challenges were headed off so easily. In 2011, following Fox's purchase of the Shine production house from Rupert Murdoch's daughter Elizabeth, trustees of two independent shareholders, The Amalgamated Bank of New York and the Central Laborers Pension Fund, filed a class action in the Delaware court claiming the price was "far above [what] any independent, disinterested party would pay" and demonstrated that "In addition to larding the executive ranks of the company with his offspring Murdoch constantly engages in transactions designed to benefit family members". [18] After a reported $7 billion fall in News Corp's market value following the hacking scandal revelations in early July 2011, they were joined by the Massachusetts Labourers' Pension Annuity Fund accusing Murdoch and the directors of causing the company to lose billions of dollars in value as a result of their failure to investigate and limit the fallout from the hacking scandal until July 2011, although the scandal first came to light in 2005. [19] In April 2013, shareholders were awarded $139 million in compensation, the largest ever cash settlement in a derivative lawsuit.

5.2 Labour Relations

Democracies depend on open debate between diverse positions. Media owners may subvert this ideal by promoting their favoured views. Control can be exercised directly through explicit instructions but is more usually secured by appointing like-minded personnel to key editorial positions and regularly reminding them of preferred positions.

Rupert Murdoch vets prospective editors of his news outlets to ensure that they share his general worldview. As Rebekah Wade, former editor of both British tabloids, attests, "he is the traditional proprietor … before my appointment, he knew me pretty well … he would be aware of my views, both my social views, cultural views and political views … [he] was absolutely aware of my views on Europe". [20]

As Andrew Neil, former *Sunday Times* editor, recalls, "he picks as his editors people like me, who are mostly on the same wavelength as he is: we started from a set of common assumptions about politics and society … Then he largely left me to get on with my work." [21]

Commenting on his exercise of control to a British Parliamentary Committee, Murdoch distinguished between his tabloid titles, where he exercises "editorial control on major issues – like which party to back in a general election or policy on Europe" and the *Times* titles where the terms of the acquisition exclude direct interventions but allow more subtle steers. [22]

Andrew Neil confirms this distinction. Working at *The Sun*, he recalls the editor "would get daily telephone calls … to make sure that on every major issue … it followed the Rupert Murdoch line. There was no question about that". [23] As he notes:

> [T]he decision to place his two Tory tabloids – the biggest selling in Britain – behind Blair and the Labour Party was entirely Rupert's. Their editors played almost no part in the decision, and many of the staff, especially on *The Sun*, were very unhappy about it. They were never consulted. [24]

As editor of *The Sunday Times*, he recalls the subtle pressures exerted by Murdoch's constant background presence "everywhere, even when he is nowhere", making "anticipation of his attitudes [and] second-guessing" his requirements essential to success. [25] To aid guesswork, Murdoch offered regular reminders of priorities and performance. He denies ever giving "instructions to the editor of *The Times* or *The Sunday Times*" but concedes that "sometimes when I was available … I would call and say 'What's the news today?' Other times I'd ring and say, 'That was a damn fine newspaper you had this week.'" [26]

Elsewhere, he has admitted to ringing the editor of *The Sunday Times* "nearly every Saturday – not to influence what he has to say at all. I am very careful always to premise any remark I made to him by saying, 'I'm just inquiring'." [27]

Editorial stances may provoke clashes with journalists struggling to adhere to the ideal of balanced coverage. Soon after acquiring the *New York Post*, Murdoch lent his full-throated support to Ed Koch's bid to become the city's mayor. When 50 of the paper's 60 reporters objected to the virulence of attacks on Koch's rivals, Murdoch reportedly invited them to resign. Twelve did.

Since then, there have been a number of high-profile resignations by journalists objecting to distorted coverage of climate change and other issues, and to the growing space given to overtly right-wing partisan commentators promoting positions that directly contradict evidence-based news reporting.

There has also been mounting criticism from female staff members of the sexism pervading News Corp's corporate culture. Stereotypical representations of female attractiveness have been a prominent feature of News Corp's tabloid style from *The Sun*'s Page 3 pin-up onwards. As Ann Rogers, a long-serving photographer for News Corp's Australian titles, has recounted, she was repeatedly instructed to "'Get a photo of a yummy mummy', or 'a pretty backpacker'" and avoid "women who were overweight or over 35" dismissed as "pigs in lipstick". [28]

Her claim that objectification and discrimination extend to the workplace is supported by successive instances of sexual harassment across News Corp's divisions. In the same month that Fox News established a Workplace

Professionalism and Inclusion Council to receive complaints of improper behaviour, the channel's star presenter, Sean Hannity "himself accused of sexual harassment, ran a series of segments claiming women invent stories of workplace mistreatment for the money". [29] In July 2016, Roger Ailes, the channel's principal architect, was forced to resign following a lawsuit filed by programme anchor Gretchen Carlson and allegations from six other female employees. In January 2022, *New York Post* journalist Michelle Gotthelf initiated legal proceedings for harassment against editor-in-chief Col Allan. [30] In December 2022, Sky News commentator Chris Smith was dismissed for mistreating female colleagues at a staff party. [31]

5.3 Networks and the Pursuit of Power

The publication of C Wright Mills' pioneering study *The Power Elite* in 1956 [32] focused renewed attention on the interactions between the people and organisations heading key nodes of power: corporate, financial, political, military, and cultural. The role of business leaders with connections spanning a range of power centres has attracted particular interest. Their networks, integrating "powerful participants from different fields", are seen as central to mediating conflicts and constructing coalitions that determine the "institutional settlements and resource flows" that maintain existing relations of power. [33] As the authors of one recent study of French elites argue, these "bridging actors" act as "hyper-agents who 'make things happen' and "constitute an 'elite of elites'". [34] As Manuel Castells, the leading theorist of contemporary capitalism as a Network Society, has argued, because the major multimedia conglomerates "are not only corporate and media actors in their own right" but control the central communicative spaces "in which power – whether it is political, economic or social – is articulated", their leaders are particularly well placed to perform the role of "bridging agents". [35] His joint research with Amelia Arsenault details the multiple ways Rupert Murdoch exploits this dual position and operates as a "switcher", a connection point linking different networks. They see this as adding an extra dimension to his power which he deploys relentlessly "in the service of NewsCorp". [36] Murdoch's offer during a lunch with Margaret Thatcher in 1981 to introduce her "to a group of 'New Right' politicians who had gathered around Daniel Moynihan during her visit to New York" is an example. She "indicated that she would be inclined to take up such an invitation if her schedule allowed". [37]

5.3.1 Connecting Webs

5.3.1.1 Company Directorships

Alongside the senior executives responsible for key administrative roles, company boards of directors recruit non-executive members to provide expertise, experience, and contacts with political and business interests.

Rupert Murdoch has been a non-executive director of several major corporations operating in areas outside communications, most notably Genie Oil and Gas. His tenure on Genie's Strategic Advisory Board cemented contacts with influential figures from finance and American politics. They have included: former US Republican vice president, Dick Cheney; former CIA director James Woolsey; former US Treasury head Larry Summers; investment banker Jacob Rothschild, and hedge fund manager Michael Steinhardt. Rupert Murdoch has also sat on the board of the leading cigarette manufacturer, Philip Morris. [38] We will return to the possible influence of these connections on communicative activity later in this chapter.

For a map of the current range and focus of the connections between News Corp and Fox Corp and key nodes of political and economic power, however, we need to examine the biographies and interests of the current non-executive directors of both companies. Their board membership delivers direct links to the other companies whose boards they sit on, secondary links to the companies those fellow board members are involved with, and contacts accumulated through past employment and careers.

5.3.1.1.1 LINKS TO POLITICIANS

Kelly Ayotte (News Corp) was Republican attorney general and later senator for New Hampshire (2011–2017). Paul Ryan (Fox Corp) was the Republican speaker of the House of Representatives (2015–2019). Jose Maria Aznar (News Corp), the former prime minister of Spain (1994–2004), is an enthusiastic proponent of privatisation and deregulation, a climate sceptic, and supported the invasion of Iraq.

5.3.1.1.2 LINKS TO FINANCIAL INSTITUTIONS

Kelly Ayotte (News Corp) sits on the boards of the Blackstone Group, one of the "Big Three" institutional investors detailed earlier, and the real-estate investment trust Boston Properties. Anna Pessoa (News Corp) is a director of Credit Suisse. Masroor Siddiqui (News Corp) is chief executive of investment firm Naya Capital Management and was previously a partner in The Children's Investment Fund, named the world's top performing hedge fund in 2022, holding significant stakes in Microsoft and Alphabet. In November 2022, he wrote to Alphabet's CEO Sundar Pichai calling for job cuts. In January 2023, 6 per cent of the workforce were laid off. Roland Hernandez (Fox Corp) is director of U.S. Bancorp.

5.3.1.1.3 LINKS TO MANUFACTURING COMPANIES

Peter Barnes (News Corp) was a senior manager at tobacco firm Philip Morris (1971–2013). Kelly Ayotte (News Corp) sits on the board of Caterpillar Inc., the world's largest construction equipment manufacturer, together with David

Calhoun, CEO of Boeing, and David Maclennan, CEO of Cargill, a leading global food company.

5.3.1.1.4 LINKS TO COMMUNICATIONS COMPANIES

Kelly Ayotte's (News Corp) fellow Blackstone board members include Ruth Porat Senior, vice president of Alphabet and Google, James Breyer, Facebook board member (2005–2013), and Rochelle Lazarus, former CEO and Chair Emeritus of the major advertising company Ogilvy and Mather. Anna Pessoa (News Corp), former senior manager at Globo, the dominant force in Brazilian television, is a partner in the Brazilian AI company Kunumi. Roland Hernandez (Fox Corp) is a board member of toy maker Take-Two Interactive Software together with Bing Gordon, co-founder of Electronic Arts and special advisor to the board of Amazon.

5.3.1.1.5 LINKS TO ADVOCACY GROUPS

Jose Maria Aznar (News Corp) is a prime mover of the Friends of Israel Initiative whose founding members include John Howard, Liberal Party prime minister of Australia, and Larry Ellison, CEO of Oracle (1977–2014).

There are several points to note about this basic map of connections.

First, it extends well beyond the communications industries with links to leading corporations in core industrial sectors: construction, food, and areas where, as we will see presently, Rupert Murdoch has long-standing personal interests.

Second, links to communication companies are primarily with leading digital operators – Alphabet, Amazon, and Microsoft – rather than "legacy" media concerns, confirming the growing centrality of digital technologies to strategies for expansion and growth.

Third, board members consolidate the close ties between News Corp and neoliberalism both in the United States, with links to senior Republicans, and internationally, typified by Jose Maria Aznar's leading role in the Friends of Israel Initiative, an influential advocacy group lobbying on behalf of the Israeli state. In an article for *The Times* in 2010, Aznar attacked the liberal erosion of Judeo-Christian values:

> by the rule of political correctness; by a multiculturalism that forces us to our knees before others; and … by jihadis promoting the most fanatical incarnation of the faith … Israel is our first line of defence … If Israel goes down, we all go down. [39]

Rupert Murdoch shares this perspective. In 2010, the New York-based Jewish NGO, the Anti-Defamation League, awarded him its International Leadership Award for his "stalwart support of Israel". As we noted in the last chapter, this support extends to personal investment in Genie Oil and Gas's right to drill in the disputed Golan Heights. As we will see in Chapter 6, Aznar's general antagonism to "liberal" values is shared by Murdoch and plays a central role in organising the authoritarian populism animating News Corp's tabloid outlets.

Lachlan Murdoch's accession as sole chair of Fox Corp in October 2023 coincided with two long-standing board members – Ann Dias, chief executive of Aragon Global Management investment, and Jacques Nasser, formerly CEO of the Ford Motor Company and chair of the leading Australian mining company BHP Billiton (formerly Broken Hill) – ending their terms of office. Anne Dias's departure was dogged by her increasing concern with Fox News's right-wing stance. Following the siege of the Capitol building by Donald Trump's supporters, she wrote to Lachlan Murdoch, urging him to "take a stance". Rupert Murdoch advised telling her that "Fox News is pivoting as fast as possible … which is not as easy as it might seem". As we have seen, the channel continued to promote false claims of election fraud that had precipitated the riot. [40]

Their nominated replacements on the board were Tony Abbot and Peggy Johnson. Abbot, Liberal Party prime minister of Australia from 2013 to 2015, is a long-standing climate change sceptic and advocate of Australia's coal and mining industries. His government repealed the Mineral Resource Rent Tax and abolished the country's carbon pricing scheme. Despite widespread condemnation of his climate denialism and homophobic and misogynistic comments, in 2020 Tony Abbot was appointed advisor to the British Board of Trade by Boris Johnson's Conservative government.

Peggy Johnson, currently CEO of Magic Leap, a leading maker of augmented reality headsets projecting 3D computer generated images on to real world objects, was previously President of Global Market Development at Qualcomm Technologies, Inc., and Vice President of Business Development at Microsoft, managing relations with venture capital. She has been a director of BlackRock since 2018.

These appointments consolidate connections between Murdoch's corporate interests and key players in digital innovation and right-of-centre politics.

5.3.1.2 Advocacy Groups

"Think Tanks" advocating policy reforms have proliferated since the early 1970s, playing a major role in orchestrating debate. In the era of neoliberalism, those promoting right-of-centre ideology have been particularly effective in securing a platform, often styling themselves as "Institutes" or "Centres" to present their partisan interventions as disinterested research and reflection.

In Australia, for over a decade, between 1986 and 2000, Rupert Murdoch was a board member of the country's leading think tank, the Institute of Public Affairs. Launched in 1943 at the instigation of the Collins House group, an exclusive Melbourne-based business network linking mining, manufacturing, and media interests, it acted as a bulwark against left-wing ideas. Murdoch's father, Keith, was one of the prime movers. As Rupert Murdoch noted in an address celebrating the Institute's seventieth anniversary, the original founders "were concerned about the drift to socialism they thought might prove a legacy of the war. My father, I am proud to say, was among these men." [41] Early success in countering proposals to nationalise the banks was later followed by promotion for neoliberal privatisation and deregulation policies and climate denialism. Substantial funding continued to come from leading mining, oil and gas, and tobacco companies.

One of the most influential US think tanks is the Cato Institute, founded in 1977 and based in Washington, DC. Rupert Murdoch's appointment to the board in 1997 gave him a stake in directing a lobby group that listed actively promoting the deregulation of the television and telephone industries as one of its priorities. In return, Cato gained a valuable popular platform for its ideas with the *New York Post* carrying a series of Cato op-eds on domestic issues following Murdoch's appointment. [42]

More recently, his membership of the Board of Overseers of Stanford University's Hoover Institute, directed by Condoleezza Rice, formerly George W. Bush's national security advisor, has attracted concerted criticism from university faculty. In an open letter to the university leadership following Fox News's continued promotion of Trump's "stolen election" lies, senior professors challenged Murdoch's appointment, asking, "Does his expertise outweigh what many find to be his dangerously deficient sense of ethics?" and why "someone who has proven himself an opponent" of the values of "honesty, truth and responsible scholarship" underpinning the university's reputation is on the board. [43]

5.3.1.3 Conferences

The annual conference organised by the World Economic Forum in Davos has established itself as a key node in the networks connecting media owners to political, financial, and business elites and emerging figures in the digital economy. Public panels provide convenient access to current thinking and priorities. Social meetings offer chances to cement relations. Rupert Murdoch has been a prominent participant. He spoke at the 2007 meeting, on doing business in a connected world, co-directed by Google's CEO Eric Schmidt. Two years later, he co-chaired the Forum.

Davos is supplemented by a range of other, more restricted fora. The exclusive annual gathering hosted by the investment bank Allen and Company in the Idaho resort town of Sun Valley, provides a protected space for discussion and deal-making. Key figures in the digital and media industries are prominently on the guest list. Sun Valley meetings are credited with laying the ground for Disney's acquisition of Capital Cities/ABC and Jeff Bezos's purchase of *The Washington Post*. Rupert Murdoch has been a regular visitor.

He has also attended the exclusive annual Washington dinners organised by the Alfalfa Club, founded in 1913 supposedly to celebrate the birthday of Confederate general Robert E. Lee. The occasion provides a privileged opportunity for members of the corporate and political elites to meet and mingle. In 2015, Murdoch shared a table with the key investor Warren Buffett, across the aisle from Jeff Bezos of Amazon.

Meetings may form the basis of durable relations. In 2003, attending an event at the Aspen Institute, Lachlan Murdoch met Viet Dinh, assistant attorney general for the Office of Legal Policy in George W. Bush's administration. Dinh was invited to join the News Corp Board, later becoming godfather to Lachlan's son and the chief lawyer for Fox Corporation. [44]

Rupert Murdoch has also been proactive, inviting key elite figures to conferences he has organised. News Corp's management conferences have functioned as major "switching" points, bringing executives from the company's global subsidiaries together with leading the politicians shaping the business environment. Invitees to the 1995 meeting held on Hayman Island in Australia included Sir Roger Douglas, the main architect of New Zealand's neoliberal policies, and the deputy prime minister of Malaysia, a key market for Star TV. Signalling Murdoch's growing discontent with John Major's Conservative government in Britain, the keynote speech was given by Labour Party leader Tony Blair. Introducing him Murdoch quipped: "If the British press is to be believed, today is all part of a Blair-Murdoch flirtation. If that flirtation is ever consummated … I suspect we will end up making love like two porcupines – very carefully." [45] Two years later, endorsed by *The Sun*, Blair was elected prime minister.

The porcupine's spines, and growing discontent with Blair, were in evidence in 2004 when the Conservative Party leader, Michael Howard, was invited to address News Corp's management conference in Cancun, Mexico.

Murdoch has also regularly hosted private meetings during the annual Consumer Electronics Show in Las Vegas. Linking News Corp personnel with leading figures in digital media, they have provided privileged access to thinking and developments in key areas of digital enterprise. The 2016 meeting included Google's CEO, the founder of Snapchat, and the head of Apple's cloud services.

5.3.1.4 Political Donations

Financial gifts to the electoral campaigns of political candidates and parties are a well-established strategy for smoothing the path to favourable treatment. The fact that News Corp's donations have not gone solely to politicians and campaigns from the right has been taken as further evidence that Murdoch's politics is instrumental rather than ideological. After examining the flow of funds, Arsenault and Castell conclude that "Murdoch's political affiliations move swiftly in accordance, not with political ideology, but with NewsCorp's bottom line", [46] adding that contributions are almost always directed to politicians with influence over News Corp's business environment. They cite the years between 1998 and 2006 dominated by the Republican presidencies of George W. Bush (2001–2009), pointing out that despite Murdoch's "outspoken support" for many of Bush's policies, the largest contributions went to Senator John Kerry, the Democrat chair of the Senate Commerce Subcommittee on Science Technology and Innovation that "plays a key role in shaping regulatory decisions critical to the NewsCorp's bottom line". [47]

Detailed records of News Corp's donations to the campaigns of Senate and Congressional candidates competing for office during the four election cycles of George W. Bush's presidencies (2002–2008) show an average of 63 per cent of monies going to Democrats. Calculations for election cycles during Barak Obama's presidencies (2010–2016) arrive at the same figure, 63 per cent. [48] At first sight, these results sit somewhat uneasily with the right-of-centre positions on public issues consistently adopted by News Corp's tabloid news outlets detailed in Chapter 6. This contradiction is more apparent than real. First, in a political system where states retain control over policy areas that impact on their locally based operations, corporations need to foster positive relations with their political representatives regardless of party affiliation. Second, the Democratic Party under Obama and Clinton and the Labour Party under Tony Blair accepted the broad parameters of the neoliberal rebalancing of the economy and did not present a concerted threat to News Corp's business interests.

5.3.1.5 Charitable Giving

Captains of industry known for their rapacious pursuit of profit and influence have long used charitable giving to lay claim to altruism and public spiritedness and receive endorsement from prestigious cultural institutions. Rupert Murdoch has made a point of donating to educational initiatives. In 1968, he was made a Knight Commander of St Gregory (a papal knighthood) after giving money to a Catholic Church education fund. The following year, he gave $10 million to the fund that supported building a Catholic cathedral in Los Angeles. In 1990, he made a significant gift to his alma mater, Oxford University, to fund an endowed chair in Language and Communication bearing his name, and he supports an annual visiting lectureship in Creative Media and a grant-giving body, the News International Fund. When questions were raised following the hacking scandal, the university decided not to sever ties since, as the Professor of English noted, there was "only residual unhappiness" among faculty and a general feeling "that we have turned bad money into good". [49]

5.3.1.6 Revolving Doors

News organisations' relations with government are reinforced by the revolving doors that see journalists taking up key political appointments and politicians writing for newspapers and presenting on radio and television.

During the 1984–1985 miners' strike in Britain, Margaret Thatcher's friend and advisor, David Hart, organised dissident miners carrying accreditation as "feature writers" on Murdoch's London *Times*. In 1989, Murdoch personally approved funds to support Hart's confidential newsletter "smearing Labour and other public figures for alleged links with communism". [50] In 1987, John O'Sullivan, previously responsible for the editorial page of Murdoch's *New York Post*, moved from his position as a leader writer for *The Times* to join Margaret Thatcher's election campaign.

In 2005, another *Times* leader writer, Michael Gove, was elected as a Conservative Party member of parliament but continued writing a regular column for the paper. As secretary of state for education, he promoted the privatisation of schools and hosted Rupert Murdoch's visit to London to explore investment opportunities. In 2016, he co-convened the Vote Leave campaign advocating Britain's exit from the European Union, a cause Murdoch enthusiastically endorsed. In 2017, with Murdoch's help, he conducted the first UK interview with President-Elect Donald Trump for *The Times*, with Murdoch sitting in.

In July 2007, while still leader of the opposition, David Cameron appointed Andy Coulson, former editor of the *News of the World*, as his director of communications and, despite warnings of Coulson's unsuitability, installed him in his private office when he was elected prime minister in 2010. In July 2014, Coulson was convicted of conspiracy to intercept voicemails and sentenced to 18 months in jail for his failure to stop hacking at the *News of the Word*.

In Australia, Scott Morrison's Liberal–National Coalition Government hired Andrew Carswell, formerly chief of staff at Murdoch's *Daily Telegraph*, as press secretary and a former editor at *The Courier Mail* as speechwriter.

In December 2021, a week after an Australian Senate Committee report had characterised News Corp as the "clearest example of a troubling media monopoly", [51] the conservative Morrison government appointed Gina Cass-Gottlieb as chair of the Australian Competition and Consumer Commission overseeing media concentration. She had been Fox Corp's leading attorney and was, at the time of the appointment, managing the firm administering the trust controlling the Murdoch family's stock holdings in News Corp and Fox Corp.

In the United States in July 2018, Bill Shine, former co-president of Fox News, was appointed President Trump's director of communications and White House deputy chief of staff.

5.3.1.7 Private Meetings

Rupert Murdoch and his senior executives have consistently enjoyed privileged private access to political leaders and key ministers in News Corp's three major English-language markets.

Tony Blair's contact with Rupert Murdoch began in September 1994 with a private dinner arranged by a News Corp executive. Reportedly, both men "revelled in being self-styled radicals, impatient with the old Britain", and

Blair reportedly assured Murdoch that “media ownership rules would not be onerous under Labour”. [52] Blair built on this base, accepting an invitation to address News Corp’s executive conference, writing a Eurosceptic piece for *The Sun* at the start of the 1997 election campaign, and securing Murdoch’s endorsement.

There is no comprehensive record of their contact during Blair’s terms as prime minister but Murdoch, consulting his own notes at the Leveson Inquiry in 2012, conceded: “I enjoyed speaking with him before, during, and after he was in office and met frequently with him. I believe the topics we discussed included European integration … Islamic terrorism, Iraq and Afghanistan”. [53]

After leaving office, Blair became godfather to Murdoch’s daughter Grace and attended her baptism at the River Jordan. The relationship between the two men cooled following unsubstantiated rumours of Blair’s affair with Murdoch’s then wife, Wendi Deng.

Officially recorded figures for the year following the formation of the British Conservative-led coalition government in May 2010 record the prime minister, David Cameron, meeting with Murdoch or his senior executives on 25 separate occasions. This was almost three times as many as representatives of *The Telegraph* (9) and over six times as many (4) as the publishers of the *Daily Mail*, the two other major right-of-centre national dailies. Adding News Corp personnel meetings with senior government ministers brings the company’s total to 86. This includes nine meetings with the culture secretary, Jeremy Hunt, who was responsible at the time for adjudicating on News International’s request to acquire a controlling interest in BSkyB. [54]

Concentrated contact with successive governments has continued. In 2018–2019, employees at Murdoch-owned companies met with Conservative government ministers and advisors 206 times, an average of 2.8 meetings in every week parliament was sitting. Rupert Murdoch personally met government ministers on five occasions including three with Prime Minister Boris Johnson, the first only 72 hours after Boris Johnson’s victory in the 2019 General Election. [55]

Rupert Murdoch was the only newspaper owner to meet with Johnson during the first three months of his premiership. Relations continued after Johnson resigned as prime minister in June 2022. In October that year, Johnson flew to the US for a business meeting. Murdoch paid for his internal air travel and provided additional staff, accommodation, and hospitality. [56]

Published records show that between October 2022 and September 2023, with a new Conservative prime minister, Rishi Sunak, in office, representatives from Murdoch’s companies met with government ministers and advisors 218 times, an average of 4.6 for each week parliament was sitting. News Corp’s national newspapers’ continuing centrality to conservative politics in Britain is underlined by the 44 meetings with staff from *The Times* and the 26 with *Sun* employees as against 35 with BBC personnel and the handful with people working for the two Labour-supporting national dailies, *The Guardian* (5) and the *Mirror* (3). Rupert Murdoch personally had 12 meetings, five with the prime minister. A dinner in December 2022 logged as discussing "the PM's priorities" was attended by the editors of *The Times* and *The Sun* and Rebekah Brooks, the CEO of News Corp's British division, News UK. [57]

As Richard Cooke has pointed out, influence accruing from political contacts and meetings is cumulative. During his career, Rupert Murdoch "has enjoyed access to nine U.S. presidents, nine British prime ministers and nine Australian prime ministers. It is not just his current power but his aggregate power over time that produces velocity." [58]

5.3.1.8 Social Ties: Family and Friends

The lavish reception for the wedding of the then *Sun* editor, Rebekah Wade, in 2009 offers a snapshot of the web of social connections linking Rupert Murdoch to the British political establishment at the time. Blair's successor as prime minister, Gordon Brown, and the then opposition leader, David Cameron, attended with "their respective followers" queuing up "to hear [Murdoch's] views, to pick up the signals, to understand what he wants, to send their own signals, to bond". Cameron had the advantage of personal connections. His older brother was at Eton with the groom, Charlie Brooks. Cameron's Oxfordshire neighbour, Matthew Freud, great-grandson of Sigmund Freud, head of the country's leading public relations firm and then married to Elisabeth Murdoch, had provided a private jet to fly Cameron to the Greek islands to meet Rupert Murdoch on his yacht. [59] Family ties were never cordial, however, and in a deliberate snub, Freud refused to invite Rupert Murdoch to his fiftieth birthday party.

In February 2016, David Cameron, who (as noted earlier) had met with Rupert Murdoch a number of times since becoming prime minister in 2010, announced a referendum on Britain's membership of the European Union and confirmed that he would campaign to remain. Murdoch, a dedicated Eurosceptic, was wholly in favour of leaving. The guest list for his wedding to Jerry Hall the following month excluded Cameron but included two leading Conservative politicians campaigning for Leave, Michael Gove, who toured the country alongside Boris Johnson, and Priti Patel, a rising figure on the right of the Party.

More recently, both Rupert Murdoch and Boris Jonnson have enjoyed hospitality provided by the Bamfords, owners of the JCB construction equipment company and major Conservative Party donors. In July 2022, the Bamfords' country estate, Daylesford House, was the venue for a lavish reception marking Boris Johnson's wedding to his new wife, Carrie, with the Bamfords bearing some of the costs. The couple also lived rent-free for a time in Bamford properties in London and Gloucestershire. In January 2023, Rupert Murdoch and his then fiancé, Ann-Lesley Smith, holidayed at the Bamford's Barbados mansion.

In March 2024, Murdoch announced his engagement to the retired molecular biologist, Elena Zhukova, whose daughter Dasha is married to Stavros Niarchos of the Greek shipping dynasty and is the former wife of Russian oligarch Roman Abramovich.

The exclusive summer party Rupert Murdoch hosts every year in prestigious venues around London offers another key point of informal contact with selected senior politicians and prominent people. Invitees invariably include the prime minister, the leader of the opposition, key ministers and parliamentarians, and leading media personnel.

In the United States, Murdoch and Wendi Deng formed a close relationship with Donald Trump's daughter Ivanka and son-in-law, Jared Kushner. For a time after Murdoch's divorce, Ivanka remained a trustee of the $300 million fortune allocated to Murdoch's daughters.

These shifting ties linking Rupert Murdoch to key actors in business and political networks simultaneously illustrate and reaffirm his role as a switcher, a bridging agent moving between different segments of the power elite, forging links and creating channels.

5.4 Taking Care of Business: Minimising Regulations

As Nick Davies, the journalist who exposed the hacking scandal, has argued, Rupert Murdoch "may be … personally possessed of some extremely right-wing opinions – but what he wants from politicians is favours for his business. In practical terms, this comes down to repeated demands to be freed from regulation." [60]

Hostility to regulation extends to self-regulation. In the late 1970s, the Australian Press Council, administered by the newspaper industry, issued a series of judgements censoring *The Australian* for its relentlessly hostile coverage of the country's Labor Party, condemning it as "irresponsible", "unfair", and "intensely partisan". In 1980, News Corp cancelled its membership. [61]

Examples of Murdoch securing favourable treatment for his businesses are not hard to find. Three instances are provided by key moments in News Corp's expansion in Britain: policing for the Wapping printers' strike, the purchase of Times Newspapers, and the acquisition of monopoly control over national satellite broadcasting. All three involved Murdoch's relations with Prime Minister Margaret Thatcher.

Andrew Neil, former *Sunday Times* editor, has questioned Murdoch's claim that he has never asked politicians for anything. In the run-up to the Wapping strike, he recalls Murdoch telling him that "he had gone to Mrs Thatcher to get her assurance that enough police would be made available to allow him to get his papers out past the massed pickets at Wapping once the dispute got underway". [62] The enhanced police presence played a key role in ensuring continuity of distribution.

The purchase of the *Times* titles provides a second example. On 4 January 1981, Murdoch lunched privately with Margaret Thatcher to inform her that he had made a firm offer for both titles and offered his negative evaluations of rival bids. The meeting was kept secret and denied for 30 years. Under the then Fair Trading Act, as already the owner of the country's best-selling national daily and Sunday titles, his bid should have automatically been referred to the Monopolies and Mergers Commission.

Notes taken by Thatcher's press secretary record that she "did no more than wish him well in his bid". [63] However, immediately after the meeting she replaced the then secretary of state for trade, John Nott, responsible for deciding on referral. Nott was a former banker, well versed in press economics. He had observed the original Thompson purchase of the *Times* titles and later, as managing director of Lazard Brothers, helped block Murdoch's 1983 attempt to acquire the *Financial Times.* His replacement, John Biffen, had no practical knowledge of the newspaper industry and accepted the misleading briefing that both titles were running at a loss. [64]

When the Cabinet met on 26 January, Margaret Thatcher reminded ministers that the secretary of state for trade could personally approve a bid without referring it, if "the newspaper in question was not economic as a going concern" and "that the case was one of urgency". [65] The first condition was judged to be met by Times Newspapers' declared annual losses of £13 million and the second by Thompson's stated refusal to extend their March deadline. Since an inquiry could not be completed before that date, it was assumed that blocking Murdoch's bid would see Britain's most famous paper, *The Times*, cease publication. The meeting duly concluded that there was "little advantage to be gained from a reference".

In response to claims that the deal gave Murdoch undue control over the national press, final approval was subject to him agreeing to keep the two titles separate and accept six independent directors to guarantee editorial independence and approve the appointment and dismissal of editors. He reneged on his promise not to interfere editorially, demanding the dismissal of the business news editor and beginning what one past *Sunday Times* editor has characterised as "the rape of the Times as an independent newspaper of unimpeachable integrity" and its conversion into "a mouthpiece of Thatcherism". [66]

As he later admitted, "you tell these bloody politicians whatever they want to hear and once the deal is done you don't worry about it. They're not going to chase you ... Otherwise, they're made to look bad, and they can't abide that." [67]

Replying to Murdoch's critics, David Elstein has argued that Thatcher's personal support was helpful, but was not decisive. [68] This is contestable. Since the substantial profits from *The Sunday Times* would have comfortably subsidised losses on *The Times*, alternative bidders could have been found. Thatcher's support of Murdoch went beyond the immediate issue of ensuring *The Times*' survival. It was rooted in a common ideological commitment to market competition and a shared self-conception as "outsiders" battling an entrenched establishment.

In October 2010, Murdoch was invited to present the inaugural tribute lecture for Margaret Thatcher organised by the Centre for Policy Studies, the think tank she had co-founded. He celebrated her as a radically disruptive force claiming that:

> Much of the Tory establishment never understood [her]. For these people, the dynamism she championed was a threat to the established order. She understood that the establishment wasn't just the landed gentry but institutions hungry for power at the expense of ordinary citizens.

He went on to cast himself in the same mould arguing that:

> We should welcome the iconoclastic and unconventional … Yet when the upstart is too successful, somehow the old interests surface, and restrictions on growth are proposed or imposed. That's an issue for my company. [69]

Murdoch's coup in gaining effective control of Britain's satellite broadcasting service offers another instance of this shared antagonism to "old interests".

Following the collapse of the original plan for a national satellite service led by the BBC, a note prepared in the prime minister's private office on 3 July 1985 envisaged opening the field to "all comers", arguing that "regulation and preferential monopolies should only be a last resort, not an instinctive response (particularly from a Conservative Government)". It noted that "a Rupert Murdoch would be able to put up his own satellite with IBA permission and sell directly to television watchers", adding "*that must be right*". [70] This indicates official support for Murdoch from an early point in the debate.

In August 1989, months after launching his Sky Television service beamed from the European Astra satellite, Murdoch delivered the prestigious McTaggart Lecture at the annual Edinburgh Television Festival. Addressing the luminaries of British broadcasting, he lambasted "those who fight to restrict choice to the current duopoly [as] … fundamentally anti-democratic". Claiming that he had "never heard a convincing definition of what public service television really is", he offered a militantly marketised redefinition, arguing that:

> anybody who, within the law of the land, provides a service which the public wants at a price it can afford is providing a public service. So if in the years ahead we can make a success of Sky Television, that will be as much a public service as ITV. [71]

His insistence that competition is always "to be preferred to monopoly" was deeply ironic, given that just over a year later, Sky secured a de facto monopoly over satellite transmission. [72]

The officially franchised satellite service BSB launched in March 1990. The initial costs of competition were ruinous. By the autumn of 1990, BSB was losing £8 million a week and Sky £2.3 million. On 29 October, Rupert Murdoch met Margaret Thatcher at Downing Street to inform her of the planned merger. As the 1982 note quoted earlier confirms, a Murdoch-led direct satellite service was viewed at the heart of government as a welcome force for introducing greater competition into the British television system, and Thatcher personally viewed Sky News as "the only unbiased news in the U.K.", countering the assumed left-wing bias of the BBC. [73]

The merger was finalised on 2 November, creating a new company, British Sky Broadcasting (BSkyB), owned 50/50 by News International and BSB's shareholders. The terms favoured Murdoch. He was installed as general manager, and BSB would contribute 70 per cent of new working capital while News International would receive 80 per cent of dividends for the first 12 years.

The 1990 Broadcasting Act, which had come into force days before the merger announcement, had extended the 1981 rule barring national newspaper proprietors and non-EU shareholders from owning more than 20 per cent of a British television company to satellite broadcasters. The government, in a significant concession, had excluded Sky on the grounds that it used a satellite based in Luxembourg. News International's 50 per cent holding in the newly merged company, however, was a clear violation of the new cross-ownership rules.

A confidential note to Margaret Thatcher on 6 November conceded that "the merger is effectively a takeover of BSB by Sky" [74] and suggested possible rebuttals to objections. It recommended stressing that since "satellite television in Britain is more viable with the new merged company than previously", rather than reducing "competition in any meaningful sense", it in fact "strengthens it". The note ends by anticipating "a vicious public campaign made up of the Good and the Great on the Left to denigrate Murdoch and everything he stands for". [75]

The new regulator, the Independent Television Commission (ITC), later instructed BSkyB to demerge or cease broadcasting by the end of 1992. Murdoch ignored the instruction and was not penalised.

Replying to critics, he traded on his self-image as an outsider battling an entrenched establishment. As he told an interviewer, "There are people who resent the existence of Sky, people who enjoyed the status quo, particularly the self-appointed elite, who saw themselves as elite and were able to project themselves as elite, and who hate anything that changes Britain." [76]

As we have seen, Murdoch has consistently employed his command over the mass circulation of positive and negative publicity to secure political compliance for his business plans.

But his relations with Thatcher suggest that, in some cases, a combination of ideological affinity and a shared sense of self presented an open door he was invited to walk through.

He enjoyed a similar free pass during Donald Trump's presidency. The FCC blocked the proposed merger between the Tribune Media Company and the Sinclair Broadcast Group, scratching plans to launch a new conservative competitor to Fox. Despite the obvious implications for market concentration, the Justice Department raised no serious antitrust objections to Fox's sale of its entertainment assets to Disney. The deal gave the senior Murdoch children $2 billion each to invest in new projects.

5.5 Politics: Making and Breaking Reputations

As Harold Evans, former editor of *The Sunday Times*, has argued, "The secret of Murdoch's power over the politicians is, of course, that he is prepared to use his newspapers to reward them for favours given and destroy them for favours denied." [77]

As Nick Davies notes, politicians have come to fear "that without his favour they will find themselves attacked, destabilised and discredited" and their electoral fortunes dashed. [78]

The pattern was established early, during Gough Whitlam's premiership in Australia.

In 1972, Murdoch threw the full weight of his titles behind Whitlam, the Labour Party's candidate for prime minister. As he later recalled:

> I ran all the election policies of my papers in Australia and got deeply, far too deeply, involved. Looking back, we did some dreadful things to the other side ... I wrote the leaders [editorials] every day in the [Sydney] *Daily Mirror*. [79]

By the beginning of 1975, increasingly dissatisfied with government policies and the refusal of his request to be appointed Ambassador to Britain, he launched a concerted editorial campaign against Whitlam. On 25 February, *The Australian* carried a front-page story reporting a breakfast meeting with two "gun-toting Arabs" to solicit funds. It was headed "Irak (sic) promises $US500,000 to pay Labor's debts, Whitlam in Secret Arab Election Deal". Attributed to a "special correspondent", the story was written by Murdoch, drawing on information supplied by Henry Fischer who had hosted the original meeting, met with Murdoch in London at the *News of the World* offices, and was paid. Whitlam admitted to a serious error of judgement but the story "would irreparably damage [his] authority within [his] party and effectively ended his parliamentary career". [80]

In October, the opposition party blocked the passage of the budget, precipitating a political crisis. Journalists on *The Australian*, protesting the relentless attacks on Whitlam, signed a statement saying they could no longer be "loyal to a propaganda sheet". [81]

Following an unprecedented constitutional move of sacking Whitlam by the Governor General, the year ended with a forced election. "Journalists on *The Australian* struck in protest at the editorial line of the newspaper, a unique event in Australia." [82]

As Murdoch recounted:

> On *The Australian*, there were still people committed to the changes Whitlam had tried. They tried to overlook the failures, and there was a clash. I deny completely that we twisted the news … Nineteen-seventy-five rather got me the reputation of being a reactionary. [83]

Speaking to an Australian Senate Inquiry into media diversity, Kevin Rudd, a former Labor prime minister, himself the target of persistent attacks, testified that Murdoch has continued to hound "opponents with a deeply personal viciousness", cultivating a pervasive "culture of fear". [84]

Addressing the same Senate inquiry, the former Liberal Party prime minister, Malcolm Turnbull, recounted the (Sydney) *Daily Telegraph*'s response to a ministerial speech linking the bushfires to global warming, a connection the Murdoch tabloids denied: "The attack … was bitter, vicious and personal. It was designed to not just punish him but also to send the message … if you step out of line, you will cop some of this too. That's the threat." [85]

Another demonstration of objections to political arguments translating into personal attacks is provided by the coverage of the British Labour Party leader Neil Kinnock during the 1992 General Election campaign. Murdoch's long-standing rejection of the party's continuing commitment to public ownership of essential utilities was reinforced by the manifesto proposal to convene an official inquiry into media concentration. In the weeks leading up to the election, Kinnock was the target of relentless personal attacks in the News Corp tabloids. Questioned at the Leveson Inquiry, Rupert Murdoch claimed not to recall them but argued they were entirely legitimate since: "He was the personification of the leadership of the Labour Party … it was fair to attack his policies, and even sometimes the way he expressed himself." [86]

A witness at an evening dinner Murdoch attended on polling day reported that when a Labour politician appeared on screen blaming defeat on media smears, Murdoch shouted, "That's me" and was delighted. [87]

The day after the election, *The Sun* greeted the victory of Kinnock's Conservative opponent, John Major, with the banner headline "It's the Sun Wot Won It". It was a gross exaggeration since the forces shaping voting preferences were multiple, but the fact that one-third of all "floating" voters with no firm party allegiance were *Sun* readers had arguably opened a significant space for persuasion. [88]

The career of Rupert Murdoch's relationship with Donald Trump offers a cautionary tale of tensions underlying Murdoch's political patronage.

Murdoch first met Trump in New York soon after purchasing the *New York Post.* Trump saw a chance to boost his public profile as a playboy mogul. Murdoch saw Trump's exploits as a source of tabloid copy. In private, however, he "regarded Trump with disdain, seeing him as a real-estate huckster and shady casino operator". [89]

When Trump initially declared his intention of running for president, Murdoch was unenthusiastic, but having secured the Republican nomination, Murdoch endorsed him. During the election campaign, Fox News's reporter Diana Falzone obtained proof that Trump was about to pay the pornographic film actress Stormy Daniels a substantial sum not to disclose their 2006 sexual relationship. The story was eminently newsworthy but never published. She was told, "Rupert wants Donald Trump to win. So just let it go." [90]

The endorsement paid dividends. Fox News was Trump's preferred broadcast platform for most of his presidency. By March 2019, he had given the channel 44 interviews compared to ten to the other main television networks combined and none to CNN. [91] He watched the network voraciously, reposting claims made on *Fox and Friends* and other major programmes on his Twitter account, and tweeting comments that fed back into the news cycle. He talked to the star anchor Sean Hannity "virtually every night" after his show ended and established a direct line to Rupert Murdoch's office for confidential conversations. Trump gained privileged access to a television audience that mapped onto his core support base. His endorsement of Fox News cemented viewers' loyalty to channel. However, as we saw in Chapter 2, this pact was broken when Fox called the election for Biden, forcing Murdoch to attempt to regain Trump's endorsement and his viewer base by promoting his claim that the election had been "stolen" by false vote counting, knowing it to be false.

5.6 Policies: Interested Interventions

Demonstrating that contacts translate into influence is problematic since, as Lance Price, Tony Blair's media advisor from 1998 to 2001, has noted, "Rupert Murdoch doesn't leave a paper trail that could ever prove his influence over policy". [92] Testifying before the Leveson Inquiry, Rupert Murdoch insisted: "In ten years of his power [I] never asked Mr Blair from anything. Nor did he receive any favours." [93]

In February 1998, however, Blair made good on his promise that his government would not interfere in Murdoch's business. In a parliamentary speech opposing a House of Lords amendment to the Competition Bill aimed at ending News Corp's use of predatory pricing, he insisted that it "would result in newspapers being prevented from competing with one another" which they are "perfectly entitled" to do. [94] There was no suggestion that competition was systematically distorted by News Corp's ability to subsidise losses from lower cover prices from the profits generated by its other businesses.

As Nick Davies has observed, Murdoch "does not have to make threats or issue instructions. He just has to exist, somewhere in the background. Everybody understands the fact of power is enough." [95] As Lance Price recalls, "When I worked in Downing Street he seemed like the 24th member of the cabinet. His voice was rarely heard, but his presence was always felt." [96] Britain's membership of the European Union was a particular point of contention.

In a speech at the Milken Institute conference in 2004, Murdoch lambasted the EU as "an awful French socialist bureaucracy stuck in Brussels, which is deterring investment in Europe". When Blair rejected a proposal to hold a referendum on any new EU constitution, the *News of the World* accused him of "surrender" and denounced him as "Traitor Tony". [97] He "soon reversed his position". Lance Price claims to have been told "by somebody who would know" that Murdoch had been assured that Labour "wouldn't change policy on Europe without talking to him first". [98]

Tony Blair's predecessor as prime minister, John Major, was subjected to direct pressure to change his policy on Europe. He recalled a dinner he arranged with Murdoch before the 1997 General Election to seek his continuing support. When the conversation turned to Europe, Major claims Murdoch was adamant "that he really didn't like our European policies. That he wished me to change our European policies. If we couldn't … his papers could not and would not support the Conservatives." [99]

Evidence for other instances of direct intervention is more problematic since they are based on unverifiable evidence. When the phone hacking scandal at the *News of the World* broke, a former minister in the Labour government of Gordon Brown claimed that he had been told that "Murdoch got in touch with a good friend who then got in touch with Brown … to get him to cool things down" and head off an official inquiry. News Corp sources deny this. [100]

Tony Blair's pledge of military support for George Bush's war with Iraq offers another disputed example. The decision provoked mass popular opposition and a bitter conflict with the BBC over claims that the dossier purporting to demonstrate that Saddam Hussein possessed "weapons of mass destruction" had been "sexed up" to make it more convincing. In March 2003, as Blair "was poised to make a final decision to back the invasion without waiting for a U.N. resolution which could have made it legal resolution", he made three phone calls to Murdoch. [101] What was discussed remains disputed. Testifying to the Leveson Inquiry, Murdoch claimed, "I don't remember the calls", but argued that Blair "wouldn't have been calling me for support" since "our position on the war had been declared very strongly in our newspapers well before that date". [102] He also denied reports that Tony Blair had rung the Italian prime minister, Romano Prodi, to discuss Murdoch's possible acquisition of Silvio Berlusconi's media holding company, Mediaset.

Testifying before the Leveson Inquiry, Rupert Murdoch insisted that "my commercial interests, such as they are, or whatever you want to describe them, never came into any consideration on where we stood on issues or political parties". [103]

He neglects to mention the possible influence exerted by his personal stakes in three economic sectors – mining, tobacco, and fossil fuels – that have attracted sustained public controversy for their adverse social and environmental impacts.

In the early 1980s, research suggesting a link between lung cancer and passive smoking prompted calls to ban smoking in public places. The tobacco industry mobilised every available channel to marginalise debate and cast doubt on the link. The leading cigarette manufacturer, Philip Morris, could already rely on News Corp. As an internal company memo in 1985 noted: "We plan to build similar relationships to those we have with Murdoch's News Limited with other newspaper proprietors. Murdoch's papers rarely publish anti-smoking articles these days." [104]

News Corp's relations with Philip Morris, a major advertiser, were reinforced by Murdoch's membership of the Morris board and other ties. Before being hired to establish Fox News, Roger Ailes's political consulting firm had counted Philip Morris among its corporate clients. In 2000, a Philip Morris employee became a "science columnist" for Fox News and began attacking research on passive smoking

Murdoch has also had long-standing interests in mineral and gas extraction. He inherited *The Barrier Miner* from his father and has had personal investments in mining from an early point in his career. In the 1960s, he negotiated shares in Lang Hancock's huge Western Australian mineral holdings in the Pilbara. Employing the leverage offered by his ownership of *The Sunday Times* in Perth and using a tactic that became part of his stock in trade, he reputedly told the politician opposing the deal: "look you can have a headline a day or a bucket of shit every day. What's it to be?" [105] The politician opted for the headline.

Murdoch's most important outside interest, however, has been his equity stake in Genie Oil and Gas Inc., purchased in 2010. The company is the gas division of Genie Energy. It administers the parent company IDT's interests in American Shale Oil and Israel Energy Initiatives Ltd. It has substantial interests in the Middle East, including a major oil exploration project in the Israeli-controlled Golan Heights, a disputed territory once held by Syria. Welcoming Murdoch's involvement, Genie's CEO heralded his "access to the expertise of the oil and gas industry and to the financial markets", noting that he was "extremely … connected to leaders in these sectors". [106] Murdoch's enthusiastic personal support for developing fracking, despite its negative environmental impacts, has been reproduced on Fox programming. On three consecutive days in April 2012, Fox Business Network promoted Genie's oil shale gas project in Israel and later featured the company's activities in Colorado. Murdoch's investment in Genie was not mentioned. [107]

His Genie stake has arguably been a factor in reinforcing both his publicly expressed scepticism towards climate science and his endorsement of Israel. [108] We will return to these stances in the next chapter when we examine News Corp's ideological influence.

References

[1] Market Screener (2023) Available at www.marketscreener.com/quote/stock/NEWS-CORPORATION-13439787/company

[2] Jennifer G. Hill (2010) 'Subverting Shareholder Rights: Lessons from News Corp.'s Migration to Delaware', *Vanderbilt Law Review*, Vol. 63, No. 1, pp. 1–51.

[3] Jennifer G. Hill, 2010, op. cit.

[4] Jennifer G Hill, 2010, op. cit.

[5] Neil Chenoweth (2013) 'Rupert's sweetest deal of all was at his family's expense', 12 November. Available at https://neilchenoweth.com/2013/12/11/ruperts-sweetest-deal-of-all-was-at-his-familys-expense

[6] Matthew Stevens (1993) 'A window on the Murdoch family wealth', *Australian Financial Review*, 21 May. Available at www.afr.com/companies/a-window-on-the-murdoch-family-wealth-19930521-kar42

[7] Alex Barker (2023) 'The Murdoch family trust: how the scions could battle for control', *Financial Times*, 9 January. Available at www.ft.com/content/58a752a3-0dad-433c-97cd-047b1ff7fe39

[8] Karlholt Pty Limited (2004) Prospectus ACN 008 483 261, 22 October, p. 9 section 2.1. Available at www.crikey.com.au/wp-content/uploads/2010/02/2005-10B3GH2BE00.pdf

[9] Alex Barker, 2023, op. cit.

[10] Cynthia Littleton (2015) 'Prince Alwaleed Cuts Stake in News Corp. But Sticks with 21st Century Fox', *Variety*, 4 February. Available at https://variety.com/2015/tv/news/prince-alwaleed-cuts-stake-in-news-corp-but-sticks-with-21st-century-fox-1201423434

[11] Jan Fichtner (2019) 'The rise of institutional investors'. In Philip Mader, Daniel Mertens, and Natascha van der Zwan, (Eds). *The Routledge International Handbook of Financialization* (2020), pp. 265–275. Routledge, 2020, https://doi.org/10.4324/9781315142876

[12] Jan Fichtner, Eelke Heemskerk, and Javier Garcia-Bernardo (2017) 'Hidden power of the Big Three? Passive Index funds, re-concentraton of corporate ownership, and new financial risk', *Business and Politics*, Vol. 19, No. 2, pp. 298–326.

[13] Market Screener. Available at www.marketscreener.com/quote/stock/NEWS-CORPORATION-13439787/company

[14] T. Rowe Price (2023) Available at www.troweprice.com/financial-intermediary/uk/en/lp/us-equities.html

[15] Jan Fichtner et al., 2017, op. cit.

[16] Quoted in Lauren Hirsch (2022) 'News Corp Investors Raise Concerns about Proposed Merger with Fox', *The New York Times*, 20 November. Available at www.nytimes.com/2022/11/20/business/dealbook/news-corp-fox-investors.html

[17] Mayne Report (2021) 'A history of shareholder resolutions against the Murdochs: Shareholder resolutions and voting results at News Corp and 21st Century Fox

since 2005', 19 November. Available at www.maynereport.com/articles/2020/01/15-1508-3012.html

[18] Quoted in Mark Sweney (2011) 'Rupert Murdoch's News Corp sued over "nepotism" in buying his daughter's firm', *The Guardian*, 17 March. Available at www.theguardian.com/media/2011/mar/17/rupert-murdoch-news-corp-shine

[19] Chief Investment Officer (2011) 'Mass Laborers' Pension Fund Joins Growing List of News Corp Plaintiffs', 21 July. Available at www.ai-cio.com/news/mass-laborers-pension-fund-joins-growing-list-of-news-corp-plaintiffs

[20] Rebekah Wade oral testimony, House of Lords (2008) Select Committee on Communications: First Report, Chapter 3: Why Does Ownership Matter? Para 133. Available at https://publications.parliament.uk/pa/ld200708/ldselect/ldcomuni/122/12202.htm

[21] Andrew Neil (1996) 'Murdoch and Me', *Vanity Fair*, December. Available at https://archive.vanityfair.com/article/1996/12/murdoch-and-me

[22] House of Lords Select Committee on Communications, op. cit., Appendix 4: Minute of the Visit to the USA, para 49.

[23] House of Lords Select Committee on Communications, op. cit., Minutes of Evidence Wednesday 23 January, Questions 1648–1659, Q 1657.

[24] House of Lords Select Committee on Communications, op. cit., First report, Chapter 3, quoted in para 124.

[25] Andrew Neil, 1996, op. cit.

[26] Leveson Inquiry, Report into the Culture, Practices and Ethics of the Press (2012) Transcript: Morning Hearing on 25 April 2012. Available at www.discoverleveson.com/hearing/2012-04-25/987/?bc=4

[27] House of Commons (2011) Oral evidence to the Culture, Media and Sport Committee, Phone Hacking, Tuesday 19 July, Q 274. Available at https://publications.parliament.uk/pa/cm201012/cmselect/cmcumeds/uc903-ii/uc90301.htm

[28] Official Committee Hansard (2021) Media Diversity in Australia. Senate Environment and Communications References Committee. Hearings Friday, 12 March 2021. Canberra, Commonwealth of Australia.

[29] Richard Cooke (2018) 'The Endless Reign of Rupert Murdoch', *The Monthly*, July. Available at www.themonthly.com.au/issue/2018/july/1530367200/richard-cooke/endless-reign-rupert-murdoch

[30] Ben Butler (2022) 'Former NY Post editor sues News Corp and Col Allan, alleging sexual harassment', *The Guardian*, 19 January. Available at www.theguardian.com/media/2022/jan/19/former-ny-post-editor-sues-news-corp-and-col-allan-alleging-harassment

[31] Zoe Samios and Karl Quinn (2022) 'Sky News and 2GB terminate Chris Smith contracts after Christmas party incident', *Sydney Morning Herald*, 13 December. Available at www.smh.com.au/business/companies/2gb-terminates-chris-smith-s-contract-after-christmas-party-incident-20221213-p5c5uq.html

[32] C. Wright Mills (1956) *The Power Elite*. Oxford. Oxford University Press.

[33] Mairi Maclean, Charles Harvey, and Gerhard Kling (2017) 'Elite Business Networks and the Field of Power: A Matter of Class?' *Theory, Culture and Society*, Vol. 34, Nos 5–6, p. 127.

[34] Mairi Maclean, Charles Harvey and Gerhard Kling, op. cit. p. 127.

[35] Amelia Arsenault and Manuel Castells (2008) 'Switching Power: Rupert Murdoch and the Global Business of Media Politics: A Sociological Analysis', *International Sociology*, Vol. 23, No. 4, pp. 488–489.

[36] Amelia Arsenault and Manuel Castells, 2008, op. cit., p. 489.
[37] Margaret Thatcher Foundation Archive, Ingham minute for MT ("Note for the Record") *["Rupert Murdoch Lunch"]* 4 January 1981. Available at www.margaretthatcher.org/document/114234
[38] Ali Cromie (1994) 'The Murdoch Succession', *Australian Financial Review*, 17 October. Available at www.afr.com/companies/the-murdoch-succession-19941017-kaskm
[39] Jose Maria Aznar (2010) 'Support Israel: if it goes down, we all go down', *The Times,* 17 June, p. 31. Available at: www.thetimes.co.uk/article/support-israel-if-it-goes-down-we-all-go-down-n596dwkh09d
[40] Quoted in Stephen Battaglio and Meg James (2023) 'With Lachlan Murdoch in charge, Fox Corp, shakes up board of directors', *Los Angeles Times*, 22 September.
[41] Rupert Murdoch (2013) 'The Morality of Markets', Lecture to the Institute of Public Affairs, 31 May. Available at https:/ipa.org.au/ipa-review-articles/the-morality-of-free-markets
[42] David McKnight (2003) '"A World Hungry for a New Philosophy": Rupert Murdoch and the rise of neo-liberalism', *Journalism Studies*, Vol. 4, No. 3, pp. 347–358.
[43] 'Why is Rupert Murdoch associated with Stanford? An Open letter to leadership', *The Stanford Daily*, 12 March 2023. Available at https://stanforddaily.com/2023/03/12/why-is-rupert-murdoch-associated-with-stanford-an-open-letter-to-leadership/
[44] Michael Wolff (2023) *The Fall: The End of the Murdoch Empire*. London. The Bridge Street Press, pp. 49–50.
[45] Sam Jones and Farrah Jassat (2011) 'Rupert Murdoch: Labour's forays into the lion's den', *The Guardian*, 12 July. Available at www.theguardian.com/politics/2011/jul/11/rupert-murdoch-labour-tony-blair
[46] Amelia Arsenault and Manuel Castells, 2008, op. cit., p. 497.
[47] Arsenault and Castells, 2008, op. cit.
[48] Kathleen Ronayne (2011) 'Murdoch's Cash Lines the Pockets of Members of Congress', *Open Secrets*, 21 July. Available at www.opensecrets.org/news/2011/07/rupert-murdoch-cash-lines-pockets
[49] Doug Lederman (2011) 'The Murdoch-Oxford Connection', *Inside Higher Ed*, 13 July. Available at www.insidehighered.com/quicktakes/2011/07/14/murdoch-oxford-connection
[50] David McKnight (2003), op. cit., p. 349.
[51] Commonwealth of Australia (2021) The Senate Environmental and Communication References Committee – Media Diversity in Australia, Executive Summary, p. xiii.
[52] Neil quoted in Leveson Inquiry, Report into the Culture, Practices and Ethics of the Press (2012) Transcript: Morning Hearing on 25 April 2012. Available at www.discoverleveson.com/hearing
[53] Levenson Inquiry, 2012, op. cit.
[54] Leveson Inquiry, 2012, op. cit. Witness Statement of Keith Rupert Murdoch; First Statement KPM1–KPM44.12 April 2012. Para 92.
[55] Hacked Off (2020) *Unelected: The Insidious Influence of Rupert Murdoch at the Heart of Government*. London: Hacked Off. Available at https://hackinginquiry.org/unelected-insidious-influence-murdoch
[56] Aletha Adu (2022) 'Boris Johnson received £276,130 plus expenses for US speech', *The Guardian*, 17 November.

[57] Hacked Off (2024) 'Murdoch's Puppet Show: Pulling on the Strings of Government'. 6 February. Available at https://hackinginquiry.org/murdochs-puppet-sho/
[58] Ricard Cooke, 2018, op. cit.
[59] Nick Davies (2014) *Hack Attack: How the Truth Caught Up with Rupert Murdoch*. London. Chatto and Windus, p. 170.
[60] Nick Davies, 2014, op. cit., p. 169.
[61] Davd McKnight, 2003, op. cit., p. 354.
[62] Quoted in PA Mediapoint (2012) 'Andrew Neil: "Did Murdoch forget he was under oath?"' Press Gazette, 11 July. Available at https://pressgazette.co.uk/publishers/nationals/andrew-neil-did-murdoch-forget-he-was-under-oath
[63] Margaret Thatcher Foundation Archive, Ingham minute for MT ("Note for the Record") *["Rupert Murdoch Lunch"]* 4 January 1981. Available at www.margaretthatcher.org/document/114234
[64] See Harold Evans (2015) 'How Thatcher and Murdoch made their secret deal', *The Guardian*, 28 April. Available at www.theguardian.com/uk-news/2015/apr/28/how-margaret-thatcher-and-rupert-murdoch-made-secret-deal
[65] Margaret Thatcher Foundation Archive, Minutes of Cabinet Economic Strategy Committee – E(81) 4th meeting ("The Times Newspapers" – extract) *[Murdoch purchase]* 26 January 1981, p. 3. Available at www.margaretthatcher.org/document/114233
[66] Harold Evans (2011) 'Ruper Murdoch is the stiletto, a man of method, a cold-eyed manipulator', *The Guardian*, 18 September. Available at www.theguardian.com/media/2011/sep/18/harold-evans-rupert-murdoch-leadership
[67] Quoted in Harold Evans, 2011, op. cit.
[68] David Elstein (2020) 'Rupert Murdoch is not an evil genius, whatever the BBC's "Dynasty" doc says', *Open Democracy*, 15 September. Available at www.opendemocracy.net/en/ourbeeb/rupert-murdoch-is-not-an-evil-genius-whatever-bbcs-dynasty-doc-says
[69] Rupert Murdoch (2010) 'Inaugural Margaret Thatcher Lecture. Free Markets and Free Minds: The Security of Opportunity', 21 October London, Centre for Policy Studies. Available at https://cps.org.uk/events/post/2010/lecture-rupert-murdoch-the-inaugural-margaret-thatcher-lecture
[70] Margaret Thatcher Foundation Archive. Warry minute for Addison ("Direct broadcasting by satellite") *["the DBS consortium has now collapsed and a year's lead on the competition gone"]* 3 July 1985. Available at www.margaretthatcher.org/document/212293
[71] Rupert Murdoch (1989) 'Freedom in Broadcasting', Text of the McTaggart Lecture delivered at the Edinburgh International Television Festival, 25 August. In Bob Franklin et al. *Television Policy: The MacTaggart Lectures*. Edinburgh: Edinburgh University Press, 2022.
[72] Rupert Murdoch, 1989, op. cit., p. 132.
[73] Scott W. Fitzgerald (2012) *Corporations and Cultural Industries: Time Warner, Bertelsmann and News Corporation*. Lanham, MD: Lexington Books, p. 340.
[74] Margaret Thatcher Foundation Archive, No. 10 Policy Unit minute to MT ("Sky-BSB merger") 6 November 1990. Available at www.margaretthatcher.org/document/212514
[75] Margaret Thatcher Foundation Archive No.10 Policy Unit minute to MT ("Sky-BSB merger") 6 November1990. Available at www.margaretthatcher.org/document/212514

[76] Bill Hagerty (1999) The BJR Interview: 'I don't do it for the money' – Rupert Murdoch', *British Journalism Review*, Vol. 10, No. 4, p. 13.
[77] Harold Evans (2011) *Good Times, Bad Times*. London. Bedford Square Books, p. xxii.
[78] Nick Davies, 2014, op. cit., p xiii.
[79] Alexander Cockburn (1976) 'Rupert Murdoch tells All', *The Village Voice*, 29 November. Available at www.villagevoice.com/rupert-murdoch-tells-all/
[80] Jenny Hocking (2012) 'Murdoch's plan to sink Whitlam over dog's breakfast', 26 August. Available at www.smh.com.au/politics/federal/murdochs-plan-to-sink-whitlam-over-dogs-breakfast-20120825-24t4e.html
[81] 'The day The Australian's reporters stopped writing lies'. Available at https://independentaustralia.net/politics/politics-display/the-day-the-australians-reporters-stopped-writing-lies,5107
[82] Alexander Cockburn, 1976, op. cit.
[83] Alexander Cockburn, 1976, op. cit.
[84] Commonwealth of Australia (2021) The Senate Environmental and Communications References Committee, *Media Diversity in Australia*, pp. 103–104.
[85] Commonwealth of Australia, 2021, op. cit., p. 87.
[86] Rupert Murdoch (2012) oral evidence to the Leveson Inquiry. Morning hearing 25 April. Available at www.discoverleveson.com/hearing/2012-04-25/987/?bc=4
[87] Rupert Murdoch (2012) oral evidence to the Levenson Inquiry, op cit.
[88] Martin Linton (1996) 'Maybe The Sun won it after all', *British Journalism Review*, Vol 7, Issue 2, pp 20–26.
[89] Martin Linton, 1996, op. cit.
[90] Jane Mayer (2019) 'The Making of the Fox News White House', *The New Yorker*, 4 March.
[91] Jane Mayer, 2019, op. cit.
[92] Lance Price (2006) 'Rupert Murdoch is effectively a member of Blair's cabinet', *The Guardian*, 1 July Available at www.theguardian.com/commentisfree/2006/jul/01/comment.rupertmurdoch
[93] Rupert Murdoch, 2012, Oral Testimony to the Levenson Inquiry, op cit.
[94] Tony Blair House of Commons speech Hansard (1998) House of Commons Parliamentary Business 11 Feb Column 365
[95] Nick Davies, 2014, op. cit., p. 178.
[96] Lance Price, 2006, op. cit.
[97] Rik Kirkland (2007) 'Rupert Murdoch', *Foreign Policy*, No. 158, January–February, p. 29.
[98] Lance Price, 2006, op. cit.
[99] John Major (2012) Witness Statement of Sir John Major to the Leveson Inquiry, 14 May. Exhibits SJM 1–10. Available at www.discoverleveson.com/search/?bc=2&q=john+major
[100] Toby Helm and James Robinson (2011) 'Phone hacking: Rupert Murdoch "urged Gordon Brown" to halt Labour' attacks', *The Guardian*, 9 April. Available at www.theguardian.com/uk/2011/apr/09/phone-hacking-rupert-murdoch-gordon-brown
[101] Nick Davies, 2014, op. cit., p. 216.
[102] Rupert Murdoch, 2012, Oral testimony to the Leveson Inquiry, op. cit.
[103] Rupert Murdoch, 2012, Oral testimony to the Leveson Inquiry, op. cit.

[104] Tobacco industry documents, available at www.industrydocuments.ucsf.edu/tobacco/docs/#id=fpfg0131

[105] Eric Beecher (2020) 'Murdoch's Power: how it works and how it debases Australia', *InDaily*, 3 November. Available at https://indaily.com.au/opinion/2020/11/03/murdochs-power-how-it-works-and-how-it-debases-australia

[106] DeSmog (2023) 'Rupert Murdoch'. Available at www.desmog.com/rupert-murdoch

[107] Sarah Pavlus (2011) 'Shale Game: Why Won't Fox Disclose Murdoch's Oil Interests?' *Media Matters*, 15 July. Available at www.mediamatters.org/fox-news/shale-game-why-wont-fox-disclose-murdochs-oil-interests

[108] Michael West Media (2020) 'Compromised: Genie Energy and the Murdoch media's climate denial', 15 January. Available at https://michaelwest.com.au/compromised-genie-energy-and-the-murdoch-medias-climate-denial

6 Ideology: Tabloid Tales and Populist Politics

6.1 A Megaphone for Market Populism

Interviewed in 1976, soon after acquiring the *New York Post*, Rupert Murdoch admitted to being:

> a bit of a political buff. I love politics ... I'm interested, fascinated by it. I'm not the ... type of newspaper proprietor, just making money out of newspapers. I get a lot of kicks out of the political side of it. [1]

Commentators have often presented Murdoch's relations with politicians as purely transactional. Support is bestowed or withheld and attacks mounted, depending on how far policies advance or impede News Corp's business interests. As we saw in the last chapter, it is not difficult to find instances of this instrumentality in action. This has led observers to conclude that commercial calculation always trumps ideological commitment. As Nick Davies argues:

> Wherever Murdoch owns outlets, theirs is the ... loudest voice calling for the state to be cut back to make way for private enterprise. They do this as though it were simply a point of political philosophy. Clearly, however, it is matter of overwhelming commercial interest. [2]

This interpretation leaves aside the cumulative impact of the right-of-centre populism that has informed the corporation's news coverage across a wide range of events and issues. This clearly meets John Thompson's useful definition of ideology as meaning mobilised in support of prevailing relations of power. [3]

As David McKnight has persuasively argued, "Murdoch is just as interested in in political influence for its own sake as he is in using it to get favourable treatment from government". [4]

Close analysis of the company's news outlets demonstrates that they are "as much about setting a diffuse political and cultural agenda over the long term" informed by Murdoch's own ideological migration "from social

DOI: 10.4324/9781003255086-6

libertarianism to a militant economic libertarianism" and neoconservatism in foreign policy. [5] This position was most overtly articulated in *The Weekly Standard* launched in 1995 and aimed squarely at the Washington political elite. Expressly intended as a vehicle for neoconservative ideas, it incurred continual losses which Murdoch covered [6] and was eventually sold to the conservative billionaire Philip Anschutz in June 2009.

Writing to the then Labor Prime Minister of Australia, Ben Chifley, Rupert's father Keith noted that his teenage son "is at present a zealous Laborite but will I think (probably) eventually travel the same course as his father" to the right of the political spectrum. [7] Subsidising the *Standard* confirmed how far he had travelled.

As Andrew Neil, former editor of *The Sunday Times*, recalls, Murdoch expected his titles to "stand broadly for … a radical-right dose of free market economics" allied to "the social agenda of the Christian Moral Majority and hard line conservative views on drugs, abortion, law and order and defence". [8]

This combination finds its political expression in the right-wing populism that has colonised the major conservative parties in News Corp's English-language markets. Organised around a binary opposition between "Us" and "Them", it claims to defend the rights and beliefs of "ordinary people" against attacks from a ruling political and cultural establishment. Its master narrative of conflict weaves together three core themes: free markets, culture wars against moral relativism, and neoconservative defence of American centrality in promoting a global order based on "Western" values.

Advocates of minimal corporate regulation have always presented markets as guarantors of personal freedom, but recent decades have seen the rise of "market populism" celebrating markets not simply as spaces of exchange but as mediums of democratic consent giving us what we want. As Thomas Frank notes, if "markets express the will of the people virtually any criticism of business could be described as an act of 'elitism' arising out of a despicable contempt for the common man". The confrontation between capital and labour disappears to be replaced by a new civil war in which "the patriotic blue collar 'silent majority' (along with their employers)" confront an elite characterised by their "contemptuous disregard for the wisdom and values of" decent ordinary citizens. [9]

This new elite comprises "liberal" and "progressive" voices within government, the universities, the arts, and the media, together with experts and scientists who challenge rationales for business as usual.

Having identified an assembly of hostile forces, right-wing populists have mounted an aggressive counter-offensive animated by the militant reassertion of sedimented conceptions of gender roles, sexuality, race, nation coupled with defence of a US-led global order. In the ensuring "culture wars", the foundational White, Anglo-Saxon, Protestant (WASP) culture of the English-speaking world has acted as a recurrent point of reference for essential values and practices. This has led in one direction to hostility to immigration, particularly from Islamic countries, and to the persistence of structural racism and assertions of white supremacy, and in another direction to anxieties around declining influence and a shift in global power from the West to the East.

These themes moved to the centre of public discourse in all three of News Corp's core markets, the United States, Australia, and Britain, finding potent political expression in the Brexit campaign to take Britain out of the European Union and Donald Trump's aggressive performative populism. [10]

Electoral support for right-wing populist platforms overlaps substantially with the core audience base for News Corp's tabloid news outlets, establishing a self-reinforcing relation. Populist themes and frames provide a ready resource for reporting and commentary. Reaffirming them in a vivid vernacular ensures their continuing purchase on public discourse. The intimate relation between Fox News and the Trump Presidency described earlier offers a particularly clear instance of this circulatory system in action, but News Corp's "upmarket" outlets have also worked extensively with populist themes.

The launch of neoliberalism as a philosophy of government in Western democracies is generally dated from Margaret Thatcher's 1979 election as British prime minister and Ronald Reagan's 1981 election as American president. Murdoch admired and supported both leaders, but his own ideological migration was shaped more by the changing political climate in Australia. Columnists writing in the pages of his national daily, *The Australian*, had been publicising core neoliberal ideas since the mid-1970s. Increasing disillusion with the right-of-centre Liberal Party governments of Malcolm Fraser (1975–1983) saw a hardening of the ideological agenda. *The Australian* actively promoted a revisionist view of where power and its abuses are located, shifting the focus from business and finance to the liberal political and cultural elites who had supposedly captured government, science, universities, and the mass media, imposing a ruling orthodoxy built around "political correctness" and hostility to private enterprise. [11] Against this constructed enemy, the paper consistently championed not only the core neoliberal economic agenda of privatisation, reduced taxes, and minimal government, but also "uncritical support for the American alliance and for Israel [and] opposition to … moral relativism". [12]

The Australian ran at a loss for the first 20 years, moved into profit between 1985 and 2007, but lost money again after the Global Financial Crash, relying on cross-subsidies from profitable ventures. As John Sinclair notes, "it is difficult not to conclude that this arrangement is structured principally for the purpose of exerting influence". [13]

The Australian's ideological offensive is widely credited with playing a major role in moving the Liberal Party "from traditional conservatism to militant liberalism", and there is "overwhelming evidence" that Murdoch's own political views "strongly determined the [paper's] outlook and ideological bias". [14]

The Wall Street Journal offers further evidence of an ideological agenda pursued beyond News Corp's tabloid outlets. Having acquired the *Journal*, Murdoch repositioned it as a competitor to *The New York Times*, adding more extensive coverage of politics and foreign affairs to the established focus on business and finance. Detailed analysis of editorials published between 2004 and 2009 revealed a marked "ideological shift to the right". Commentary became "significantly more pro-Republican," "significantly more negative towards Democrats", and much less likely to support government intervention. [15] This shift accelerated following Murdoch's endorsement of Donald Trump, before and after his election as president, with increasing contributions to the opinion column from members of the administration and committed Trump supporters. Their interventions frequently misrepresented available evidence on contentious issues that had been carefully investigated by the news desk. In July 2020, resentment boiled over when 280 journalists from the *Journal* and other Dow Jones outlets wrote to the CEO Almar Latour protesting that their reporting was being devalued, claiming that: "Opinion's lack of fact-checking and transparency, and its apparent disregard for evidence, undermines our readers' trust and our ability to gain credibility with sources", leaving reporters facing "questions about the Journal's accuracy and fairness". [16]

In a combative response, the *Journal*'s editorial board issued a "Note to Readers", assuring them that "these pages won't wilt under cancel culture pressure". [17] The phrase "cancel culture" is routinely deployed by right-wing populists to characterise the supposed capture of cultural institutions by "liberal" forces and their silencing of conservative voices. Its use points to the *Journal*'s accommodation of populist frames.

In October 2021, the paper attracted further criticism when it published a letter from Trump reasserting his false claim that the 2020 Presidential election had been "rigged" against him, a claim comprehensively disproved by *Journal* reporters. Giving an uncontested platform to proven lies is a major break from accepted practice. As a former *Journal* managing editor noted, "if someone is going to spout a bunch of falsehoods, the editor usually feels an obligation to trim these out, or publish a contemporaneous response … [T]he editorial page chose not to do this in this case." [18]

Normalising Trump and core populist themes prompted substantial numbers of senior journalists covering foreign affairs, national security, and the White House to leave the paper, accepting buy-outs or moving to rival titles. [19]

New Corp's orchestration of populist themes emerges clearly in detailed analyses of coverage in four central areas of contention: culture wars, defining who belongs with "the people" and who doesn't, responses to the changing global order, and coverage of the climate crisis.

6.2 Culture Wars

6.2.1 Public Service Broadcasting

News Corp's assault on "liberal" elites has made a particular point of attacking the public service broadcasting (PSB) institutions that play a central cultural role in both Britain (the BBC) and Australia (the ABC). Financed out of taxation, operating under government charter, and staffed by an educated elite, they present advocates of market populism with a perfect target.

Addressing the Edinburgh Television Festival in 2009, James Murdoch, responsible for News Corp's European interests at the time, launched an aggressive assault arguing: "We are on the wrong path – but we can find the right one. The right path is all about trusting and empowering consumers. It is about embracing private enterprise and profit as a driver of investment, innovation and independence." [20]

This argument is underpinned by a clear commercial rationale articulated in classic market populist terms. PSB occupies spectrum space and commands audiences that should be used for subscription and advertising-based services because the liberal elite responsible for programming, far from "serving" the public, are condescending, paternalistic, and arrogant, and insist on imposing their own values and tastes.

Versions of this argument have been widely promoted in News Corp's press titles, particularly those directed at opinion formers and decision makers. *The Times* and *The Australian* have consistently championed neoliberal voices accusing PSB of left-wing bias and calling variously for full or partial privatisation or an exclusive focus on programming that commercial providers are uninterested in making.

Systematic analysis of British press reporting and commentary in selected years between 1990 and 2011 recorded News International titles publishing 54 per cent more articles about the BBC than rival titles, and at least twice as many negative pieces supported by editorial comment that was 70 per cent hostile. [21] As journalism lecturer John Jewell has argued, "one thing you can be sure of, historically, is that when the BBC is up for discussion, it's *The Times* and *Sunday Times* which like to believe they are setting the agenda". [22] He notes the same pattern repeated in Australia with News Corp's "flagship newspapers" keeping up "a barrage of criticism against the ABC – questioning its funding, its scope, and regularly, its bias". [23]

Licence to question is not extended to public broadcasters, however, with News Corp repeatedly accusing PBS coverage of its operations of bias. In 2020, Rupert Murdoch lodged an official complaint against a BBC documentary series, *The Rise of the Murdoch Dynasty*, alleging that it gave too much airtime to his opponents, failed to give sufficient weight to his business successes, and implied that he posed a threat to liberal democracy. The BBC rejected the complaint but the Corporation's Australian channel, carried on Murdoch's Foxtel network, "chose not to air [denying] this was due to its relationship with Murdoch's business". [24]

In 2021 ABC's major current affairs programme *Four Corners* screened a critical analysis of Fox News' relations with Donald Trump. In the following two days, News Corp's Australian titles published 45 articles attacking the broadcaster. *The Australian* carried a front-page editorial headed "The ABC's big lie and the madness of Four Corners". Fox News followed up with a letter threatening legal action, claiming that the ABC had clearly exhibited "bias and a failure to maintain any level of impartiality in the presentation of news and information". [25]

Market populism abolishes public service broadcasting's central missions, first to "educate" in the original Latin sense of going beyond what people already know and like, to introduce unfamiliar ideas and experiences, and second to cultivate a culture of informed citizenship. Commercial provision addresses audiences first and foremost as consumers. It consistently fails to deliver the full range of cultural resources supportive of citizenship: comprehensive information on key events and issues, authoritative analysis of their causes and likely consequences, spaces of respectful deliberation, and diverse imaginative representations of plural histories and ways of living that cultivate empathy and solidarity. It is precisely these essential supports for a fully functioning participatory democracy that News Corp's most successful television services, led by Fox News, have subverted. James Murdoch belatedly arrived at this conclusion himself when he resigned from News Corp, citing disagreements with editorial policies.

6.2.2 Critical Intellectuals

Populist culture wars are waged against any critical voice with a public platform. University teachers and researchers are another prime target. Content analysis of *The Australian* from 2009 to 2015 reveals a pattern "of aggressive news stories that attack the expertise and social legitimacy of academics the newspaper seemingly regards as ideological enemies". [26] Speaking at a conference for journalism educators, *The Australian*'s former science and rural affairs reporter claimed that the paper's editor-in-chief, Chris Mitchell, controlled stories to reflect his personal hostility to theories of anthropogenic climate change. Following tweets she posted commenting on the paper, journalism lecturer Julie Posetti was subjected to sustained vilification in print and threatened with legal action for defamation. As she later remarked, "what kind of editor, invested in freedom of expression, threatens to sue for defamation over a fair report of public proceedings and then mounts his case against an individual via screaming headlines in his own newspaper?" [27]

6.3 Defining "The People": Belonging and Exclusion

Within the moral universe of right-wing populism, full membership of "the people" can never be taken for granted. It has to be earned by honest toil and commitment to core values. Perceived failure to meet either test incurs automatic disqualification.

Welfare claimants are permanently suspected of deliberately avoiding work and spending hard-earned tax income on feckless lifestyles. They are cast as the new "undeserving poor" and castigated as "scroungers" and "skivers". Immigrants who continue to embrace "alien" cultures and values are placed under permanent suspicion.

Both groups have figured prominently in News Corp's orchestration of populism.

6.3.1 The Undeserving Poor: Welfare Claimants

Stigmatising those forced to rely on welfare has a history stretching back to the Victorian workhouse, [28] but recent years have seen penalisation intensify as neoliberal policies have sought to slash state expenditure and transfer responsibility for welfare to individuals and voluntary agencies.

Stigmatisation is universal, but its relative prominence varies by political affiliation and market position. Research reveals a clear pattern with News Corp's tabloid newspapers in both countries playing a central role.

In Britain, *The Sun* has been far more likely than any other national title to feature stigmatising content. Detailed analysis of national press coverage of claimants between 1995 and 2011 found that 81.7 per cent of *Sun* items featured one or more negative themes compared to 61.1 per cent in its main tabloid rival, the left-leaning *Daily Mirror*, and 43.5 per cent in New Corp's national daily broadsheet *The Times*. Only 13.3 per cent of *Sun* stories focused on genuine need or disability compared to 38.9 per cent in the *Mirror* and 38.8 per cent in *The Times*. [29]

This pattern of attention is repeated in Neil Gavin's analysis of British press treatment of benefit fraud between January 2008 and December 2017. Again, negative coverage was most extensive in *The Sun*, with 848 items containing references to fraud, cheat, scam, or fiddle compared to 593 in the *Mirror* and 207 in *The Times*. [30] Readers' sense of being taken advantage of is easily stoked by items featuring people like themselves gaming the system. The *Sun* story from 16 June 2018 headed "Sun, Sand and Swindle: Benefits scrounger rakes in thousand while going on luxury holidays" is prototypical. In 2012, the paper sought to mobilise popular suspicion with its "Beat the Cheats" campaign, urging readers to report any neighbour "who claim [s] to be too sick for work but enjoys sports and nights out down the pub".

Research on Australia's five most-read newspapers between 2001 to 2016 revealed a similar pattern. News reporting of the disability pension rose sharply over the period, coinciding with an increased political "focus on the economics of welfare and budget sustainability". [31] News Corp titles carried markedly more stories than their competitors: 775 in *The Australian* and 728 in *The Daily Telegraph* compared to 579 in *The Age* and 521 in the *Sydney Morning Herald.* [32] They were also more likely to use fraud language, leading the authors to conclude that "Diagnosed illnesses no longer shielded" recipients "from scepticism about the validity of their claims". [33]

In 2016, as part of a drive to reduce state expenditure, Australia's right-of-centre Coalition government introduced a new automated system to identify and recover "overpayments" made to social security recipients. It relied on a simple algorithm that averaged earnings over the year "data-matching historic records of benefit payments with past income tax returns" to identify discrepancies. [34] Popularly dubbed "Robodebt", it aimed to recover AU$1.7 billion over five years. From the outset, it generated multiple false estimates of money owing, causing widespread social distress and culminating in September 2019 in the government refunding AU$720 million to over 400,000 individuals unlawfully designated as debtors.

This official admission of catastrophic policy failure came at the end of a protracted struggle for public opinion in which the Murdoch press played a central role in supporting the government. As Rachelle Miller, the media advisor responsible for government press liaison, explained in her evidence to Royal Commission hearings on Robodebt, in response to early stories criticising the scheme in "what we described as the 'left-wing' media i.e. *The Guardian, Age/SMH, ABC*" [35]:

> [We ran] a counter narrative in more friendly media such as *The Australian* and the tabloids, which we knew were interested in running stories about welfare system integrity, and the supposed "dole-bludgers" [and supported] cracking down on people who were cheating the welfare system … This strategy was very effective [and was framed around] protecting taxpayers' dollars. [36]

In Australia and elsewhere, the loss to the public purse from benefit fraud is a fraction of the sum lost to tax evasion and avoidance by companies and high net worth individuals exploiting legal loopholes and tax havens. Stigmatising claimants as "undeserving" of either sympathy or solidarity recasts them as enemies of the people, directing attention away from corporate abuses and bolstering the neoliberal case for transferring responsibilities for welfare from ineffective state agencies to private providers.

6.3.2 Immigration and Islamophobia

Immigration presents a problem for right-wing populism. On the one hand, neoliberal economics champions the free movement of labour as an essential driver of economic growth. On the other hand, combatants in the "culture wars" see the influx of "alien" bodies and ideas as a corrosive force, displacing established hierarchies, ways of life, and beliefs.

Neoliberal policies of globalisation, both economic and political have resulted in "the mass movement of people around the globe", prompting renewed reassertion of physical and cultural boundaries. [37]

In September 2010, Rupert Murdoch appeared before the US House of Representatives Subcommittee on Immigration. He conceded that: "Many people worry that immigrants will take their jobs, challenge their culture, or change their community", but "as an immigrant", he felt "an obligation to speak up for immigration that will keep America the most economically robust, creative and freedom loving nation in the world". [38]

In opposition to voices demanding mass deportation of "illegals", he called for a recognised path to citizenship for "responsible, law-abiding immigrants" currently in the US without authorisation, and for visa rules to be relaxed to make it easier for foreign students with high-end skills to stay and work in the US after completing their studies.

He returned to the economic benefits of immigration in October 2013 in a lecture to the Lowry Institute, the right-of-centre Sydney think tank launched by Frank Lowry, the immigrant founder of the global Westfield shopping centre chain, originally from Slovakia via Israel: "Immigration adds its own dynamism to any economy … The more people we have with ties to other parts of the world, the greater our advantage when we seek trade relationships." [39]

This positive economic case confronted a resistant political climate. Right-of-centre parties in News Corp's three core English-speaking markets were fostering an increasingly "hostile environment" for migrants, with calls for strict limits on numbers, deportations to offshore holding camps, protective walls, and outright bans. As Murdoch explained in his Lowy lecture, in making a positive case he was referring specifically to "immigrants who understand and share our values" – those who "will certainly create greater value for all Australians". [40]

Demands to share "our" values require migrants to relinquish "alien" beliefs and practices. "Multiculturalism", based on respect for difference, is replaced by mandatory assimilation to the dominant culture. As Murdoch had argued in August 2013, on his Twitter page, launched in 2011: "Let's put multiculturalism behind us. Societies have to integrate. Muslims find it hardest," [41]

Nominating Muslim migrants as a particular problem draws on the long tradition of Orientalism in Western thought celebrating the inherent superiority of "Occidental" Western culture and operating to justify "dominating, restructuring, and having authority over the Orient". [42]

Emphasis on the incompatibility of Islamic culture and practices with dominant Western values remained a constant focus of commentary, but following the 9/11 destruction of the New York Twin Towers by aircraft hijacked by jihadist militants and President Bush's subsequent declaration of a global "War on Terror", endorsed by both Britain and Australia, it was joined by an emphasis on violent threats. Murdoch endorsed this framing in tweets he posted in January 2015 in the wake of the fatal attack on journalists working for the satirical magazine, *Charlie Hebdo* in Paris: "Maybe most Moslems peaceful, but until they recognize and destroy their growing jihadist cancer they must be held responsible." [43]

The colonial spelling "Moslems" carries strong Orientalist connotations of cultural subordination and is similar to the Arabic word for "oppressor". Adding the qualifier "maybe" evokes doubt and assigns collective responsibility, placing all Muslims under permanent suspicion of being potentially violent "enemies of the people".

This threat frame joined the earlier cultural incompatibility frame to dominate coverage of Islam and Muslims across News Corp's tabloid news outlets.

Analysis of articles containing the words "Islam" and "Muslim" published in the three years following the 9/11 attacks found that less than a quarter (24%) published in News Corp's *Herald Sun* could be classified as positive compared to 50 per cent in *The Age*, its main rival in Victoria. [44]

Analysis of the company's five leading Australian titles over the year 2017 found attitudes had hardened, with 80 per cent of items referring to Islam or Muslims "alongside words like violence, extremism, terrorism or radical", again, considerably more than in rival Fairfax publications. [45] The increasingly alarmist tone of imminent threat was typified by an opinion column in the *Herald Sun* in July 2016 headed "The Enemy Within", claiming: "We have among us small groups of young men, predominantly Australian born and bred, who loathe Australia and the West so much so that they are willing to sacrifice their own lives to attack us." [46]

Reaction to a post on Australian activist Yassmin Abdel-Magied's personal Facebook page is prototypical of the overall emphasis on "alienness". Designed to call attention to the refugee crises, it was captioned, "Lest We Forget", a phrase associated with ANZAC Day. Although it was taken down and retracted within an hour, the post prompted over 100 condemnatory articles and five front pages in News Corp Australian titles dramatising her supposed disloyalty. [47] Her activities were also mobilised to undermine the ABC with a *Daily Telegraph* front page captioned, "Un-Australian Broadcasting Corporation backs activist who demeans out war heroes", a calculated reference to the House Un-American Activities Committee charged with identifying disloyalty and subversion in American universities, cultural industries, and public institutions at the height of the Cold War. [48]

In Britain, research has identified *The Sun* as the "paper most likely to construct a unified consensus about Islam as a threat to the British 'values' and the paper … least likely to see any elements of counter discourses". [49]

This construction finds particularly potent expressions in arguments over face covering. Analysis of *Sun* coverage in 2006 revealed a consistent presentation of veiling as a calculated rejection of British culture aided by an over-tolerant multiculturalism that has allowed a minority to impose "their" way of life on "us", fostering the "extremism" that animates terrorism. [50]

This argument was put in particularly strident and abusive language in an opinion column on 24 June 2009 complaining, "We let shroud-swishing zombies flout OUR standards of freedom and tolerance every day" (Capitals in the original). [51]

On 18 July 2016, in the wake of the terrorist attack in Nice, *The Sun* printed a column by the former editor, Kelvin MacKenzie, attacking Channel 4 for having a Muslim presenter wearing a hijab report on the incident. Asking, "Was it appropriate for her to be on camera when there has been yet another shocking slaughter by a Muslim?" implied that she is guilty by association by virtue of her faith and that "the rest of us are reasonably entitled to have concerns about what is beating in their religious hearts". [52]

The sense of ever-present threat from violent jihadism had been amplified in Britain by the 7 July 2005 (7/7) bombs detonated on a London bus and in the Underground system by young Muslim men born and brought up in Britain, cementing "Islamic terrorism" as a central political concern. [53]

In November 2015, the paper carried a photo of a masked man brandishing a knife alongside a banner headline "Shock Poll: 1 in 5 Brit Muslims' sympathy for jihadists". The survey question had asked respondents about their sympathy for "young Muslims who leave the UK to join fighters in Syria" without mentioning Islamist groups. The press regulator judged the headline to be "seriously misleading" and demanded a correction. The story belonged to a wider pattern of coverage which stripped discussion of possible motivations for terrorist acts of their historical and political contexts and attached them to religious belief, placing all Muslim under permanent suspicion. [54]

Replying to Maxine Waters, representative from California, during the Congressional hearings mentioned earlier, Murdoch denied that Fox News was anti-immigrant.

> *Waters:* You are here with a basically decent proposal ... but I don't see that being promoted on Fox. As a matter of fact, I am often stunned by what I hear on Fox.
>
> *Murdoch:* We are not anti-immigrant on Fox.
>
> *Waters:* What do you do to promote the same views that you are here talking with us about?
>
> *Murdoch:* We do it in the *Wall Street Journal* every day. [55]

While the positive economic case for immigration may have found space in *The Wall Street Journal*, aimed squarely at the business class, research demonstrates that Fox News has consistently demonised Muslim immigrants to the United States.

Analysis of editions of *Fox News* and *Fox News Sunday* broadcast between March 2007 and March 2009, found 345 out of the 428 sampled comments from hosts, guests, and correspondents framed Islam and Muslims in negative terms, reaffirming prevailing suspicions and antagonisms. [56] Front-page stories posted on the channel's foxnews.com website in 2007 and 2008 promoted a sense of pervasive threat by repeatedly stressing "the core incompatibility of Islamic customs with western ones; and the impending loss of cultural institutions if assimilation continues". [57] A cumulative patchwork of items dramatised the impact on everyday life with stories of Mohammed becoming the most popular name for newborn boys in Britain, hospital beds turned to face Mecca, and a ban on the children's story of the Three Little Pigs.

Democratic politicians were particular targets for accusations of disloyalty to America and its cultural foundations. In March 2019, Fox presenter Jeanine Pirro's suggested that Congresswoman Ilhan Omar's decision to wear the hijab proved her allegiance to a culture and legal system openly antagonistic to American values: "Think about it. Omar wears a hijab … Is her adherence to this Islamic doctrine indicative of her adherence to Sharia law which in itself is antithetical to the United States Constitution?" [58]

From an early point in his bid for the presidency, accusations that Barak Obama, whose father was Kenyan and his mother a white American, was Muslim not Christian, were mobilised to undermine his legitimacy. A few weeks after he had accepted the Democratic Party nomination, Steve Dooley the co-host of the *Fox & Friends* morning show recycled a story from a right-wing fringe publication claiming that Obama had spent "the first decade of his life raised by his Muslim father as a Muslim and was educated in a madrassa [teaching] the religion that pretty much hates us". [59] Following his convincing victory, Obama was subjected to accusations that he had been born outside the United States and was Constitutionally barred from being president. This "Birther" claim was repeatedly promoted by Fox presenters and enthusiastically adopted by Donald Trump in his campaign for the presidency. When Obama released his birth certificate proving that he was born in Hawaii, a US state, Trump denounced it as fake.

Research on American news coverage of the 11 terrorist attacks on US soil between October 2001 and January 2010 revealed a consistent pattern in Fox coverage. Representations of international terrorists were dominated by images of predominantly Muslim or Arab actors "working together in organised cells against a 'Christian America'" and intent on lethal violence. In marked contrast, domestic terrorism was presented as a minor threat comprised of isolated incidents committed by troubled individuals driven by attention seeking, or the desire to create fear or send anti-government message. [60]

A later study of Fox News coverage between 2012 and 2022 confirmed a continuing skew in attention. Despite "the significant increase in incidents of right-wing domestic terror over the sample period", the channel's coverage "placed the blame almost entirely on radical Islamic terror and leftwing domestic terror" and "commonly portrayed right-wing extremists, as being unfairly targeted and framed" by the FBI and other intelligence agencies. [61]

In 2019, News Corp senior vice president, Joseph Azam, from a family of Afghan refugees, admitted that his mounting concern over negative coverage of Muslims had prompted him to resign from the company: "Scaring people. Demonising immigrants … It fundamentally bothered me on a lot of days and I think I probably wasn't the only one." [62]

6.3.3 Marginalising First Nation Peoples: The Australian Voice Referendum

One of the most extraordinary demonstrations of News Corp's animating right-wing populism was displayed during the months of campaigning around the referendum to establish a constitutional "voice" for Australia's First Nations peoples who have endured a history marked by colonisation and dispossession, leading to aberrant conditions in health, employment and well-being, and high incarceration rates. Efforts to bridge the gaps in life chances between Indigenous Australians and the rest of the population have consistently failed over the years. A "yes" vote in the referendum would have acknowledged Aboriginal and Torres Strait Islander peoples in the Australian constitution and created an Indigenous body to advise the government and parliament on issues and policies affecting their welfare. Negative coverage strongly emphasised claims that a successful voice referendum would strip the Australian parliament of its power. This was factually inaccurate. The referendum amendment explicitly stated that parliament would retain the authority to enact laws pertaining to Aboriginal peoples and Torres Strait Islanders.

Analysis of referendum coverage in News Corp's main tabloid outlets found the vast majority of words used were deployed in support of "No" arguments: over three-quarters (77%) in both the *Herald Sun* and *Sky News* and 69 per cent in the *Daily Telegraph*. [63] Sky News launched a 24/7 channel dedicated to the campaign consistently promoting a "no vote" agenda and spreading misinformation about the implications of the referendum. [64] Presenting it as a Labor Government policy effectively erased the voices of the First Nations peoples who had originally proposed it and erected a platform for calls for the prime minister, Anthony Albanese, to resign. The "no" vote in the referendum resulted in a paradigmatic failure that will impede similar breakthroughs in Australia for years to come.

6.4 The Shifting International Order

6.4.1 Special Relations: Brexit

Britain sees itself positioned at the intersection of three geopolitical "circles" led by the United States and the wider English-speaking world, with Continental Europe some way behind. [65] Accepting an honorary degree in the USA in 1946, Winston Churchill laid claim to "a special relationship" between Britain, the Commonwealth, and the United States based on the shared language and culture of "the English-speaking peoples". [66]

With the collapse of the British empire and preferential trade, joining the European common market became an economic imperative, but moves to greater political integration were fiercely opposed by Eurosceptics. They imagined Britain's future revolving around relations with the US and the major

English-speaking nations and saw any proposed European "law or treaty change" as an assault on national self-determination "by a devious centralising project". [67] Murdoch shared this basic scepticism. Interviewed by the BBC in 2003, he rejected "any more abdication of our sovereignty over economic affairs or anything else". [68] As noted earlier, in 1997 he threatened to withdraw support from Britain's Conservative government if Prime Minister John Major did not alter his policy. Cultural attachments formed by living and working among Churchill's "English-speaking peoples" and his personal admiration for America may partly explain his antipathy to the European Union, but it was also informed by economic calculation. Lacking the political connections and mass news outlets he commanded in Britain and the US placed him at a disadvantage in securing concessions in Europe. As he told a journalist, "When I go to Downing Street they do what I say; when I go to Brussels they take no notice." [69]

His scepticism was reproduced in *The Sun*'s jingoistic populism memorably captured by the 1 November 1990 front cover opposing the common currency proposed by the European Commission President, Jaques Delors. The banner headline "Up Yours Delors" was accompanied by a photograph of a hand making the classic V sign emerging from the Union Jack flag. Readers were urged to assemble the next day, face the Continent, and raise their collective fingers to "tell the French fool where to stuff his ECU". *The Times*'s was less strident but "consistently presented … the EU as a threat to the National Interest" and applauded British government refusals of greater integration. [70]

Faced with mounting pressure from Eurosceptics, in 2016 Conservative Prime Minister David Cameron called a referendum on whether Britain should leave the EU (Brexit). *The Sun* and other right-of-centre dailies supported "Leave". *The Times*, read by a corporate elite concerned with likely damage to the economy, joined the *Financial Times*, and the centre-left *Guardian* and tabloid *Daily Mirror* in endorsing "Remain". [71]

The Leave campaign employed the classic populist opposition between the elite and the "people". *The Sun* and other Leave-supporting outlets mentioned "The Establishment" in 547 articles and "elites" in 636. [72] Leave supporters dismissed remainers' predictions of economic damage as "Project Fear" with *The Sun* claiming that projections of a "Brexit 'catastrophe' is a Hitler-style Big lie" (18 April).

The economy accounted for almost half (48%) of all articles published in the British press followed by 30 per cent devoted to immigration. However, over a third (38%) of articles mentioning the economy also mentioned immigration. This figure rises to 46 per cent for *The Sun.* The salience of immigration was further boosted by the 99 front-page leads devoted to it, compared to 81 for the economy. [73] Of these, 14 appeared in *The Sun*. Building on the central Leave campaign slogan, "Take Back Control", of borders and law making, *The Sun* greeted voting day as "Independence Day".

6.4.2 Defending American Ascendency

Outside of the Communist bloc, the global order installed in the wake of World War II was based around international institutions that secured American ascendency, supported by Britain and Australia. As Rupert Murdoch noted in his Lowy lecture:

> The United States remains our number one alliance. For good reason: Americans share our deepest values, as well as 100 years of history shedding blood with each other in wars for the cause of democracy, both close to home and afar. [74]

For a brief period following the final collapse of the Soviet Union, America's position as the pre-eminent global power appeared unassailable, with emerging states expected to follow the Western model combining market capitalism with democratic politics. This assumption was challenged by two major ruptures: the destruction of New York's Twin Towers and China's rise as a global power. Both challenges evoked a concerted response.

The populist tone of News Corp's tabloid war reporting had been on full display in *The Sun*'s earlier coverage of Britain's war with Argentina to repossess the Falklands/Malvinas Islands. Accusing "other papers of treason and treachery when they expressed doubts about the course of the war", it celebrated the disputed torpedoing of the *Belgrano* with a front-page headlined "GOTCHA" and a photo of the battleship engulfed in flames, "sponsored a missile with 'Stick this Up Your Junta' inscribed on its side", and "paid £5 for every 'anti-Argie' joke sent in by readers". [75]

6.4.3 The Iraq War

A central plank in George Bush's response to 9/11 centred on his decision to invade Iraq and depose the regime of Saddam Hussein. There was no evidence that Iraq had been involved in the attacks, but neoconservative thinking on foreign policy provided "intellectual justification for direct military intervention in nations perceived to be hostile to the interests of the United States". [76] The proposed Iraq invasion split public opinion in Britain and Australia, with mass protest demonstrations in the streets and substantial numbers either opposing armed intervention outright or demanding a mandate from the United Nations. Dissenting voices were swept aside and the case for war promoted on the basis of inaccurate, false, and outdated intelligence, quickly dubbed the "dodgy dossier", claiming that Saddam possessed "weapons of mass destruction". Since Iraq had been subjected to stringent sanctions since its invasion of Kuwait and United Nations inspectors had found no trace of any alleged weapons, the claim was always suspect. Germany and France declined to join the "coalition of the willing" supporting Bush. Britain and Australia signed up.

Against a background of popular doubt and distrust, News Corp outlets played a central role in mobilising support for war. Rupert Murdoch reaffirmed his unequivocal personal commitment in the *Sydney Morning Telegraph*: "We can't back down now, where you hand over the whole of the Middle East to Saddam … I think Bush is acting very morally, very correctly, and I think he is going to go on with it." [77]

This justification rested on a clear economic base. As Murdoch had explained in an earlier interview with *Fortune* magazine, taking control of Iraq's extensive oil reserves would deliver major gains to business: "Once it [Iraq] is behind us, the whole world will benefit from cheaper oil, which will be a bigger stimulus than anything else." [78]

As Andrew Calabrese has noted, Fox News "set the standard for patriotic television with an editorial policy that echoed the Bush administration's official stance, making any challenge to the White House's plans for war seem tantamount to treason". [79] The Channel's presentation of foreign policy increasingly relied on neoconservatives, allowing them to promote their views with little or no challenge or qualification.

Elsewhere, as Roy Greenslade noted at the time, support for the war was promoted across almost all of News Corp's 175 press titles on three continents. The single exception was the Hobart *Mercury* with an editorial on 12 September 2002 arguing that "It would be wrong for the us to pre-emptively attack Iraq" and warning, presciently, that throwing a "blazing ember in the powder key would be a dream scenario for the future rise of Islamic fascist fundamentalism". [80]

The paper received a written instruction to alter its position. It complied.

In News Corp's titles, Australians opposed to the war were labelled in classic culture war terms typified by the *Herald Sun*'s denunciation of "our growing church of appeasers … Cultural relativists, ageing Marxists … cause junkies and far Left agitators". Multiple "editorials and articles – many very intemperate – attacked the [Labour Party leader] Simon Crean's unwillingness to support an invasion of Iraq without UN sanction". [81]

In contrast, the Fairfax-owned *Sydney Morning Herald* was far more likely to provide a platform for critical voices. Scepticism carried over into the coverage of the conflict with 41 per cent of items carried by the *Sydney Morning Herald* during the first week of the invasion negative or questioning and only 19 per cent positive. In News Corp's flagship title, *The Australian*, these figures were almost reversed with the 23 per cent of negative stories comprehensively outweighed by the 38 per cent of positive and celebratory postings. [82]

In Britain, *The Sun*'s main tabloid competitor, the *Daily Mirror*, mounted a concerted opposition to the war, challenging the arguments advanced by the US and UK governments, launching "No War" petitions, distributing anti-war posters, and supporting the million-strong anti-war march in London on 15 February 2003. [83]

6.4.4 Yellow Perils: China Rising

Recent years have seen America's economic and political dominance challenged by a resurgent China. The massive death toll and economic disruption caused by COVID-19, the worst global pandemic for over a century, prompted concerted efforts to identify causes and apportion blame.

The pandemic's origins will probably never be identified with 100 per cent certainty, but the majority of scientific research points to zoonotic transmission from bats to humans by way of an intermediate wild animal host sold in the Wuhan wet market in central China where the initial outbreak originated. This explanation locates the causes with agribusiness corporations and accelerating deforestation and industrialised farming. [84] An alternative explanation, directly hostile to the Chinese state, asserts that the virus was assembled in Wuhan's virology laboratory and released either accidentally or deliberately and the facts deliberately concealed. More extreme versions claim it was manufactured as a biological weapon. News Corp news outlets played a prominent role in publicising the laboratory leak conspiracy.

In January 2020, as the first COVID cases were recorded in the US, the fringe right-wing publication, the *Washington Times*, owned by the Unification Movement (the "Moonies") carried a story headlined "Coronavirus May Have Originated in Lab Linked to China's Biowarfare". By early April, various versions of the lab leak theory, most posted by Trump supporters, were logging over five million views on Twitter. [85] On 2 April in Britain, *The Sun*'s website posted a story on the Wuhan lab's long-standing research on bats as virus carriers sourced extensively from the *Washington Times*. Headed "Bat out Hell", it featured a video showing a "virus expert catching bats", fuelling speculation that the coronavirus originated with the activities of "Wuhan scientists". On 30 April, during a White House press briefing, President Trump endorsed the leak claim, saying he had a "high degree of confidence" that the virus originated in the Wuhan lab but declined to name his sources. On 2 May, the Saturday edition of News Corp's *Daily Telegraph* in Australia carried a "World Exclusive" headed "China's Batty Science: Bombshell dossier lays out case against the People's Republic", claiming that intelligence "compiled by concerned western governments" strongly supported the lab leak claim. A subhead noted that the dossier "claims incurable virus invented at lab with links to Australia".

Research unravelling COVID-19's genome sequence, the essential foundation for effective vaccines, was a collaborative effort between researchers at Wuhan and the University of Sydney. Far from celebrating their life-saving expertise, however, News Corp reports "effectively impugned the loyalty the Australians involved" with headlines such as "China's great science swindle" and "Red Army Virus" fostering a climate of suspicion and blame that led to members of the research team receiving death threats. [86]

The *New York Post* built on the *Telegraph* article, explicitly naming the "Five Eyes" intelligence network linking Australia, the US, Britain, Canada, and New Zealand as the dossier's source. Hosting Sharri Markson, who had filed the original story, on *Tonight on Fox News*, Tucker Carlson hailed her claim as "the most substantial confirmation of what we've suspected", asserting that because it was based on a "multinational effort … it would be hard to dismiss it as a political document". [87] Markson labelled sceptical voices as further proof of the culture wars waged by "left wing sections of the media". In a scenario with strong echoes of the Iraq War "dodgy dossier", the document turned out not to be a classified Five Eyes text but a background briefing report on the outbreak of the virus compiled from publicly available material and widely circulated within the US State Department. This was revealed by the ABC, Australia's public service broadcaster, but by then the false claims had been promoted across News Corp news outlets. [88]

6.5 Climate Change Denialism

Analysis of News Corp's coverage of global warming has identified a dominant scepticism dating to 1997 when Murdoch joined the board of the Cato Institute, bringing him into contact with leading climate change deniers. Cato's co-founder, Charles Koch, was the CEO of Koch Industries, the largest private oil company in the United States. Between 1997 and 2018, the Koch Family Foundation spent more than US$145 million directly financing groups attacking climate science and decarbonisation policies. [89] This is more than three times the US$39.2 million spent by Exxon Mobil, the second largest funder of climate disinformation between 1998 and 2020. [90]

Mobilising a culture wars frame, News Corp coverage presented the scientific consensus on human-made climate change as orthodoxy imposed by left-wing "political correctness" and cast sceptics as courageous "dissidents". [91]

Denial of global warming was a frequent theme in the tabloid *New York Post*, but Fox News, expressly launched to counter the imagined tyranny of the "liberal" elite, offered the most widely distributed platform. The opinions voiced by hosts and contributors were "almost uniformly sceptical of climate change", dismissing the scientific consensus, in Sean Hannity's pithy phrase, as "phony science from the left" [92] or presenting it as simply one position among others. As Bill O'Reilly told viewers in 2001, "some scientists say emissions from the earth are making the planet hotter. Other scientists say sunspots or some other natural occurrence is in motion and the heat will soon subside." [93]

In Britain, *The Sun* offered a mass circulation platform to influential climate deniers. They included the paper's popular motoring correspondent, Jeremy Clarkson, with 16 columns ridiculing climate concerns from 1998 to 2006. He dismissed the views of the "half a dozen scientists [who] say carbon dioxide emissions from cars are causing global warming" as "rubbish" and railed "at 'eco-mentalists' [who] say we must stop burning oil and gas immediately and go back to living in caves". In 2000, writing for *The Sunday Times*, he insisted: "There is no such thing as man-made global warming. It does not exist." [94]

Debate around the climate crisis has been particularly "polarised and strident" in Australia where News Corp dominates the daily press. [95] Australia emits more greenhouse gases than any other country in the OECD but with an economy substantially based on extraction, mining for metals, minerals and coal that continues to play a central role in shaping national self-perceptions. A comparative study of media coverage in six countries, including the UK and USA, found that "Australia had the highest number of articles with sceptics" denying or questioning the evidence linking the climate crisis to human activity. [96] News Corp's news outlets have consistently promoted scepticism, directing attention away from the urgent need for fundamental intervention.

Between 1997 and 2007, *The Australian* lent strong support to John Howard's national government, "a key ally of the Bush White House on climate". [97] Once again, a culture wars frame depicted climate science as a "new orthodoxy, which was stifling dissent".

In July 2006, in a move commentators took as signalling a major shift in position, Murdoch invited Al Gore to the Corporation's meeting at Pebble Beach, California, to screen his Oscar-winning film on climate change, *An Inconvenient Truth.* The following year, Murdoch announced that News Corp would "weave this issue into our content … to inspire people to change their behaviour" and aim to be carbon neutral by 2010. [98] Despite these commitments, scepticism continued to play a central organising role in coverage.

Analysis of climate science coverage in ten Australian newspapers in 2011 and 2012 found 32 per cent of articles refusing to "accept the scientific consensus that human beings are major contributors to global warming". [99] News Corp's *Herald Sun* and *The Daily Telegraph*, the country's two best-selling papers, were markedly more sceptical with 81 per cent and 73 per cent of words respectively challenging the scientific consensus. Both hardly mentioned relevant peer-reviewed research. Articles appearing as commentary rather than reporting (65% in the *Herald Sun*) offered additional space for scepticism. [100]

Speaking at the Corporation's AGM in 2019, Murdoch highlighted the economic benefits of moving to carbon neutrality, noting that company energy costs had been cut by US$18 million since 2014. Answering a shareholder question, he insisted: "There are no climate change deniers around I can assure you". [101] There is a fine line between denial and scepticism, however.

In a tweet in August 2015, Murdoch described himself as "A climate change sceptic not a denier" but went on to dismiss reports of accelerating global warming from the UN Intergovernmental Panel as "alarmist nonsense". His tweet read: "Sept UN meets in NY with endless alarmist nonsense from u know whom! Pessimists always seen as sages" (27 August 2015).

Analysis of News Corp publications between April 2019 and March 2020 found 45 per cent of all items either rejecting or casting doubt on the scientific consensus, but with reporting and comment sharply divided. While 89 per cent of reportage accepted climate science findings, 65 per cent of opinion pieces expressed scepticism. [102]

Fifty-five per cent of all sources used came from financial, fossil fuel, and other mining interests. Scientists contributed only 6 per cent, public interest groups engaged with climate issues 4 per cent, and voices from First Nation groups, often subjected to the most severe impact of climate change, only 0.2 per cent. [103]

In marked contrast to the populist general coverage, 95 per cent of business-themed items, both news and features, accepted the conclusions of climate science and just over half (55%) were positive towards mitigation efforts. [104]

Over nine months in 2019 and 2020, devastating forest fires in Australia killed 33 people and over a billion animals, and released more carbon dioxide than the country's annual total. Analysis found that News Corp publications produced 75 per cent of all articles denying the influence of climate change [105] and, despite a conspicuous lack of evidence, allocated more space than other media organisations to promoting arson as a possible cause, directing attention away from the urgent need to reduce reliance on fossil fuels. Confronting what she saw as "dangerous and damaging" coverage, senior executive, Emily Townsend, sent an open letter to News Corp staff, stating that she found it:

> unconscionable to continue working for this company, knowing I am contributing to the spread of climate change denial and lies … News Corp's decision to take this approach in such a devastating time for our country, communities and environment is a step too far. [106]

6.6 Conclusion

The evidence presented in this chapter argues against the common perception of News Corp's relations with politicians and the political system as purely transactional, driven solely by business interests. It points beyond financial calculations to the consistent promotion of a right-wing populist platform across a range of issues in the company's three major markets: the United States, Australia, and Britain. The denialism and scepticism in reporting the climate crisis offers a particularly clear example of prioritising ideology over facts and evidence. Given the central role the corporation continues to play in these three countries' news systems, this raises major concerns about its distorting influence on public debate and democratic processes.

References

[1] Alexander Cockburn (1976) 'Rupert Murdoch Tells All', *The Village Voice*, 29 November. Available at www.villagevoice.com/2019/11/29/rupert-murdoch-tells-all

[2] Nick Davies (2014) *Hack Attack: How the Truth Caught Up with Rupert Murdoch.* London. Chatto and Windus, pp. 169–170.

[3] John B. Thompson (1984) *Studies in the Theory of Ideology*. Cambridge: Polity Press, pp. 130–131.
[4] David McKnight (2012) 'Henry Mayer Lecture 2012: The Market Populism of Rupert Murdoch', *Media International Australia*, No. 144, August, p. 6.
[5] David McKnight (2010) 'Rupert Murdoch's News Corporation: A media institution with a mission', *Historical Journal of Film, Radio and Television*, Vol. 30, No. 3, p. 304.
[6] Stefan Halper and Jonathan Clarke (2004) *America Alone: The Neo-Conservatives and the Global Order*. New York. Cambridge University Press, p. 187.
[7] Sally Young (2023) 'Rupert Murdoch: how a 22-year-old 'zealous Laborite' turned into a tabloid tsar", *The Conversation*, 29 May. Available at https://theconversation.com/rupert-murdoch-how-a-22-year-old-zealous-laborite-turned-into-a-tabloid-tsar-204914
[8] Andrew Neil (1996) *Full Disclosure*. London: Macmillan, p. 165.
[9] Thomas Frank (2000) 'The Rise of Market Populism', *The Nation*, 12 October. Available at www.thenation.com/article/archive/rise-market-populism
[10] Graham Murdock (2020) 'Profits of Deceit: Performing Populism in Polarized Times', *European Journal of Cultural Studies*, Vol. 23, No. 6, pp. 874–899.
[11] S. Scalmer and M. Goot (2004) 'Elites constructing elites'. In M. Sawer and B. Hindess (Eds) *Us and Them: Anti-Elitism in Australia*. Perth: API Network, pp. 137–159.
[12] Robert Manne (2011) Bad News: Murdoch's *Australian* and the shaping of the nation, *Quarterly Essay*, No. 43, p. 3.
[13] John Sinclair (2016) 'Political economy and discourse in Murdoch's flagship newspaper *The Australian*', *The Political Economy of Communication*, Vol. 4, No. 2, p. 4.
[14] David McKnight (2003) '"A World Hungry for a New Philosophy": Rupert Murdoch and the rise of neo-liberalism', *Journalism Studies*, Vol. 4, No. 3, 350–356.
[15] Michael W. Wagner and Timothy P. Collins (2014) 'Does Ownership Matter? The Case of Rupert Murdoch's purchase of the *Wall Street Journal*', *Journalism Practice*, Vol. 8, No. 6, pp. 765–766.
[16] Bruce Harding (2020) 'Wall Street Journal, Dow Jones Editors/Reporters Complain of "Misinformation" in Opinion Columns', *Deadline*, 22 July. Available at https://deadline.com/2020/07/wall-street-journal-editors-reporters-letter-cites-misinformation-in-opinion-columns-1202992550
[17] The Wall Street Journal Editorial Board (2020) 'A Note to Readers', *The Wall Street Journal*, 23 July. Available at www.wsj.com/articles/a-note-to-readers-11595547898
[18] Jeremy Barr (2021) 'Wall Street Journal publishes letter from Trump claiming "rigged" election', *The Washington Post*, 27 October. Available at www.washingtonpost.com/media/2021/10/27/trump-letter-wall-street-journal-election
[19] Lucia Graves (2017) 'The Wall Street Journal's Trump problem', *The Guardian*, 10 September. Available at www.theguardian.com/media/2017/sep/10/the-wall-street-journals-trump-problem
[20] James Murdoch (2009) 'The Absence of Trust', *Edinburgh International Television Festival MacTaggart Lecture*. 28 August, pp. 4–5. Available at: https://image.guardian.co.uk/sys-files/Media/documents/2009/08/28/JamesMurdochMacTaggartLecture.pdf

[21] Rachel Langworth (2020) *Media ownership and the exploitation of media power for corporate self-interest: a case study of News International's coverage of the BBC and Ofcom*. Unpublished PhD thesis. University of Westminster.

[22] John Jewell (2015) 'Bad news week for the BBC as Murdoch press sharpens claws', *The Conversation*, 14 July Available at https://theconversation.com/bad-news-week-for-bbc-as-murdoch-press-sharpens-claws-44621

[23] John Jewell, 2015, op. cit., p. 2.

[24] Jim Waterson (2021) 'BBC inquiry dismisses Rupert Murdoch complaints about documentary series', *The Guardian*, 20 August. Available at www.theguardian.com/media/2021/aug/20/rupert-murdoch-complains-bbc-doc-suggests-he-is-threat-to-liberal-democracy

[25] Quoted in Amanda Meade (2021) 'Murdoch empire strikes back at ABC Four Corners documentary on Fox News' championing of Trump', *The Guardian*, 26 August. Available at www.theguardian.com/media/2021/aug/25/murdoch-empire-strikes-back-at-abcs-documentary-on-fox-news-championing-of-trump

[26] Mitchell Hobbs and Stephen Owen (2016) 'Stifling dissent: the Murdoch press and its campaign against its 'critics', *Communication Research and Practice*, Vol. 2, No. 2, p. 138.

[27] Mitchell Hobbs and Stephen Owen, 2016, op. cit., p. 144.

[28] Peter Golding and Sue Middleton (1982) *Images of Welfare: Press and Public Attitudes to Poverty*. London. Robertson.

[29] Ben Baumberg, Kate Bell, and Decian Gaffney (2012) *Benefit Stigma in Britain*. Turn2us. Available at www.turn2us.org.uk/T2UWebsite/media/Documents/Benefits-Stigma-in-Britain.pdf

[30] Neil T. Gavin (2021) 'Below the radar: A UK benefit fraud media coverage tsunami-Impact, ideology, and society', *British Journal of Sociology*, Vol. 72, pp. 707–724.

[31] Sonia Martin, Timothy Schofield, and Peter Butterworth (2022) 'News media representations of people receiving income support and the production of stigma power: An empirical analysis of reporting on two Australian welfare payments', *Critical Social Policy*, Vol. 42, No. 4, pp. 648–670.

[32] Sonia Martin et al., 2022, op. cit., Table 1, p. 658.

[33] Sonia Martin et al., 2022, op. cit., p. 663.

[34] Peter Whiteford (2021) 'Debt by design: The anatomy of a social policy fiasco – Or was it something worse?", *Australian Journal of Public Policy*, Vol. 80, pp. 340–360.

[35] Royal Commission into the Robodebt Scheme (2023) Block 3 – Response by Rachelle Miller, p. 6. Available at https://robodebt.royalcommission.gov.au/publications/exhibit-3-4305-rmi999900010002-230118-hearing-block-3-response-rachelle-miller-ntg-0147

[36] Royal Commission into the Robodebt Scheme, op. cit., p. 7.

[37] Elizabeth Poole (2011) 'Change and Continuity in the Representation of British Muslims Before and After 9/11: The UK Context', *Global Media Journal-Canadian Edition*, Vol. 4, No. 2, pp. 49–62.

[38] Rupert Murdoch (2010) 'Role of immigration in Strengthening America's Economy', Hearing Before the Subcommittee on Immigration, Citizenship, Refugees, Border Security and International Law of the Committee on the Judiciary, House of Representatives, One Hundred and Eleventh Congress Second Session. 30 September Serial No. 111-155. p. 10. Available at www.govinfo.gov/content/pkg/CHRG-111hhrg58480/html/CHRG-111hhrg58480.htm

[39] Rupert Murdoch (2013) *Annual Lowy Lecture: 2013 Address by Rupert Murdoch, AC*. Sydney. Town Hall, 31 October. Available at www.lowyinstitute.org/publications/annual-lowy-lecture-2013-address-rupert-murdoch-ac

[40] Rupert Murdoch, 2013, Annual Lowy Lecture, op. cit.

[41] Rupert Murdoch Twitter post, 20 August 2013. Available at twittercom/rupertmudoch/status/369583753502265344

[42] Edward Said (1978) *Orientalism*. New York. Vintage Books, p. 3.

[43] Rupert Murdoch Twitter post, 10 January 2015. Available at twittercom/rupertmurdoch/status/553734788881076225

[44] Shahram Akbarzadeh and Bianca Smith (2005) *The Representation of Islam and Muslims in the Media: The Age and Herald Sun Newspapers*. Monash University, School of Political and Social Inquiry, p. 14.

[45] OnePathNetwork (2018) 'Islam in the Media 2017'. Table p. 3. Available at https://onepathnetwork.com/islam-in-the-media-2017

[46] Rita Panahi (2016) 'The Enemy Within', *Herald Sun*, 15 July. Available at https://heraldsun.com.au/rita-panahi/colun-the-enemy-within/news-story/da8f448coaega8a2ca9c276747acaea5

[47] One PathNetwork, 2018, op. cit., p. 11.

[48] OnePathNetwork, 2018, op. cit., p. 11.

[49] Elizabeth Poole (2002) *Reporting Islam: Media Representations of British Muslims*. London. I.B. Tauris, p. 81.

[50] Gholam Khiabany and Milly Williamson (2008) 'Veiled bodies – naked racism: Culture, politics and race in the *Sun*', *Race and Class*, Vol. 50, No. 2, p. 71.

[51] Quoted in Paul Baker, Costas Gabrielators, and Tony McEnery (2013) *Representations of Islam in the British Press 1998–2009*. Lancaster University, ESRC Centre for Corpus Approaches to Social Science (CASS), p. 12.

[52] Slaman Al-Azami (2021) 'Language of Islamophobia in Right-Wing British Newspapers', *Journal of Media and Religion*, Vol. 20, No. 4, pp. 168–169.

[53] Elizabeth Poole, 2011, op. cit., p. 55.

[54] Elizabeth Poole, 2011, op. cit., p. 55.

[55] Rupert Murdoch, 2010, Hearing Before the Subcommittee on Immigration, op. cit., pp. 16–17.

[56] Fred Vultee (2009) 'Jump Back Jack. Mohammed's Here: Fox News and the construction of Islamic peril', *Journalism Studies*, Vol. 10, No. 5, Table 2. See also Sadia Pervez and Shazia Saeed (2010) 'Portrayal of Muslims and Islam in the talk shows of CNN and Fox News', *Journal of Media Studies*, Vol. 25, No. 2, pp. 122–140.

[57] Fred Vultee, 2009, op. cit., p. 628.

[58] Quoted in Mobashra Tazamal (2019) 'Fox News: A Megaphone for Anti-Muslim Hatred', *Georgetown University Bridge*, 18 March. Available at https://bridge.georgetown.edu/research/fox-news-megaphone-for-anti-muslim-hatred

[59] Michael D Giardina (2010) 'Barak Obama, Islamophobia, and the 2008 U.S. Presidential Election Media Spectacle', *Counterpoints*, Vol. 346, p. 137.

[60] Kimberly A. Powell (2011) 'Framing Islam: An Analysis of U.S Media Coverage of Terrorism Since 9/11', *Communication Studies*, Vol. 62, No. 1, p. 91.

[61] Jesse Wiles (2023) *What does the Fox say? A mixed-method framing analysis of Fox News' coverage of domestic terrorism, 2012-2022*. Unpublished Master's dissertation in Global Studies SIMZ23. Lund University. Faculty of Social Sciences.

[62] David Folkenflik (2019) 'Former Media Executive Says He Quit Over Fox's Anti-Muslim Rhetoric, *National Public Radio*, 21 March. Available at www.npr.org/2019/03/21/705441083/former-murdoch-executive-says-he-quit-over-foxs-anti-muslim-rhetoric

[63] Victoria Fielding (2023) *Under the Facade of Journalism: How News Corp Used Fear, Manipulation and Division to Campaign Against the Indigenous Voice to Parliament*. Available at https://murdochroyalcommission.org.au/wp-content/uploads/Under-the-Facade-of-Journalism.pdf

[64] Malcolm Turnbull and Sharan Burrow (2023) 'Sky News spreading fear and falsehoods on Indigenous voice is an affront to Australian democracy', *The Guardian*, 25 July. Available at www.theguardian.com/commentisfree/2023/jul/25/indigenous-voice-to-parliament-sky-news-falsehoods-referendum

[65] Oliver Daddow (2013) 'Margaret Thatcher, Tony Blair and the Eurosceptic Tradition in Britain', *British Journal of Politics and International Relations*, Vol. 14, p. 213.

[66] Graham Murdock (2021) 'Special Relations: Trump, Brexit and the British Media', in Yahya R. Kamalipour (ed.) *Global Media Perceptions of the United States: The Trump Effect.* London. Rowman and Littlefield, p. 114.

[67] Oliver Daddow (2012) 'The UK media and Europe: From permissive consensus to destructive dissent', *International Affairs*, Vol. 88, No. 6, p. 1220.

[68] Quoted in Paul Rowinski (2016) 'Euroscepticism in the Berlusconi and Murdoch press', *Journalism*, Vol. 17, p. 984.

[69] Quoted in Newstalk (2016) 'Why does Rupert Murdoch want a Brexit?', *Newstalk*, 15 January. Available at www.newstalk.com/business/why-does-rupert-murdoch-want-a-brexit-592236

[70] Paul Rowinski, 2016, op. cit., p. 993.

[71] David A.L. Levy, Billur Aslan, and Diego Bironzo (2016) *UK Press Coverage of the EU Referendum.* University of Oxford, Reuters Institute for the Study of Journalism, p. 18.

[72] Martin Moore and Gordon Ramsay (2017) *UK Media Coverage of the 2016 EU Referendum Campaign*. London: Kings College Policy Institute, p. 10.

[73] Martin Moore and Gordon Ramsay, 2017, op. cit., pp. 27–37.

[74] Rupert Murdoch, 2013, Annual Lowy Lecture, op. cit.

[75] Alan Rusbridger (1983) 'Down Among the Press Lords', *London Review of Books*, Vol. 5, No. 4, 3 March. Available at www.lrb.co.uk/the-paper/v05/n04/alan-rusbridger/down-among-the-press-lords

[76] Mitchell Hobbs (2010) 'Neo-conned: The Murdoch press and the Iraq War', *International Journal of Media and Cultural Politics,* September. Available at https://intellectdiscover.com/content/journals/10.1386/mcp.6.2.187_1

[77] Quoted in Roy Greenslade (2003) 'Their master's voice', *The Guardian*, 17 February. Available at www.theguardian.com/media/2003/feb/17/mondaymediasection.iraq

[78] Quoted in Roy Greenslade, 2003, op. cit.

[79] Andrew Calabrese (2004) 'Profits and Patriots: US Media Coverage of the Iraq War', *Media Development*, Vol. 51, No. 3, pp. 34–38.

[80] Quoted in Robert Manne (2005) 'Murdoch's War', *The Monthly*, July. Available at www.themonthly.com.au/node/62/wrap-xhr

[81] Robert Manne, 2005, op. cit.

[82] Judith Betts (2015) *The Battle of the Narratives; Australian Media Agendas and the Iraq War.* Unpublished PhD Thesis. Sydney University. Department of Government and International Relations. Table 5.13, p. 154.

[83] John Jewell (2016) 'Tony Blair took Britain to war in 2003 – but most of Fleet Street marched with him', *The Conversation*, 5 July. Available at https://theconversation.com/tony-blair-took-britain-to-war-in-2003-but-most-of-fleet-street-marched-with-him-62065

[84] Graham Murdock (2021) 'Killing Fields: Pandemics, geopolitics and environmental emergency', in Stuart Price and Ben Harbisher (eds) *Power, Media and the COVID-19 Pandemic: Framing Public Discourse*. London. Routledge, pp. 3–21.

[85] Timothy Graham, Axel Bruns, Guangnan Zhu, and Rod Campbell (2020) *Like a Virus: The Coordinated Spread of Coronavirus Disinformation*. Canberra: The Australian Institute Centre for Responsible Technology, May.

[86] Commonwealth of Australia (2021) The Senate Environmental and Communications References Committee, *Media Diversity in Australia*, p. 16.

[87] Daniel Hurst (2020) 'A dodgy dossier? How News Corp hyped a US government reading list into a China coronavirus "bombshell"', *The Guardian*, 26 May. Available at www.theguardian.com/us-news/2020/may/26/a-dodgy-dossier-how-news-corp-hyped-a-us-government-reading-list-into-a-china-coronavirus-bombshell

[88] Daniel Hurst, 2020, op. cit.

[89] GreenPeace (2018) 'Koch Industries: Secretly Funding the Climate Denial Machine'. Available at https://greenpeace.org/usa/fighting-climate-chaos/climate-deniers/koch-industries

[90] Union of Concerned Scientists (2022) 'It's time for Charles Koch to Testify About His Climate Change Disinformation Campaign', *The Equation*, 31 March.

[91] David McKnight (2010) 'A change in the climate? The journalism of opinion at News Corporation', *Journalism*, Vol. 11, No. 6, p. 694.

[92] David McKnight, 2010, op. cit., p. 697.

[93] David McKnight, 2010, op. cit., p. 697.

[94] David McKnight, 2010, op. cit., pp. 701–702.

[95] Wendy Bacon (2013) *Sceptical Climate Part 2: Climate Science in Australian Newspapers*. Australian Centre for Independent Journalism, p. 5.

[96] James Painter (2013) *Climate Change in the Media: Reporting Risk and Uncertainty*. London. I.B. Tauris, p. ix.

[97] David McKnight, 2010, op. cit., p. 699.

[98] David McKnight, 2010, op. cit., p. 693.

[99] Wendy Bacon, 2013, op. cit., p. 11.

[100] Wendy Bacon, 2013, op. cit., pp. 13–17.

[101] Quoted in Graham Readfern (2019) 'Rupert Murdoch says "there are no climate change deniers" around News Corp', *The Guardian*, 21 November. Available at www.theguardian.com/media/2019/nov/21/news-corps-rupert-murdoch-says-there-are-no-climate-change-deniers-around-here

[102] Wendy Bacon and Aruna Jegan (2020) *Lies, Debates and Silences: How News Corp Produces Climate Scepticism in Australia*. GetUp, p. 7.

[103] Wendy Bacon and Aruna Jegan, 2020, op. cit., p. 9.

[104] Wendy Bacon and Aruna Jegan, 2020, op. cit., p. 8.

[105] Louis Brailsford et al. (2020) *Dirty Power Burnt Country: How the fossil fuel industry, News Corp, and the Federal Government hijacked the Black Summer bushfires to prevent action on climate change*. Sydney: Greenpeace Australia, p. 21.

[106] Quoted in Michael West Media (2020) 'Compromised: Genie Energy and the Murdoch media's climate denial', 15 January. Available at https://michaelwest.com.au/compromised-genie-energy-and-the-murdoch-medias-climate-denial

7 Revaluations

In an episode of Fox's popular animation series, *The Simpsons*, Homer, the embodiment of News Corp's core tabloid audience, mistakenly enters a private box at the Superbowl, the grand finale of the American football season. He encounters Rupert Murdoch who introduces himself as "the billionaire tyrant", neatly encapsulating the sharply divided opinions on his corporate career.

7.1 Murdoch the Billionaire

Supporters of Murdoch, exemplified by David Elstein, former head of programming at BSkyB, emphasise his "remarkable business success". [1] They point to his acquisition of *The Sun* at a minimal cost, transforming it into the UK's top-selling newspaper, his disruption of the US broadcast industry's three-channel dominance, the creation of Fox from scratch, and the launch of a British satellite TV service that significantly expanded viewer choices.

This admiring reading attributes News Corp's successes almost entirely to Rupert Murdoch's business acumen, risk taking, and determination to disrupt prevailing arrangements. It neglects to mention his serial disregard of agreements.

In 1981, having failed to acquire the publisher William Collins, he promised the company's chief executive and deputy chair that he "would never again make a hostile bid". He later broke his pledge and bought the company out. As Harold Evans, the former *Sunday Times* editor, has argued, the double-cross was typical of a recurrent pattern of broken promises across three continents, with Murdoch playing "the Houdini of agreements. With one bound he is free." [2]

Laudatory accounts of Murdoch's business career also tend to avoid sustained engagement with the changing economic and political environment that created the conditions for his success.

Murdoch has been astute, and at times ruthless, in exploiting the spaces opened by marketisation. He has pursued a relentless strategy of horizontal integration, buying up properties at the same point in production chains to consolidate his position in the British and Australian newspaper and American television markets. Successive acquisitions have cemented vertically integrated

DOI: 10.4324/9781003255086-7

relations between production and distribution. Profits from one sector have been deployed to finance diversification into new areas. These moves were made possible by the wider political turn against the interventionist state and the concerted shift to neoliberal governance. He was the right man, in the right places at the right time, trading on an image as an outsider and iconoclast that resonated strongly with Margaret Thatcher's sense of herself as disrupting the old Conservative establishment and Ronald Reagan's origins in Hollywood rather than the traditional Republican heartlands.

The neoliberal retreat from public interest regulation has been decisive in News Corp's development. Key instances include:

- in the UK, Thatcher's endorsement of the purchase of *The Times* and *Sunday Times* and Sky's monopolisation of British direct satellite broadcasting
- in the US, the waivers on ownership paving the way for a fourth television network in the US and the space created for Fox News's opinion-driven programming by the abolition of the Fairness Doctrine
- in Australia, the 2017 Broadcasting Services Act removal of the '2 out of 3' cross-media control and the 75 per cent audience reach rules allowing News Corp to own radio stations and newspapers in each capital city, regional newspapers and a majority share of the Foxtel news network.

As Murdoch once remarked tongue in cheek, "Monopolies are a terrible thing … unless you have one." [3]

Also absent from many accounts is any detailed discussion of the missed opportunities, misreadings of globalisation, and uneven responses to digitalisation that have marked News Corp's development.

Despite an assertive strategy of diversification, the company failed to establish a significant presence in two major markets: video games and recorded music. In marked contrast to Bertelsmann which controls the world's fourth largest music company, BMG, alongside the world's leading book publishing concern, Penguin Random House, and the multiple RTL broadcast channels, having once owned a record company News Corp missed the opportunity to build a major international label. It also failed to capitalise on its brief ownership of a major early online gaming site.

In common with other enthusiasts of marketised globalisation, Murdoch saw the retreat from state management in emerging economies, led by China and India, ushering in a borderless world of expanding and exploitable markets. He underestimated the resilience of national interests. News Corp's attempts to establish a core presence in newly commercialised television systems using satellite distribution consistently bumped up against government ambitions for national investment and control, forcing the company to abandon its ventures in China and Japan and accept co-investment from the major national industrial conglomerate, Tata, in India.

The commitment to satellite systems was one strand in a wider ideological conviction that emerging digital technologies were creating major new opportunities for profit generation. As we detailed in Chapter 3 and 4, however, News Corp consistently failed to take full advantage of the opportunities on offer. The mismanagement and sale of the pioneering Delphi internet service provider and MySpace social media site represent major failures to capitalise on first mover advantages.

Later digital investments have enjoyed mixed fortunes. The video advertising concern Unruly (2019) and the social media aggregator Knewz (2021) were both sold after brief unsuccessful tenures. On the other hand, the Dow Jones financial services, the REA property services, and OPIS have been major successes and become core profit centres.

How far recent ventures into blockchain and artificial intelligence will deliver the anticipated boosts in revenues remains an open question.

7.2 Murdoch the Tyrant

In marked contrast to the celebration of Murdoch's business acumen, critics have focused on the central role played by his tabloid media in debasing the public sphere, a view memorably encapsulated in the television playwright Dennis Potter's decision to name his terminal cancer tumour "Rupert". As he explained in his last interview:

> I call it Rupert, so I can get close to it. I would shoot the bugger if I could. There is no one person more responsible for the pollution of what was already a fairly polluted press, and the pollution of the British press is an important part of the pollution of British political life. [4]

As we noted at the outset, Rupert Murdoch has repeatedly cited his father's account of the military debacle at Gallipoli to present himself as continuing the family tradition of an outsider challenging entrenched power. Rather than interrogating abuses of corporate power, News Corp's animating ideology of market populism has systematically directed attention elsewhere. It organises accounts around two central lessons from Keith Murdoch's newspaper career: the power of publicity to pressure politicians to support the company's business and ideological interests and the market success of aggressive tabloidisation.

Throughout his career, Rupert Murdoch has used his news outlets to undermine the reputations and credibility of politicians whose policies threatened his business interests or whose views he opposes while throwing his full weight behind those prepared to relax regulatory restraints and promote positions he endorses. The attacks on Gough Whitlam and Neil Kinnock and the free pass given to Donald Trump, despite Murdoch's personal reservations, stand as prominent examples.

His interventions have played a central role in promoting the right-wing populism that has colonised conservative politics in the company's major English-speaking markets. His tabloid outlets have consistently tapped into common-sense understandings and prejudices, articulated them in resonant language and imagery, dramatised them in immediately recognisable examples, and returned them, renovated and reinforced, to everyday conversation and action. It has been both a highly successful commercial strategy and an ideological project.

Scope for ideological intervention has been significantly increased by the expanded space allocated to comment and opinion, generating tensions with news reporting teams adhering to accepted journalistic standards of evidence. Endorsing right-wing populism reached its apogee with Fox News's continuing promotion of Donald Trump's "stolen election" claims, knowing them to be false. The immediate rationale was commercial, protecting revenues by retaining the channel's core audience. But as the evidence we have presented demonstrates, Trump's claims were rooted in a wider populist world view that the company's news outlets have promoted for decades across a range of core issues. It has defined News Corp's tabloid outlets but has also permeated the flagship *Wall Street Journal* and *Australian.* As recent commentary has concluded:

> The Murdoch empire did not cause the right-wing populist wave. But more than any single media company, it enabled it, promoted it and profited from it. Across the English-speaking world, the family's outlets have helped elevate marginal demagogues, mainstream ethnonationalism and politicize the very notion of truth … It may not have been the family's mission to destabilize democracies around the world, but that has been its most consequential legacy. [5]

News Corp's effectiveness in promoting populism relies on its development of an assertive style of tabloidisation that combines sensation, titillation, puns and jokes, and opinion couched in the language of the bar and the work break. It claims to speak for the "people" against the "powers that be" but withholds the comprehensive information, analysis, and deliberation required to understand where real power lies or how it operates. It is an exercise in misdirection, denial, and scapegoating. The intensifying search for saleable sensation led directly to the hacking scandal, one of the defining events in the corporation's development. As a former senior Murdoch executive told Carl Bernstein, co-author of the Watergate revelations that brought down President Richard Nixon:

> This scandal … could not have happened anywhere else … More than anyone Murdoch invented and established this culture in the newsroom, where you do whatever it takes to get a story, take no prisoners, destroy the competition, and the end will justify the means. [6]

There is a direct line of descent from Keith Murdoch's sensationalist coverage of the murdered teenage girl in Gun Alley to the hack on the phone of Milly Dowler.

The ruthless disregard for the personal damage done is exemplified by *The Sun*'s treatment of another teenager, the then 13-year-old singing star Charlotte Church. Invited to perform for Rupert Murdoch's wedding to Wendi Deng, Church waived a fee in return for the promise of career-boosting coverage in News Corp's papers. The promise was immediately broken. *The Sun* featured a clock counting down to her sixteenth birthday (the age of sexual consent) and revealed that she was pregnant "before she told her parents – almost certainly because her phone was hacked". [7]

Injuries to targets of tabloid abuse have been accompanied by the wider corruption of political debate on central issues of public concern. Unquestioning blanket support for the Iraq War and consistent climate denialism, both responsible for uncountable avoidable deaths and destruction, offer dramatic demonstrations. The leading climate scientist Michael Mann has claimed that Murdoch "will go down in history as one of the greatest climate villains". [8] The research evidence lends this damning verdict strong support.

Concern with News Corp's role in the degradation of democracy has been particularly vocal and organised in Australia where the company dominates the press and operates a highly successful Sky News Australia national television service modelled on Fox News. The campaign to hold News Corp to account has been headed by two former prime ministers, Kevin Rudd from the Labor Party and Malcolm Turnbull from the opposition Liberal Party, united across the political divide in viewing Murdoch's influence as "a cancer on democracy … withering away the vitality of the body politic". [9]

In 2020, Rudd uploaded a video asking his social media followers to sign a petition calling for a Royal Commission to investigate News Corp. It gathered more than half a million signatures and prompted a parliamentary inquiry into media diversity, collecting evidence from politicians and former News Corp employees. [10] The Campaign for a Royal Commission remains active, chaired now by Turnbull after Rudd's appointment as ambassador to the United States.

7.3 Succession

Rupert Murdoch's decision to relinquish leadership of both News Corp and Fox Corp and hand responsibilities to his son Lachlan sets in motion the struggle for succession. The outcome is uncertain. On Rupert Murdoch's death, his votes in the family trust will be distributed among the four senior children, giving each two votes in total. Any decision on the company's future direction and leadership requires a majority vote. There is no guarantee that the present corporate structure will be retained or that Lachlan Murdoch's present control will be confirmed. James Murdoch has a very different vision for the company's future to his brother. [11] Independent investors are pressing for assets to be sold. The longer-term impacts of generative AI and the recent shift in company profits from media to data services are open questions and there is always the possibility of a hostile takeover bid.

When asked about the forces shaping News Corp, Rupert Murdoch had no hesitation in claiming that "for better or worse, [it] is a reflection of my thinking, my character, my values". [12] How far that thinking and those values will survive the succession, when it comes, will determine the company's future.

References

[1] David Elstein (2020) 'Rupert Murdoch is not an evil genius, whatever the BBC's "Dynasty" doc says', openDemocracy, 15 September. Available at www.opendemocracy.net/en/ourbeeb/rupert-murdoch-is-not-an-evil-genius-whatever-bbcs-dynasty-doc-says

[2] Harold Evans (2011) 'Rupert Murdoch is the stiletto, a man of method, a cold-eyed manipulator', *The Guardian*, 18 September. Available at www.theguardian.com/media/2011/sep/18/harold-evans-rupert-murdoch-leadership

[3] Quoted in Andrew Neil (1996) *Full Disclosure*. London: Pan Books, p. xiii.

[4] Melvyn Bragg (2007) 'We tend to forget that life can only be defined in the present tense', *The Guardian*, 12 September. Available at www.theguardian.com/theguardian/2007/sep/12/greatinterviews

[5] Jonathan Mahler and Jim Rutenberg (2019) 'How Rupert Murdoch's Empire of Influence Remade the World. Part One: Imperial Expansion', *The New York Times*, 3 April. Available at www.nytimes.com/interactive/2019/04/03/magazine/rupert-murdoch-fox-news-trump.html

[6] Carl Bernstein (2011) 'Is Phone-Hacking Scandal Murdoch's Watergate', *Newsweek*, 7 September. Available at www.newsweek.com/carl-bernstein-phone-hacking-scandal-murdochs-watergate-68411

[7] On this, see David McKnight (2012) 'Henry Mayer Lecture 2012: The Market Populism of Rupert Murdoch', *Media International Australia*, No. 144, August, p. 9.

[8] Quoted in Gaham Readfearn and Adam Morton (2023) '"Climate villain": scientist says Rupert Murdoch wielded his media empire to sow confusion and doubt', *The Guardian*, 23 September. Available at www.theguardian.com/media/2023/sep/23/rupert-murdoch-climate-change-denial

[9] Hacked Off (2020) Interview with Kevin Rudd, 21 December. Available at https://hackinginquiry.org/36055-2

[10] The Senate (2021) Media Diversity in Australia, The Senate Environmental and Communications References Committee, December, Canberra, Commonwealth of Australia.

[11] See Michael Wolff (2023) *The Fall: The End of the Murdoch Empire*. London. Bridge Street Press, pp. 289–295.

[12] Richard Cooke (2018) 'The Endless Reign of Rupert Murdoch', *The Monthly*, July. Available at www.themonthly.com.au/issue/2018/july/1530367200/richard-cooke/endless-reign-rupert-murdoch#mtr

Index

For Product Safety Concerns and Information please contact our EU
representative GPSR@taylorandfrancis.com
Taylor & Francis Verlag GmbH, Kaufingerstraße 24, 80331 München, Germany

www.ingramcontent.com/pod-product-compliance
Lightning Source LLC
LaVergne TN
LVHW010917110826
845149LV00013B/2392